S

1ˢᵗ ᴇᴅ

1360

CRY COMANCHE

THE 2nd U.S. CAVALRY IN TEXAS, 1855-1861

Some Other Books By
COLONEL HAROLD B. SIMPSON

———————————

BRAWLING BRASS, NORTH AND SOUTH
GAINES' MILL TO APPOMATTOX
TEXAS IN THE WAR, 1861-1865 (COMP.)
TOUCHED WITH VALOR (ED.)
THE MARSHALL GUARDS
RED GRANITE FOR GRAY HEROES
ROBERT E. LEE (ED.)
HISTORY OF HOOD'S TEXAS BRIGADE (4 VOLS.)
AUDIE MURPHY, AMERICAN SOLDIER

CRY COMANCHE

THE 2nd U.S. CAVALRY IN TEXAS, 1855-1861

The neighing troop, the flashing blade,
    The bugle's stirring blast,
The charge, the dreadful fusilade
    The din and shout are past.
Nor war's wild note nor glory's peal
    Shall thrill with fierce delight
Those breasts that never more may feel
    The raptures of the fight.

               —Theodore O'Hara

By

COLONEL HAROLD B. SIMPSON

Hill Jr. College Press   •   Hillsboro, Texas   •   1979

Copyright 1979
Hill Junior College Press
Hillsboro, Texas

Published by
Hill Junior College Press

Library of Congress Catalog Card Number
79-91577

_____

I.S.B.N.
0-912172-25-8

Composed By
LEWAY COMPOSING COMPANY
Ft. Worth, Texas

Printed By
DAVIS BROTHERS PRINTING COMPANY
Waco, Texas

Bound By
LIBRARY BINDING COMPANY
Waco, Texas

DEDICATED TO

THE LATE ODIS "DOLLY" GRAY
A GOOD FRIEND
PRESIDENT, BOARD OF REGENTS, HILL JR. COLLEGE
1968-70

X v X

Preface

This volume is concerned only with the history of the original 2nd U.S. Cavalry Regiment authorized in March, 1855, and its assignment in Texas during the years 1855-1861. The elite regiment in just a few years indelibly inscribed its name on the pages of United States History, not only for its exploits along the Texas border and frontier in the late 1850's but also for the great number of general officers that it contributed to both armies during the Civil War. The original 2nd Cavalry had a life span of only six years and five months. In August of 1861, the six Regular mounted regiments in the United States Army at the time, the 1st and 2nd Dragoons, the Mounted Rifles and the 1st, 2nd and 3rd Cavalry were re-numbered as cavalry regiments according to seniority of authorization. In this re-designation of numbers the 2nd Cavalry became the 5th U.S. Cavalry Regiment and has retained this number until the present time.

The 2nd U.S. Cavalry Regiment was authorized by an Act of Congress on March 3, 1855. Often referred to as "Jeff Davis's Own," the unit was an elite organization — perhaps the finest regiment to be organized in the American Army. The officers assigned to the 2nd Cavalry were hand picked by Secretary of War Jefferson Davis; the majority of them, like Davis, were Southerners by birth and West Point graduates by education. The non-commissioned officers were specially selected from the other mounted regiments, and the privates were recruited mainly from Mid-Western and Southern States. Horses for the Regiment were purchased by a special team of 2nd Cavalry officers who were authorized to buy the best blooded stock available in Kentucky, Indiana and Ohio. For purposes of appearance and to engender *esprit de corps* each company was assigned horses of one color. In concert with the high standards set in selecting the men and mounts the Regiment was furnished the newest and best arms, accouterments and equipment.

The senior officers appointed to the 2nd Cavalry had outstanding records and the captains and lieutenants were young men of great promise. In order to obtain the best officers possible, several proven leaders were selected from civilian life, most of these, like Albert Brackett, William Chambliss, Walter Jenifer and

William Royall had fine Mexican War records. The Texas Rangers were tapped for one man — Charles E. Travis, the only son of the commander of the Alamo, Colonel William Barrett Travis. Colonel Albert Sidney Johnston of Texas was selected to command the Regiment and Lieutenant-Colonel Robert E. Lee of Virginia was designated as the second-in-command. William J. Hardee, a Georgian, was assigned as the senior major and George H. Thomas another Virginian, was appointed the junior major of the Regiment. Earl Van Dorn of Mississippi was the senior captain and commanded Company A. Numbered among the other captains were E. Kirby Smith of Florida and George Stoneman, Jr. of New York. Both Nathan "Shanks" Evans of South Carolina and John Bell Hood of Kentucky were selected as lieutenants in the 2nd Cavalry. Sixteen Civil War generals came from the rolls of the Regiment, eleven fought with the Confederacy and five for the Union. The original 2nd cavalry provided Jefferson Davis with one-half or four of his full generals — A. J. Johnston, Lee, E.K. Smith and Hood.

Although the headquarters for Johnston's Regiment was established at Louisville, Kentucky in April, 1855, the Regiment was actually formed during the summer and early fall of that year at Jefferson Barracks, Missouri. Here the companies were organized and trained and their officers assigned. Some difficulties were experienced at Jefferson Barracks during the organizational period — cholera made a brief appearance, quartermaster stores were late in arriving and military restraints and daily drills caused some dissatisfaction and a great number of desertions. In late September orders were received transferring the Regiment to the Texas frontier; however, it would be another month before the 2nd Cavalry left Jefferson Barracks.

The trek for Texas commenced on the morning of October 27 and proceeded by easy marches across the country to Fort Belknap, Texas. All company equipment and property, surplus baggage of the officers and the company laundresses were sent to Texas by water via New Orleans to Indianola. Except for the usual disciplinary problems and foraging escapades, the movement to the Southwest was uneventful — no hostile Indians, no epidemics and no serious losses of men, horses or wagons. The column rode through Missouri, across the northwest corner of Arkansas, through the Indian Territory and crossed over the Red River into

Texas at Preston on December 15, 1855.

The five years that the Regiment was stationed in Texas were years of action. The War Department had changed its strategy in regard to frontier warfare in Texas. As had been the case earlier in the decade, the mounted garrisons no longer merely maintained a defensive patrol cordon and reacted only to Indian aggression. This defensive policy had hobbled the activities of both the 2nd Dragoons and Mounted Rifles who had patrolled the Lone Star State earlier in the decade. With the posting of the 2nd Cavalry along the frontier in 1856 the War Department advocated a policy of long range scouting to ferret out the marauding Indians. Patrol, pursue, and punish was the new strategic concept. Keep as many reconnaissance and scouting forces in the field as possible, find the Comanches, Kiowa and Apache trails, follow them relentlessly, and bring the raiders to battle. This policy was advocated by the Department Commander and followed religiously by the Post Commanders, and by 1861 the red raiders had been brought to battle dozens of times and their area of manueverability greatly restricted.

The Regiment was involved in forty engagements, scores of patrols, several long reconnaissance missions and numerous escort parties during its five year tenure in Texas. All but four battle actions occurred within the borders of the Lone Star State. Twice, once in 1858 and again in 1859, dashing Earl Van Dorn penetrated deep into the Indian heartland north of the Red River to engage hostile Comanches and in 1859 and 1860 George Stoneman, Jr., led raids south of the Rio Grande against both Indians and Mexican bandits. The greatest number of casualties suffered by the Regiment in one engagement was at Wichita Village (Indian Territory) on October 1, 1858, when five cavalrymen were killed and ten wounded. Fortunately in only three other engagements did the dead and wounded total as many as a half dozen. Altogether the 2nd Cavalry had thirteen men killed and fifty-eight wounded while guarding the Texas frontier in the half decade prior to the Civil War. Another thirteen troopers died of other causes while on duty in the State.

As was the custom of the day, the officers led the men into battle; consequently several officers were numbered among the killed and wounded. Second Lieutenant Cornelius Van Camp was killed instantly with an arrow through his heart while leading a charge at Wichita Village. Major George H. Thomas, Captains Earl Van Dorn and E. Kirby Smith and Lieutenants John B. Hood, Fitzhugh Lee, James B. Witherell and Robert C. Wood, Jr., were wounded, several of them seriously. Van Dorn was wounded the most number of times, four, and also was wounded the most seriously. At Wichita Village an arrow was shot through Van Dorn's body from side to side. It passed through his rib cage twice, cut his left lung and went through the upper part of his stomach.

One of the real strengths of the elite Regiment was the high caliber of its non-commissioned officers — the backbone of any military unit and the unsung heroes of the Indian Fighting Army. Fittingly, a sergeant led the last contingent of the 2nd Cavalry to see action in Texas, and many of the Regiment's most successful encounters were led by two and three stripers. Of the forty encounters in which the Regiment was involved, non-commissioned officers led the cavalrymen into battle ten times, and many of the casualties of the 2nd Cavalry wore stripes on their sleeves. Three non-commissioned officers (all sergeants) were killed in battle and eight were wounded. Several sergeants and corporals were cited in official orders for "conspicuous gallantry and unflinching courage." First Sergeants Walter McDonald (Company D) and John W. Spangler (Company H), were specifically cited for such conduct on two occasions. The fine quality of the non-commissioned officers in the Regiment is best borne out by the fact that twelve of the sergeants won officer's commissions later in their careers.

Not only were the officers and non-commissioned officers of superior caliber, but the privates appeared to be a cut above the average recruit of the day. Time and again, the gallant conduct of the private trooper in action was cited in General Orders and company commander's battle reports. One company commander in particular was profuse in his praise of the enlisted men of his unit, writing that he did "not believe that a more superior lot of men could be found in the army" than those constituting his company. "About forty of them," he continued, "weighed from one hundred and forty to one hundred and fifty pounds . . . . Each was an excellent horseman, afraid of nothing, never tired, and always cheerful, and always willing to endure fatigue and hardship . . . ."

X   x   X

The bulk of the enlisted men were Irish and German immigrants, two nationalities that flooded the United States in the two decades before the Civil War. A survey of the 118 enlisted men in Companies A and F stationed at Fort Mason in 1860 showed that the majority of them, 52%, were from Ireland (43) and Germany (18). Seven of the enlisted men, 6%, were from the British Isles other than Ireland. Other foreign countries represented were, France, Mexico and Denmark. Forty-one of the troopers, 35%, were native born, three of these being born in Texas. These statistics were probably about the same in the other eight companies of the Regiment.

The 2nd Cavalry was commanded at one time or another by Albert Sidney Johnston, Robert E. Lee, George H. Thomas and Earl Van Dorn during its deployment in Texas. Johnston commanded the famed unit until July, 1857, when he was ordered to Washington and given command of the Utah Expedition against the Mormons. Robert E. Lee succeeded Johnston as commander, but within three months he was granted an extended leave of absence to Virginia and was replaced by Major George H. Thomas. When Thomas was granted a year's leave of absence in November, 1860, he was replaced by Captain Van Dorn. Lee again assumed command of the Regiment on Christmas Eve, 1860, and retained command until he was ordered to Washington by General Scott in mid-February, 1861. The great Virginian was the last official commander of the 2nd Cavalry while it was stationed in Texas, and it was the last command that Lee held in the United States Army.

When Texas voted to secede from the Union on February 1, 1861, General David Emanuel Twiggs, Commander of the Department of Texas, was induced, without too much persuasion, to surrender all of the Federal military installations in Texas to State authorities. Thus was perpetrated one of the biggest giveaway programs in American military history. Twenty-one military installations, between 1.5 and 3 million dollars worth of military stores and supplies and about $23,000 in cash were seized by State military forces. Too, some 2,500 troops, fifteen percent of the Regular Army at the time, were temporarily put out of action.

The commanderless cavalry regiment, like the other Federal units in the State, in compliance with Twiggs' order abandoned their stations. The exodus of the mounted units from Texas began in late February, continued through March and was completed in early April. The companies of the 2nd Cavalry, per instructions, were ordered to ride from their widely separated posts and rendezvous at Green Lake in western Calhoun County. From here they were to march the 30 miles to Indianola where they were to embark on ships for the North. The Regiment left the State in two contingents or battalions. Six companies under the command of Captain Innis Palmer sailed on the steamship *Coatzacoalcos* for New York where they arrived on April 11. Headquarters and the remaining four companies under the command of Captain Charles Whiting boarded the steamer *Empire City* on April 12, reaching New York on the 20th. This completed the movement of the 2nd U.S. Cavalry Regiment from Texas.

I wish to acknowledge the assistance of the following persons in the preparation of this book: my two secretaries Mrs. Annielee Wright and Mrs. Olene Powell for the typing of the manuscript; Miss Judith Swearingen for reading and suggesting grammatical changes to the manuscript; and student research assistants Pamela Porter, Leisha Caffe, James Hickox and Mario Huerta for indexing the book and preparing the Bibliography. I also wish to acknowledge the following persons who were responsible for the production of the book, Mrs. LeNelle Campbell, Mrs. Mary Terry, Joyce Parkhurst, Mrs. Dianne Long and Bernie DuPree of LeWay Composing Service of Fort Worth; Billy Don Shirley and Robert Davis of the Davis Publishing Company of Waco; Clarence Kedrowski and Frank Jasek of the Library Binding Company also of Waco. Too, I wish to thank the Board of Regents of Hill Junior College and the President of the College, Dr. Elbert Hutchins, for providing a grant to publish the book, and I particularly want to thank my wife, Vera Muriel, for her constant encouragement and support. Without these fine people there would be no *CRY COMANCHE.*

Harold B. Simpson

Hillsboro, Texas
October 20, 1979

CONTENTS

ILLUSTRATIONS
Follow Page 120

MAPS

CONTENTS

CHAPTERS

ILLUSTRATIONS
Follow Page 120

Uniforms of The 2nd U. S. Cavalry Regiment

Albert Sidney Johnston

Robert E. Lee

E. Kirby Smith

John Bell Hood

William J. Hardee
Earl Van Dorn
Fitzhugh Lee
Charles W. Field

Nathan G. Evans
George B. Cosby
James P. Major
George H. Thomas

George Stoneman, Jr.
Kenner Garrard
Richard W. Johnson
Innis N. Palmer

David E. Twiggs

MAPS

Important Rivers of Central and West Texas

Major Posts Garrisoned by the 2nd Cavalry,   1855-1861

Important Engagements Fought by the 2nd Cavalry, 1855-1861

CHAPTER ONE

EARLY HISTORY OF THE U.S. HORSE SOLDIER

Oh! the dragoon bold he knows no care,
As he rides along with his uncropped hair;
Himself in the saddle he lightly throws,
And on the weekly scout he goes.[1]

Although the vastness of the country would dictate otherwise, there was very little attention given to the cavalry arm of the United States Army before 1833. Horse units were normally recruited only for emergencies, then speedily disbanded when their services were no longer needed.

The American cavalryman was born during the Revolutionary War, and a very precarious birth it was. Washington himself had doubts about the value of the mounted arm, doubts which stemmed from his service with the British Army during the French and Indian War.[2] This thinking apparently prevailed in Congress, for few mounted regiments were raised or used. Thus, the cavalry was too weak to play a significant part in the war. Only in the southern theater, near the end of the war, was the mounted arm properly used, and did it play an important combat role.[3]

In 1777, the Continental Congress authorized the formation of four regiments of dragoons, each regiment to be comprised of six troops with a total regimental strength of 279 officers and men. These four regiments of dragoons, which were numbered one through four, later in the war were organized into a cavalry corps. The first commander of the corps was Count Casimir Pulaski, the colorful Polish nobleman and soldier of fortune who had embraced the American cause. Pulaski was killed charging the

---

[1] A verse from the "Song of the 2nd Dragoons." James M. Merrill. **Spurs to Glory, The Story of the United States Cavalry.** New York: Rand McNally & Co., 1966. p. 38. Hereafter referred to as **Merrill.**
[2] Richard Wormser. **The Yellowlegs, the Story of the United States Cavalry.** Garden City (N.Y.): Doubleday and Co., 1966. p. 1. Hereafter referred to as **Wormser.**
[3] John K. Kerr and Edward S. Wallace. **The Story of the U.S. Cavalry,** Boston: Little, Brown & Co., 1953. p. 4. Hereafter referred to as **Kerr.**

British artillery at Savannah, Georgia, in 1779. The cavalry corps did little in the Revolutionary War to excite the military historian. The men of the four regiments were generally poorly armed, equipped and mounted and spent most of their time on courier service and as escorts for general officers.[4]

Probably the two most successful leaders of Regular or Continental cavalry units were Henry "Light Horse Harry" Lee and William Washington. Lee, the father of Robert E. Lee, did yeoman work at Valley Forge during the winter of 1777-78, keeping Washington's army alive. He proved that a cavalry unit could be properly fed and mounted and carry out its mission during the most adverse conditions.[5] Washington, impressed with the young cavalry leader, made Lee commander of "Lee's Legion," a mixed body of cavalry and infantry. It was a colorful unit; the men wore green jackets and doeskin breeches in contrast to the regular blue and buff of the Continentals. The Legion later was called "Lee's Light Horse" and thus provided the leader with his famous sobriquet.[6] Lee did especially fine service for General Nathaniel Greene in 1780 and 1781 during the Greene's retreat through the Carolinas prior to the *coup de grace* at Yorktown. Colonel William Washington, a distant cousin of the American commander-in-chief, like Lee, provided Greene with outstanding cavalry support during the southern campaign of 1779-81. Washington with his 80 dragoons, in particular, played an important part in the British defeat at Cowpens, January 8, 1780.[7]

Throughout the Revolutionary War numerous irregular or partisan cavalry units were organized and commanded by such men as Francis Marion, Thomas Sumter, Andrew Pickens and Allan McLane. All of these except McLane fought in the South. McLane, a Philadelphian, operated primarily in the eastern Pennsylvania area. One story is told that McLane and his "Rough Riders" completely broke up a sumptuous dinner and farewell party being given for General Sir William Howe by Philadelphia Society. McLane and a mixed force of cavalry and infantry attack-

---

[4] Kerr, pp. 6-8
[5] Wormser, p. 5
[6] Ibid., pp. 5-7
[7] The British cavalry leader in the southern campaign, was Colonel, later General, Banastre Tarleton, the Oxford educated son of the mayor of Liverpool. Tarleton, who was nicknamed "the Butcher," for his ruthless tactics, confronted Lee and Washington on several occasions.

ed, by hurling kettles full of explosives at the sentries and the doors, the mansion where the party was being held, and putting the General and his guests to rout.[8]

As far as can be ascertained none of these partisan leaders were members of the Continental or national army, but rather received their commissions and support from their native states. Most of this irregular cavalry operated against British supply columns and lightly held outposts. They were paid little, if at all, had body servants to look after their horses, and would return to their homes between scouting forays or raids.

One colorful but little known American cavalry leader was Captain Casimo de Medici of South Carolina who commanded two troops of volunteer cavalry. As the Continental currency was practically worthless and of little inducement for recruitment, the captain, a large slaveholder, gave pay and bounty to his men in "grown" and "small" Negroes. A copy of his payroll on file in the War Department shows that he owed a Captain Barnett, "39-3/4 grown Negroes."[9] It would be interesting to know how Barnett was paid off.

Of all the partisan leaders, the "Swamp-Fox," Francis Marion, was the most successful and best known. Marion, a veteran of the Cherokee Insurrection of 1761, was commissioned a brigadier-general by Governor John Rutledge of South Carolina. He called his small force of horsemen, "Marion's Legion" and armed them with rifles instead of muskets. They had no uniforms but were well mounted. Their sabers were beaten out of sawmill blades. Marion and his men harrassed General Cornwallis' flanks and scouting parties regularly with hit and run tactics and then dispersed in the swamps when pursued. One of Cornwallis' cavalry officers, a Major McIlraith, accused the "Swamp Fox" of ungentlemanly tactics and unmilitary conduct and challenged him to stand and fight. Marion said he would be glad to send twenty of his picked men against twenty of McIlraith's men, the fight to take place on open ground at an agreed upon hour. The British major accepted the challenge but failed to appear for the dual.[10]

For the fifty years following the Revolutionary War there was no mounted force established on a permanent basis. Wormser

---

[8] Kerr, p. 9.
[9] Ibid., pp. 11-12.
[10] Ibid., pp. 11-12.

gives two main reasons for this. First, it was surmised that wars would come from only three sources, Spanish Florida, British Canada and on the sea. There were dense woods in the North, swamps and tropical undergrowth in the South and no fear of an invasion from the sea. Strange as it may seem, the Indians to the west were not considered a threat. Second, George Washington was the man consulted on standing armies, and he was opposed to horse soldiers. His thoughts governed high-level military thinking for years after his death. Perhaps if Henry Lee and Francis Marion, two successful cavalrymen, had not married wealthy women and retired to plantation life his thinking might have been different.[11] Too, horse regiments are expensive to raise and maintain, and so Congress was only too happy to go along with this thinking.

The first mounted force organized under the new government was authorized by Congress on March 5, 1792. This act gave the President the power to raise at his discretion a "squadron" of dragoons to serve for three years. The squadron, commanded by a major, was to be made up of four companies; each company to consist of one captain, one lieutenant, one cornet (2nd lieutenant), six sergeants, six corporals, one farrier, one saddler, one trumpeter and sixty-five dragoons.[12] The pay did little to aid recruiting, considering the fact that the trooper not only had to take care of himself and his arms but also his horse and its equipage and trappings. The major, commanding the squadron, received $55 per month; captains, $40; lieutenants, $26; cornets, $20; sergeants, $6; corporals, $5; trumpeters, $4; and privates, $3 per month. Farriers and saddlers were often civilians under contract at the lowest going wage.[13] This unit was activated at Pittsburg, Pennsylvania, in the summer of 1793, and was commanded by a Major William Winston of Virginia. The squadron fought at Fort Recovery and at Fallen Timbers with "Mad Anthony" Wayne in 1794. One of its officers, Cornet Daniel Torrey, was killed defending Fort Recovery. Torrey was the first United States cavalry officer to die in battle.[14] The most effective mounted unit at Fallen Timbers was a force of 1,400 militia horsemen from the

---

[11] Wormser, p. 38.
[12] Brackett, p. 14.
[13] Ibid.
[14] Ibid., p. 15

frontier armed with knives and rifles. They chased Chief Little Turtle and his Miamis through the fallen trees with knives and clubbed guns.[15] This would have been one instance where the saber could have been effectively used against Indians.

The squadron authorized in 1792 was de-activated, except for two small companies, during 1795 and 1796 when its three year term of service expired. On July 16, 1798, during the Quasi-War with France, a concerned Congress approved six troops of light dragoons, which, with the two from the 1792 authorization, formed a small regiment. The "new" six troops, by legislation, were to exist only as long as we had "differences" with France. On March 2, 1799, while still sparring with our ally of the Revolution, Congress authorized three more regiments of cavalry. However, these three regiments were only partially recruited. In May 1800, after our problems with France had been settled, all mounted troops raised during the emergency were disbanded, leaving only the two original companies, authorized in March, 1792. In March, 1802, when Jefferson was President these two dragoon companies were legislated out of service, leaving the nation without a mounted service for the next six years.[16]

On the 12th of April, 1808, Congress authorized a regiment of light dragoons comprised of eight troops. These troops were to serve as infantry until mounted. Wade Hampton of South Carolina, father of the Confederate general by the same name, was appointed colonel of this dismounted-mounted regiment. Hampton's command was the only semblance of a "ready" cavalry unit in the United States Army when the War of 1812 was declared and it was more foot than horse. Congress, on January 11, 1812, added a second light dragoon regiment of twelve companies to the army. However, it was not recruited for service until after the war commenced in June.[17]

During the early part of the second war with Great Britain the two dragoon regiments saw little action and on March 30, 1814, they were consolidated into one regiment. This regiment was comprised of eight troops, each troop to consist of five officers and 116 enlisted men. Colonel James Burns of the dragoon regiment authorized January, 1812, commanded the new

[15] Wormser, p. 37
[16] Brackett, pp. 20-21
[17] Ibid., p. 23.

consolidated regiment.[18] A squadron (three companies) of this regiment served with some distinction at the battles of Chippewa and Lundy's Lane in 1814, but the regiment was not employed otherwise during the war.

Several volunteer mounted units were raised during the War of 1812 but were used sparingly, fighting only effectively at the battles of the Thames and Horseshoe Bend.[19] In the former engagement, Colonel Richard W. Johnson, later Vice-President of the United States, with some 1,000 mounted Kentuckians in a gallant charge drove the British under Colonel Proctor and the Indians under Tecumseh from the field. Johnson's mounted frontiersmen, armed with knives and rifles, were dressed in hunting shirts fringed with red, and wore round hats with long plumes of white tipped with red. The Indians thought that they were safe when they retreated into the brush, and with ordinary cavalry they would have been, but the howling Kentuckians, following closely, leaped from their horses and did fearful execution with their long hunting knives. Johnson's men referred to this technique as a "stab-and-scalp" attack.[20] It is not surprising that such a tactic was never included in a cavalry training manual — perhaps it should have been. Brackett calls the charge of Johnson's mounted militia at the Thames "the only movement worthy the name of a cavalry charge" that occurred during the War of 1812.[21]

At the battle of Horseshoe Bend, March 28, 1814, General Jackson with a mixed force of regular and volunteer infantry and a volunteer cavalry regiment under General John Coffee attacked the Creek stronghold on the Tallapoosa River in northern Alabama. Under their chief Weatherford, some 800 Creeks had fortified a strong position on the Horseshoe Bend of the river. General Coffee and his 700 mounted volunteers, plus 600 friendly Cherokees, cut off the Creek retreat north of the river bend. Meanwhile, Jackson, and the foot troops with the 39th U.S. Infantry Regiment in the center, broke through the breastworks and slaughtered the defenders, giving no quarter. General Coffee remarked, "The slaughter was greater than we had ever done

---

[18] Ibid., p. 32.
[19] Kerr, pp. 20-21
[20] Wormser, p. 39; Merrill, p. 8
[21] Brackett, p. 25

before," 557 dead bodies were counted within the Creek breast-works.[22] Coffee's cavalry had effectively blocked any avenue of escape for Chief Weatherford and his braves. Sam Houston, an ensign in the 39th Infantry, was wounded seriously, with an arrow in the thigh and a musket ball in the shoulder.

Outside of the few instances noted the regular mounted arm was of little use during the War, and on June 15, 1815, Congress disbanded the dragoon regiment. The army once again was without a mounted unit. It would not be until the summer of 1832, when Andrew Jackson was president, that the horse soldiers would again become a part of the national military establishment.

The United States Cavalry as a permanent part of the army dates from the authorization by Congress on June 15, 1832 of a battalion of "Mounted Rangers" to guard the frontier and serve in the Blackhawk War.[23] The battalion, commanded by Major Henry Dodge, was composed of six companies. Dodge's Battalion was an elite unit. The men enlisted for only a year and were paid $1 per day. This was more than a 1st Sergeant in the army received.[24] One of the company commanders of the Rangers was Nathan Boone, son of Daniel Boone. The battalion saw only limited service on the frontier as the Blackhawk War was over soon after it started. The United States Rangers were merged into the 1st Regiment of Dragoons, authorized by a Congressional Act of March 2, 1833.[25]

The 1st Dragoon Regiment was established "for duty on the frontier to cope with the mounted Indians of the Great Plains."[26] According to Price, "with the activation of this mounted regiment a system of promotion was established and a career was opened to officers with a reasonable certainty of retaining their position and by faithful services gaining increased rank with advancing

---

22 Henry Adams. The War of 1812. Washington: The Infantry Journal, 1944. pp. 126-27.
23 The term "Ranger" was probably used to overcome the aversion of the public to professional mounted soldiers. A Ranger has generally been looked upon as a civilian cavalryman who furnished his own horse and equipment and who returned to civilian life after short emergency service.
24 Wormser, p. 44
25 Brackett, pp. 34-35. The reason for disbanding the Rangers and establishing a dragoon regiment to replace it was probably due to the cost factor. Secretary of War Lewis Cass, in his annual Report for 1832, pointed out the folly of a one year enlistment and the fact that the "cost of the Rangers was $150,000 annually greater than a regular dragoon regiment." Merrill, p. 17.
26 Kerr, p. 24

years."[27] The 1st Dragoons were organized at Jefferson Barracks. Dodge was made colonel of the regiment, and Stephen Watts Kearny, lieutenant colonel. Several of the officers of the new regiment came from the old Mounted Rangers, including Nathan Boone, the rest of the officers transferred in from infantry and artillery units. Recruitment was slow and by the spring of 1834, the Regiment was still far short of authorized strength.[28] Nevertheless, during the summer of 1834, Colonel Dodge led the dragoons on their first expedition into Indian country. It was a near disaster, after eighty miles most of the column had to turn back. The weather was hot, up to 114°, too hot for the heavy uniforms, most of the horses had the heat staggers, and many of the men were sick from fever, dysentery and sunstroke. Dodge, with 200 of his dragoons, pressed on and succeeded in stopping the Kiowa-Osage War, which was his primary objective.[29] After this initial expedition, the 1st Dragoons were employed in the West. The Regiment made several marches through Indian country toward the Rockies and as far southwest as the Red River prior to their service in the Mexican War.

The 2nd Dragoons Regiment was authorized by Congress May 23, 1836. This regiment came into being partly because of the Texas-Mexican trouble but more so because of the Seminole uprising in Florida. The 2nd Dragoons were organized and recruited at Jefferson Barracks, during the summer of 1836. The Seminole affair blossomed into a full scale war in mid-1836, so the 2nd Dragoons were sent to Florida where they remained for several years among the swamps, live-oak trees, and mangrove bushes chasing the illusive Osceola. Swamps and tropical vegetation were not suited for horsemen and the dragoons served primarily as escorts, scouts or messengers.[30] David E. Twiggs, who transferred from the 4th Infantry into the 2nd Dragoons was colonel of the Regiment and William S. Harney was the lieutenant-colonel.[31] According to Brackett, the 2nd Dragoons had "more dash" than the 1st Dragoons, but the latter had "a steadiness of purpose and a determination [which had] made many an enemy

---

[27] George F. Price. **Across The Continent With The Fifth Cavalry.** New York: Antiquarian Press, 1959, reprint, p. 13. Hereafter referred to as **Price.**
[28] **Wormser,** p. 45; **Brackett,** pp. 35-36.
[29] **Wormser,** pp. 47-48.
[30] **Ibid.,** p. 58.
[31] **Brackett,** pp. 37-38.

quail on many a field."[32] Following the Seminole War, Congress did an unkind thing to the 2nd Dragoons: the legislators dismounted the horse soldiers and forced them to serve as riflemen. The act was passed on August 23, 1842 to take effect March 4 of the next year. This ill-advised economy act was rectified in 1844 when Congress returned the horses to the dragoons.[33]

From 1842 until the war with Mexico, the mounted arm was free from war fare. During this period, the dragoon regiments were employed primarily in building forts and encampments along the frontier and conducting expeditions and reconnaisance operations from Fort Snelling (Minnesota Territory) in the North to Fort Jessup (Louisiana) in the South and westward as far as the foothills of the Rockies.[34] The most ambitious of these undertakings being Kearny's Expedition to the Oregon Territory in the summer of 1844. With five companies of the 1st Dragoons, Kearny rode northwest from Fort Leavenworth to provide a show of force in the Oregon Territory then disputed by United States and England and to clear hostile Indians from the Oregon Trail. The expedition reached about 300 miles past Fort Laramie, some two-thirds the way across the present state of Wyoming, before it turned back. After ninety-nine days and 2,200 miles, the 250 jaded troopers and horses returned to Fort Leavenworth. A peace treaty with the Teton Sioux was the only result of their efforts.[35]

The United States declared war against Mexico on May 13, 1846. During this conflict Congress approved two more regular mounted regiments, the Mounted Rifles and the 3rd Dragoons. The former was established by a legislative act passed on May 19, 1846, and the latter regiment was created by an act of February 11, 1847.[36] The Mounted Rifles Regiment was originally established to garrison forts along the Oregon Trail, but the war with Mexico was of greater importance, so the Rifles, after being

---

[32] Ibid., p. 38.
[33] Ibid., p. 46; Wormser, p. 61
[34] In 1841 when the 2nd Dragoons were stationed at Fort Jessup, two companies were trained as lancers, but the innovation did not succeed, as American troopers could never properly master the weapon. These two companies of the 2nd Dragoons were the only two companies in the Regular Army to ever use the lance. Herr. p. 31.
[35] Wormser, p. 63; Merrill, p. 39.
[36] Brackett, pp. 60, 84.

organized, were sent to Mexico.[37] Persifer F. Smith of Louisiana was appointed colonel of the regiment and John C. Fremont of the Topographical Engineers, lieutenant colonel. Fremont, at the time of his appointment was involved in military operations in northern California and never served with the Mounted Rifles.[38] Smith's Regiment was assigned to Scott's Army and participated in the successful drive on Mexico City, particularly distinguishing itself at Cerro Gordo, April 17-18, 1847, and at Mexico City on September 13. The Mounted Rifle Regiment was retained in the regular service after the war.

The 3rd Dragoon Regiment, as stated in its activation order, was raised only for the war with Mexico.[39] Edward G.W. Butler of Louisiana, a West Point graduate, Class of 1820, was appointed colonel of the regiment and Thomas P. Moore of Kentucky, the lieutenant colonel. The 3rd Dragoon Regiment saw only limited action in Mexico. It joined Scott as his army was nearing Mexico City; one company of the regiment was engaged at Churumbusco on August 20, 1847, and part of another company fought at Molino del Rey on September 8.[40] The Regiment disbanded shortly after the Treaty of Guadalupe Hidalgo ending the war was ratified in mid-1848. The 3rd Dragoon's greatest claim to fame were its two politically important majors, William Polk, brother of the President and Lewis Cass, Jr., son of the former governor of the Michigan Territory and later senator from Michigan.[41]

The 1st and 2nd Dragoons played important reconnaissance roles in the Mexican War and both were committed to minor combat actions on numerous occasions. Five of the companies of the 1st Dragoons rode with General Stephen W. Kearny's Army of the West from Fort Leavenworth to Santa Fe, and two companies continued on with him to California in the conquest of that Mexican province. Other companies of the 1st Dragoons fought with Zachary Taylor's Army along the Rio Grande in North Mexico and

---

[37] Herr, p. 29; Unfortunately, most of the horses of the regiment were lost in a shipwreck in the Gulf of Mexico, so, except for two companies that were mounted, the rest of the Rifles served in Mexico as infantrymen. Brackett. p. 60.
[38] Ibid.
[39] Ibid. p. 84
[40] Ibid. pp. 95, 98. On the march from the seacoast to join Scott's Army the regiment performed well at a small engagement at National Bridge against Mexican irregulars. Ibid., pp. 90-91.
[41] Ibid. pp. 84-85.

then later with Winfield Scott's Army in Central Mexico. Companies of the 2nd Dragoons were equally scattered, riding first with John Wool's Army in northwestern Mexico and then fighting later with both Taylor and Scott's Armies. The two Dragoon regiments were present at most of the major battles fought during General Scott's drive from Vera Cruz to Mexico City during the spring and summer of 1847. Both the 1st and 2nd Dragoons fought at Contreras and Churumbusco on August 19 and 20, and the 2nd Dragoons did yeoman work at the bloody battle of Molino del Rey, on the outskirts of Mexico City.[42] Too, several companies of both the 1st and 2nd Dragoons fought with Zachary Taylor's Army at the battle of Buena Vista, February 22-23, 1847.[43]

Seven mounted volunteer regiments saw service in the Mexican War. When the President called for twelve months volunteers, mounted militia regiments were raised by five states for the war. Kentucky sent one regiment of cavalry under Colonel Humphrey Marshall and Tennessee another commanded by Colonel Jonas E. Thomas. Missouri supplied two, the 1st Missouri Mounted Volunteer Regiment under Colonel Alexander W. Doniphan and the 2nd Missouri under Colonel Sterling Price. Arkansas raised a cavalry regiment under Colonel Archibald Yell, and Texas organized two mounted volunteer cavalry regiments, one from East Texas commanded by Colonel George T. Wood, Governor of the State, and another from the Texas frontier under Colonel John C. "Coffee Jack" Hays.[44] Several of these volunteer cavalry regiments saw much service, particularly Coffee Jack Hays' Texans who fought at Monterey with Zachary Taylor and then later with Winfield Scott on his conquest of Mexico City.

Undoubtedly, the two most spectacular feats performed by the mounted arm during the Mexican War were General Stephen W. Kearny's 2,000 mile march from Fort Leavenworth, Kansas, to California and Colonel Alexander W. Doniphan's 2,500 mile ride from Fort Leavenworth via Chihuahua City to Buena Vista, Mexico. These were two of the most extraordinary marches in modern military history. Kearny, commander of the Army of the West, comprised of some 1,700 men, left Fort Leavenworth in

[42] Ibid., pp. 85-100.
[43] Ibid., pp. 81-83.
[44] Ibid., p. 60.

late June, 1846. His initial objective was Santa Fe, ancient northern outpost of Mexico. The city was taken on August 18, without a fight.[45] After resting and refitting and a reconnaissance of the regions down the Rio Grande, Kearny set out for California. He left Santa Fe in mid-September with two companies of the 1st Dragoons. The Dragoons, mounted mostly on mules, rode through the desert wasteland of what is today the southern part of New Mexico and Arizona. Hunger, thirst and the loss of mounts made the march miserable. Kearny's exhausted force in rags and half starved, reached California early in December, 1846.[46] As the debilitated dragoons neared San Diego they were attacked by a superior force of Mexican lancers and lariat throwers under General Andres Pico and forced to fight for survival. Kearny's command was finally rescued by a naval contingent sent from San Diego by Commodore Robert F. Stockton.[47] The conquest of California was complete when General Kearny, leading a mixed force of dragoons and sailors, captured Los Angeles on January 10, 1847.

The march of "Doniphan's Thousand" from Santa Fe to Buena Vista in North-Central Mexico was even more remarkable than Kearny's march to the West Coast. Colonel Doniphan and his 1st Missouri Mounted Volunteer Regiment had been a part of the Army of the West and had made the march to Santa Fe from Fort Leavenworth with Kearny. Several weeks after reaching Santa Fe, Doniphan was ordered to march directly south to Chihuahua City, Mexico. Here he was to rendezvous with General John E. Wool's Army of the Center coming down from San Antonio, Texas. Doniphan, whose command consisted primarily of his own regiment, left Valverde, New Mexico, south of Santa Fe in mid-December, 1846. He reached Chihuahua City via El Paso del Norte on March 2, 1847, only to find that there was no American Army there. General Wool, after he had gone as far south as Monclova,

---

[45] Although the capture of Santa Fe was bloodless the march from Fort Leavenworth to the Mexican outpost cost the U.S. Quartermaster-General heavily. It took 1,556 wagons; the services of 459 horses, 3,658 draft mules and 516 pack mules; and 14,904 oxen to transport and maintain Kearny's Army and its reinforcements during the march to Santa Fe. Ex. Doc., 1, Sen., 30th Cong., 1st session, p. 454.
[46] Wormser, pp. 69-74. The men were so hungry that seven dragoons were said to have devoured an entire sheep. Ibid., p. 74
[47] Merrill, pp. 71-74.

had been diverted to Buena Vista to join Taylor's Army.[48] It had been a long 500 mile march through waterless wasteland in hostile country for Doniphan. The march was not without military action, a brisk affair being fought some eighteen miles north of Chihuahua City where the El Paso road crossed the Sacramento River. In a brilliant maneuver, Doniphan out flanked a well built and heavily manned fortification and put to flight the Mexican defenders.[49] The Missouri volunteer cavalry, after occupying Chihuahua City for fifty-nine days, was ordered to join the main American Army near Buena Vista, 600 miles to the southeast. Doniphan left the City on April 28, 1847, and on May 22, after riding through rugged, hostile country, the regiment arrived at General Wool's headquarters at Buena Vista. Five days later, the tattered horse soldiers were reviewed by Zachary Taylor at his headquarters near Monterey. The 1st Missouri Mounted Volunteers then continued on to the Rio Grande, thence by ship to New Orleans and finally back to Missouri.[50] The lean, tanned survivors of the regiment arrived home in early July after a 5,000 mile Odyssey to complete their one year voluntary enlistment. No American cavalry unit, regular or volunteer, had ever performed better.

Even though individual horse units had performed well in all theaters of operation during the Mexican War, neither Scott or Taylor had used the mounted arm to any great extent except for reconnaissance. In battle, even where the terrain was excellent, neither commander committed the horse soldiers to a major action.[51] Only Kearny, in a minor theater of combat, used the cavalry properly in battle and he had little choice at San Pasqual for all he had was cavalry.

With the ratification of the Treaty of Guadalupe Hidalgo in the summer of 1848, the New Mexico Territory and California were transferred to the United States. These vast territorial acquisitions along with the annexation of Texas just prior to the war increased the area of the country by one-third. Much of this

---

[48] Henry, p. 402. When Doniphan entered Chihuahua City he described his force as "rough, ragged and ready." Ibid., p. 235.
[49] Henry, pp. 233-34. This engagement, fought on February 28, 1847, in which one American and some 300 Mexicans were killed is known as the Battle of Sacramento. Ibid., pp. 234-35.
[50] Ibid., pp. 236-37.
[51] Merrill, p. 76.

was wild territory inhabitated by bands of nomadic unfriendly Indians. With settlements constantly expanding westward, the families of the frontiersmen needed protection as did the wagon trains of emigrants going to California and Oregon. Mounted troops were the only force that could cope with the hard riding Plains Indians that constantly raided the frontier and harassed the wagon trains.

Both settlers and military officers criticized the government for not increasing the size of the army. Those on the western frontier, in particular, implored Congress for more horse soldiers as the infantry had proven to be next to worthless in combating the mounted Redmen. The *Daily Missouri Democrat* made this crystal clear in an editorial in the early 1850's which read, "As well might we send boys into a cornfield to catch marauding crows with hopes of success as to start footsoldiers in pursuit of Indians."[52] Congress, finally aware of the fact that more and better frontier protection was needed, authorized two additional mounted units in the spring of 1855, the 1st and 2nd U.S. Cavalry Regiments.[53] Both regiments were destined for frontier service, the 1st Cavalry on the Kansas-Nebraska frontier, the 2nd Cavalry on the Southwest frontier in Texas. This is the story of the regiment that rode to Texas.

---

[52] Ibid., p. 76.
[53] As early as the winter of 1855, there had been serious talk within the War Department about merging the regiments of dragoons, mounted riflemen and cavalry into a single mounted corps. However, nothing developed along this line prior to the Civil War. Randy Steffen. **The Horse Soldier, 1776-1943.** Norman (Okla.): University of Oklahoma Press, 1978, Vol. II, p. 67. Hereafter referred to as **Steffen.**

CHAPTER TWO

"JEFF DAVIS'S OWN"

The Second Cavalry was a cadre regiment that supplied more officers to high command than any other in military history, and it would be the most striking of coincidences if it had not been planned by Jefferson Davis. [1]

General Winfield Scott, Senator James Shields of Illinois, Secretary of War Jefferson Davis and President Franklin Pierce all played a part in establishing the 2nd U.S. Cavalry Regiment, with Davis playing the key role. Winfield Scott, commanding general of the United States Army, included in his lengthy "Report of Operations" for the year 1853, a request that the Army be substantially increased in order to better protect the country's vast frontiers. He requested that at least four regiments, two mounted and two foot, be added to the regular service. [2] Although "Old Fuss and Feathers" never attached much importance to the mounted arm during his campaigns, he frequently commended their valuable service. Secretary Davis, in his "Annual Report" to Congress in 1853, concurred in General Scott's request for an increase in the regular establishment although differing with the General somewhat on its composition. [3] A parsimonious Congress, however, failed to act on the Secretary's recommendation. Although the lawmakers discussed the augmentation at some length, they took no action.

Davis, in his "Annual Report" of the following year (1854), specifically requested that Congress authorize an addition of four regiments, two mounted and two foot, to the regular service thus echoing Scott's sentiments of the previous year. Davis also included in his report an estimate of the bleak military situation in Texas, a section of the nation's frontier that was particularly in

---

[1] Richard O'Connor. Thomas: Rock of Chickamauga. New York: Prentice-Hall, Inc., 1948. p. 89. Hereafter cited as O'Connor.

[2] George F. Price, Across the Continent With the Fifth Cavalry. New York: Antiquarian Press, 1959, Reprint. p. 13. Hereafter cited as Price.

[3] "Report of the Secretary of War," Dec. 1, 1853, 33rd Congress, 1st Session, Ex. Doc. No. 1, Washington, D.C.

need of more protection. He estimated "the Indian frontier in Texas to be nearly 2,000 miles, the lines of communication through the Indian country at more than 1,200 miles and the nomadic and predatory Indians at 30,000; while the army in that Department (Texas) was only 2,886 officers and men . . ."[4] The Regular Army at the time was understrength and was comprised of but 13,821 officers and enlisted men assigned to fifteen regiments, three mounted, eight infantry and four artillery.[5] President Pierce, in his "Annual Message" to Congress the same year, recommended that favorable action be taken on Davis' request.[6]

Although the general reaction of the legislators to the President's request for an increase in Army strength was favorable, Congress debated the question with much feeling. General Scott was called before the House Military Affairs Committee and questioned at length on the need for expanding the Army. To the question, "What should be the strength of the Army in view of our extended seaboard, foreign frontiers, and prospective relations with Indian tribes," the old general answered,

> The increase of the strength of the Army as provided for by the bill submitted by the War Department, now under consideration by this Committee, I deem highly necessary. The bill proposes that there shall be two additional regiments of infantry and two regiments of cavalry. This, I consider, is the minimum force that is essential to be added to the Army to protect the frontiers against the hostilities of the Indians, the present force on the frontiers being entirely inadequate for that purpose. In Texas, the Indian hostilities have been more destructive than at other points, principally on account of the small forces stationed in that country. The troops are constantly engaged in encounters with hostile Indians, and the loss of men, when successful, is always in the inverse ratio of our inferior numbers. Hence, the proposed increase, simply in reference to Indian frontiers, seems to be dictated by considerations both of policy and humanity, in order that adequate protection may be afforded to our border inhabitants without a useless sacrifice of our brave detachments. The increase proposed of two regiments of Cavalry, organized like the present force (Dragoons) and characterized by the like zeal

---

[4] Ibid., Dec. 4, 1854, 33rd Congress, 2nd Session, Ex. Doc. No. 1, Washington, D.C.
[5] Emory Upton. The Military Policy of the United States. Washington, D.C. Government Printing Office, 1912. p. 223. Hereafter cited as Upton.
[6] Price. pp. 14-15.

and activity, would, in my opinion, give reasonable protection to our frontiers and overland travels.[7]

The request for an increase in the Army was reported favorably out of committee and went to the floor of the House. Here there was token opposition. No difference of opinion existed in the House in regard to the necessity for the increase but some differences of opinion was expressed as to what form the increase should take. As finally written, the House Bill approved of an augmentation comprised of both regular and volunteer elements. The Army Appropriation Bill for 1855, including the augmentation amendment, passed the House December 7, 1854, and was immediately taken up by the Senate.

In the Senate debate on the augmentation amendment was both long and bitter. The Bill was reported favorably to the floor of the Senate from the Committee on Ways and Means, January 9, 1855. The group in the Upper House who was opposed to the increase in the Regular Army was led by Senators Sam Houston of Texas and Thomas H. Benton of Missouri. Both were outspoken critics of the Regular Army, preferring volunteers raised for short periods of service (like the Texas Rangers), as being safer and less expensive. Benton, in particular, disliked Pierce and Davis and implied that they had some ulterior motive in building up the Regular Army.[8] On January 29, Senator James Shields of Illinois proposed an amendment to the bill authorizing the President to add two regiments of cavalry and two of infantry to the Army.[9] The bill as amended by Shields finally passed the Senate and was reported back to the House on February 2. After a lengthy debate which centered around the "regulars versus volunteers"

---

[7] Ibid., pp. 15-16. The Indians were particularly active on the western frontier just prior to the Civil War. According to the Office of Indian Affairs. Department of the Interior, twenty-two distinct Indian "wars" or disturbances occurred during the decade of the 1850's. Oliver L. Spaulding. The United States Army in War and Peace. New York: G.P. Putnam's Sons, 1937 pp. 230-31. Hereafter cited as Spaulding.

[8] Price., pp. 16-18.

[9] Ibid., p. 16. Shields was one of the most remarkable Irish-Americans of the 19th Century. He fought in three wars: the Blackhawk War (1832), the Mexican War (1846-48), and the Civil War (1861-65), serving as a general in the last two wars. He was the only man to represent three different states in the United States Senate (Illinois, Minnesota and California). Shields also served as Governor of the Oregon Territory. Dictionary of American Biography. Dumas Malone (ed). New York: Charles Scribner's Sons, 1961. Vol. XI. pp. 230-31.

question, the House passed the bill with the Shields' Amendment on March 3, 1855, and the President signed it into law the following day.[10] The two mounted units were designated as the 1st and 2nd Cavalry Regiments and the two foot units as the 9th and 10th Infantry Regiments.

Never before in the United States, during peacetime conditions, had two mounted regiments been authorized at the same time. "Such generosity by Congress," wrote one military historian, "was looked upon as almost a miracle; but the necessities of the country demanded it, and our lawmakers widely acquiesed."[11] The annexation of Texas and the gaining of extensive new territory following the Mexican War demanded increased protection for the thousands of people that poured into the newly acquired areas. Texas alone had "a thousand miles of an international border and an additional thousand miles of Indian frontier" to protect.[12]

The War Department took immediate steps to complete the organization of the new regiments. On March 26, 1855, General Orders No. 4 was issued to the Army which carried into operation the provisions of the Congressional Act of March 4, 1855.[13] Outstanding officers and senior non-commissioned officers were selected from the other regiments of the regular establishment and transferred to the 1st and 2nd Cavalry. The Secretary directed that "Boards of Examination" be convened at the headquarters of the 1st and 2nd Dragoon Regiments and the Mounted Rifles to test the fitness of the young officers appointed directly from civilian life. "The utmost care was taken," wrote Price, "to make the new

---

[10] Price, p. 17. Also included in the Army Appropriations Bill that was signed by President Pierce on March 4, 1855, was another amendment proposed by Senator Shields. The Illinois Senator's second amendment provided a sum of $30,000 to purchase and import "camels and dromedaries" to be employed for military purposes. This interesting experiment involving some seventy-five camels imported into Texas was carried out between 1856-61, and enjoyed considerable success until the Civil War put an end to it. The importation of camels for army use in the Southwest had long been advocated by Jefferson Davis, first as a Senator and later as Secretary of War. Lewis B. Lesley. Uncle Sam's Camels. Cambridge (Mass): Harvard University Press, 1929. p. 6.

[11] Albert G. Brackett. History of the United States Cavalry. New York: Argonaut Press, 1965. p. 140. Hereafter cited as Brackett.

[12] W.C. Holden. "Frontier Defense, 1841-1860." West Texas State Historical Association Yearbook. Vol. VI (1930). p. 38. Hereafter cited as Holden.

[13] War Department, Adjutant General's Office, General Orders No. 4, Washington, D.C., March 26, 1855.

regiments creditable in every respect to their patron saint, Secretary Davis, with whom this arm of the service was a favorite."[14]

Davis interpreted the law of March 4, 1855, as giving him the authority to raise and maintain the two regiments of cavalry as a separate arm of the service, just as the Dragoons and Mounted Rifles were maintained as separate arms. This permitted him to staff the 2nd Cavalry on the merit system rather than the time worn seniority system that plagued the Regular Army. Thus Davis could select the best men in and out of the service, regardless of seniority, and, as Brackett wrote, "could secure promotions for his favorite officers;"[15] Davis proceeded to do both.

By design, or as O'Connor wrote, "by a striking coincidence,"[16] the 2nd Cavalry was staffed primarily with officers born in Southern states, the majority of whom were graduates of West Point. The fact that Jefferson Davis was a Southerner and a West Point graduate,[17] and played the major role in selecting the officers of the 2nd Cavalry the Regiment became popularly known as, "Jeff Davis's Own." It has long been argued among military historians as to whether or not Davis purposely assigned to the 2nd Cavalry outstanding officers of Southern birth and trained at West Point. Those who support this theory contend that the Secretary of War saw the coming conflict and visualized the officers of the Regiment being used as a cadre for a future Southern army.[18] George H. Thomas, a major in the 2nd Cavalry and a Federal general during the Civil War, was one of those who enter-

---

[14] Price. pp. 21-22. Davis spent the last two years of his abbreviated Regular Army career (1828-35) as a 1st lieutenant in the 1st Dragoons. William H. Powell. List of Officers of the Army of the United States From 1779 to 1900. New York: L.R. Hamersly & Co., 1900. p. 274. Hereafter cited as Powell.

[15] Brackett, p. 160.

[16] O'Connor, p. 89.

[17] Davis was born in Kentucky, grew up in Mississippi and was graduated from the United States Military Academy in the Class of 1828. Register of Graduates and Former Graduates, United States Military Academy, 1802-1946. New York: The West Point Alumni Foundation, Inc. 1946. p. 123. Hereafter cited as Register of Graduates.

[18] While Davis was organizing the 2nd Cavalry in 1855 the country was in the midst of a bitter sectional dispute over the Kansas Territory. The Kansas-Nebraska Act of 1854, promoted the theory of "popular sovereignty" allowing both the freeholders and the slaveholders to settle the Territory. The result was "Bleeding Kansas" where Americans, from North and South, fought each for the control of the Kansas Territory. This guerilla warfare lasted for ten years, through the Civil War. It would not be too far fetched to say that the American Civil War actually started in Kansas in 1855.

tained this opinion. "Thomas," one of his biographers wrote, "always believed that Mr. Davis had regard to a probable war between the Northern and Southern states in organizing that regiment (2nd Cavalry)."[19] Thomas, a Virginian, was one of the few Southern officers in the Regiment who did not resign his commission in 1861.

Davis, in his autobiography, states that in selecting the officers from the Regular Army he was assisted by Colonel Samuel Cooper, the Adjutant-General. "When the first list [of officers to be transferred to the 1st and 2nd Cavalry Regiments] was made out to be submitted to the President," Davis wrote,

> A difficulty was found to exist, which had not occurred either to Colonel Cooper or myself. This was, that the officers selected purely on their military record did not constitute a roster conforming to that distribution among the different states, which, for political consideration, it was thought desirable to observe — that is to say, the number of such officers of Southern birth was found to be disproportionately great. Under instructions from the President, the list was, therefore, revised and modified in accordance with this new element of geographical distribution.[20]

Apparently the first list of officers for the 2nd Cavalry was comprised almost wholly of Southern officers, for after complying with the President's request the Regiment still contained a "disproportionate" number of Southerners. This was particularly true in the higher ranks as the colonel, lieutenant-colonel and both majors of the Regiment were from the South as well as the two ranking captains, and all of them were graduates of West Point.

Not having knowledge of the original list of officers submitted by the Secretary for the President's approval it is impossible to determine the changes that Davis made to comply with Pierce's request. One must conclude, however, after examining the rosters of the two regiments that most of the changes must have been made in the proposed list of officers for the 1st Cavalry. The 1st Cavalry Regiment was by far the more balanced geographically of the two; in fact it was comprised of more officers born in the

---

[19] Thomas B. Van Horne. The Life of Major-General George H. Thomas, New York: Charles Scribner's & Sons, 1882. p. 13. Hereafter cited as Van Horne.
[20] Jefferson Davis. The Rise and Fall of the Confederate Government. New York: Thomas Yoseloff, 1958 (re-print). p. 24. Hereafter cited as Davis.

North than in the South, especially those filling higher ranks.[21]

Davis' background as a professional soldier, Southern states-man and leader of the Confederate States is well known. Colonel Samuel Cooper, the man who helped compile the list of officers selected for the 2nd Cavalry, is not so well known. Cooper, a West Point graduate of 1815, resigned his commission in 1861, and joined the Confederacy. Although from New York, Cooper had married the sister of Senator James M. Mason of Virginia and thereafter identified himself with the Old Dominion State. Davis, as the Confederate President, made Cooper the ranking officer in the Southern Army and appointed him the Adjutant and Inspector-General, a position that Cooper held throughout the war.[22]

Whether by design or by "striking coincidences," the facts show that the 2nd U.S. Cavalry Regiment was staffed with a dis-proportionate number of officers born in Southern states. The majority of these Southerners were graduated from West Point and most of them proved to be outstanding soldiers. Rupert Richardson, succinctly expressed the opinion of other military historians when he wrote, "the officer's corps of the Regiment [2nd Cavalry] consisted of the greatest aggregation of fighting men that ever represented the United States Army in the Old West."[23] Of the thirty-four officers who were initially assigned to the Regi-ment or who joined it at Jefferson Barracks prior to its march to Texas, twenty-four were from Southern states, and twenty of these were West Point graduates. Sixteen of the thirty-four officers became general officers, eleven in the Southern Army. Of these eleven, four became full generals in the Confederate Army, thus supplying Davis with one-half of his full generals.[24] One Southern-er of great promise, George H. Thomas of Virginia, the junior major of the Regiment, as noted previously did not resign his

[21] The field grade officers of the 1st Cavalry were: Col. Edwin V. Sumner (Mass), Lt-Colonel Joseph E. Johnston (Va.), Maj. William H. Emory (Md), and Maj. John Sedgewick (Conn.). The four senior captains, in order of rank were: Delos B. Sackett (N.Y.), Thomas J. Wood (Ky), George B. McClellan (Pa.), and Samuel D. Sturgis (Pa.). Thus, of the eight ranking officers in the 1st Cavalry, five were from the North, one from a Southern state, and two from border states. Brackett. pp. 141-44.
[22] Ezra J. Warner. Generals in Gray. Baton Rouge: Louisiana State Univer-sity Press, 1959. p. 62. Hereafter referred to as Warner.
[23] Rupert N. Richardson. Texas: The Lone Star State. Englewood Cliffs, N.J.: Prentice Hall, Inc., 1958, p. 151. Cited hereafter as Richardson.
[24] Albert Sidney Johnston, Robert E. Lee, E. Kirby Smith, and John Bell Hood.

commission as probably expected. Thomas remained with the Federal Army during the Civil War, was promoted to major-general, and earned fame as the "Rock of Chickamauga." Besides Thomas, Lieutenants William B. Royall, William P. Chambliss and James E. Harrison [who joined the Regiment in June of 1856] were the only officers of the 2nd Cavalry born in a seceding state who remained in the Federal Army during the Civil War. It is interesting to note that all four of these officers were born in Virginia.

Major Albert Sidney Johnston, a Kentuckian by birth but a Texan by choice, a paymaster in the Army, a West Point graduate, Class of 1826; Texas Ranger, and a former Secretary of War for the Republic of Texas was appointed the Colonel of the Regiment. Johnston was a logical and a fine choice. It was almost a surety that the 2nd Cavalry would be assigned to the Texas frontier; therefore, Texas state officials and Federal congressional members from the Lone Star State were consulted on the appointment of the regimental commander. Johnston was the unanimous choice of the Texas State Legislature, the choice of Governor E.M. Pease, Lieutenant Governor David C. Dickson, and U.S. Senator T.J. Rusk.[25] Other considerations in Johnston's favor were his friendship with both Davis and Pierce, particularly the former,[26] and the fact that his current assignment was paymaster for the "middle Federal forts" on the Texas frontier.[27] No one knew the

---

[25] Price. p. 26; William Preston Johnston. The Life of Albert Sidney Johnston. New York: D. Appleton & Co., 1879. pp. 184-85. Cited hereafter as Johnston.

[26] According to one of Davis's biographies, Johnston was Jefferson Davis's "college day idol." Hudson Strode. Jefferson Davis; American Patriot, 1808-1861. New York: Harcourt, Brace & Co., p. 274. The Secretary of War and Albert Sidney Johnston had met previously on several occasions. Their careers at West Point had overlapped, Johnston graduating with the Class of 1826, and Davis two years later. Both were stationed at Jefferson Barracks in the early 1830's and fought in the Blackhawk War, Davis with the 1st Infantry and Johnston with the 6th Infantry Regiment. At Monterrey during the Mexican War they had been associated in negotiating surrender terms for the city, Davis as colonel of the 1st Misissippi Rifles and Johnston as colonel of the 1st Texas Rifles. Powell., pp. 274-401; Register of Graduates, pp. 121-123; and Charles P. Roland and Richard C. Robbins (eds.). "The Diary of Eliza (Mrs. Albert Sidney) Johnston. SWHQ. Vol. 60, No. 4 (April 1957), p. 464. Cited hereafter as Eliza Johnston.

[27] Johnston's duties as paymaster involved the paying of troops at Forts Groghan, McKavett, Chadbourne, Phantom Hill, Belknap, Fort Worth, Graham and Gates on a 620 mile circuit every two months. Each of these circuits took about one month. His duties also took him to New Orleans

Texas frontier better than Johnston and he was an excellent soldier with a fine military record.

Ben McCulloch, the famous Texas Ranger, desired the colonelcy of the 2nd Cavalry and several of his influential friends promoted his cause to no avail. As a consolation prize McCulloch was offered a major's commission in the 1st Cavalry. This was a high compliment, for he was the only field officer in both cavalry regiments to be selected from civilian life. Unfortunately, McCulloch's pride was hurt when he failed to secure the higher rank, and he refused the major's commission. However, he had the generosity to admit long before his death at Pea Ridge (March 7, 1862), that Davis had acted wisely in preferring Johnston for the top command.[28]

Robert E. Lee, with whom Davis had become well acquainted when the Virginian was the Superintendent of the United States Military Academy (1852-1855), was selected as the lieutenant-colonel of the 2nd Cavalry. This was a promotion for Lee, as it had been for Johnston. The son of "Light Horse Harry" Lee of Revolutionary War fame held only the brevet rank of lieutenant-colonel when he was at West Point. Lee was a Southerner; a West Point Graduate, Class of 1829, and had achieved a brilliant record during the Mexican War as one of Scott's engineering officers. Scott, seeing the list of officers recommended for assignment to the 2nd Cavalry, thought that Johnston's and Lee's positions should have been reversed.[29]

The two majors selected for new elite regiment were William J. Hardee from Georgia and William H. Emory of Maryland. Emory, however never served with the 2nd Cavalry, he was transferred to the 1st Cavalry, May 26, 1855, and was replaced by a Virginian, George H. Thomas.[30] Hardee, the senior or ranking

---

three times a year to receive the money for the payroll. Charles C. Roland. **Albert Sidney Johnston, Soldier of Three Republics.** Austin: University of Texas Press, 1964, p. 157. Hereafter cited as **Roland**; Craig C. Watson (ed.). **The Johnston Journal**, Newsletter, Albert Sidney Johnston Camp No. 57, Houston, Texas, April, 1979.

[28] Johnston. p. 185.

[29] Ibid. This was natural as Scott knew Lee much better than he did Johnston, Lee having been a member of Scott's "Little Cabinet" during the Mexican War. In 1858 Scott referred to Lee as "The very best soldier that I ever saw in the field." Douglas S. Freeman. R.E. Lee. New York: Charles Scribner's Sons, 1934. Vol. I, pp. 294-295. Hereafter cited as **Freeman, R. E. Lee.**

[30] Braxton Bragg, from North Carolina, a senior captain in the 3rd Artillery Regiment had been offered Emory's vacancy first. However, Bragg, declin-

major of the Regiment had graduated from West Point with the Class of 1838; Thomas had graduated two years later. Hardee had transferred to the Regiment from the 2nd Dragoons and Thomas from the 3rd Artillery Regiment.[31] Thus all of the field grade officers of "Jeff Davis's Own" were Southerners and graduates of West Point.

Of the company commanders, half or five of them were from states south of the Mason-Dixon Line or extension west of the Line. These were: Captains Earl Van Dorn (Mississippi), Edmund Kirby Smith (Florida), Theodore O'Hara (Kentucky), William R. Bradfute (Tennessee), and Charles E. Travis (Texas). The remaining company commanders were: Captains James Oakes (Pennsylvania), Innis N. Palmer (New York), George Stoneman, Jr. (New York), Albert G. Brackett (Indiana), and Charles J. Whiting (Maine). Six of the ten company commanders were graduates of the United States Military Academy — Van Dorn, Smith, Oakes, Palmer, Stoneman, and Whiting.[32] Fourteen of the twenty lieutenants originally assigned to the Regiment were either appointed from Southern states or from border states. Ten of the lieutenants, the five ranking 1st and 2nd lieutenants, were graduates of West Point. At least two of the company grade officers assigned to the Regiment had illustrious forebears; Captain Charles. E. Travis, Company H, was the son of Colonel William B. Travis, commander at the Alamo, and 2nd Lieutenant Robert C. "Bud" Wood, Jr., Company B, was the grandson of General and later President Zachary Taylor. Wood, who had entered West Point in 1854, resigned from the Academy to accept a 2nd lieutenantcy in the 2nd Cavalry.[33]

Of the thirty-four officers first appointed to the Regiment, twenty-four were from Southern states or border slave states and could reasonably be expected to fight with the South in the event

---

ed the appointment as he had plans to leave the service and recommended that Captain George Thomas of the same regiment be given the appointment. Price. pp. 27-28.

[31] Powell, pp. 301, 355, 626. Thomas was the lowest ranking captain in the Artillery when he was appointed a major in the 2nd Cavalry. Van Horn. p. 12.

[32] Register of Graduates. Indexed by name; Richard W. Johnson. A Soldier's Reminisces in Peace and War. Philadelphia: J.B. Lippincott, 1886. p. 89. Hereafter cited as Johnson.

[33] Joseph H. Parks. General Edmund Kirby Smith. Baton Rouge: Louisiana State University Press. 1962. p. 88. Hereafter cited as Parks.

of war. Twenty of the thirty-four officers were graduates of the U.S. Military Academy. These statistics bear out the fact that the 2nd Cavalry was primarily staffed with men who fit the pattern of Jefferson Davis's concept of an outstanding officer — a man with a good military record, born in the South and a graduate of West Point.

CHAPTER THREE

ORGANIZING THE REGIMENT

*When the officers were not drilling their own
troops, he [Hardee] had officer's drill.
Between drilling their companies, reciting
tactical lessons, or being drilled in the manual
of the sabre and carbine, there was no leisure
time for anyone from reveille to tattoo.*[1]

Regimental Headquarters for the 2nd Cavalry was established
at Louisville, Kentucky on March 26, 1855.[2] Recruiting was to be
conducted under the supervision of the Regimental Commander,
and all officers assigned to the new unit were ordered by letter to
report immediately and to give their current address.[3] Colonel
Johnston, who had to travel from Austin, Texas, did not reach
Louisville until May 28.[4] Lee, who was at Arlington, Virginia,
having the shorter distance to travel, arrived at Louisville on May
20, and took temporary command of the Regiment. This was the
first time in Lee's military career of twenty-six years that he had
direct command of troops.[5]

As the senior officer present, one of Lee's first duties was to
dispatch various regimental officers to recruit troops in specifically
designated cities and areas throughout the country. This was no
easy task as each company was authorized 74 privates, an
aggregate of 740 for the ten companies of the Regiment.[6] Captain

[1] Richard W. Johnson. **A Soldier's Reminiscences in Peace and War.**
Philadelphia: J. B. Lippincott Co., 1866, p. 98. Hereafter cited as **Johnson.**
[2] War Department, General Orders No. 4, Adjutant-General's office,
Washington, D. C., March 26, 1855.
[3] Ibid.
[4] Charles P. Roland. **Albert Sidney Johnston: Soldier of Three Republics.**
Austin: University of Texas Press, 1964, p. 171. Hereafter cited as **Roland.**
[5] Douglas Southall Freeman. **R. E. Lee, A Biography.** New York: Charles
Scribner's Sons, 194--, Vol. I, p. 368. Hereafter cited as **Freeman.**
[6] Upton, p. 223. There were nine non-commissioned officers and two
musicians also authorized each company. Thus a company at full strength,
including the three officers (Captain, 1st and 2nd lieutenants) would be
eighty-eight. Few, if any, companies in the pre-Civil War army were
recruited to full strength.

Earl Van Dorn recruited for Company A at Mobile, Alabama; Lieutenant Walter H. Jenifer for Company B at Winchester, Virginia; Captain James Oakes for Company C in Western Pennsylvania; Captain Innis Palmer for Company D at Baltimore, Maryland; and 1st Lieutenant William P. Chamblis for the same company at Memphis, Tennessee; 1st Lieutenant Robert N. Eagle recruited for Company E at St. Louis, Missouri; Captain Theodore O'Hara for Company F at Louisville, Kentucky; Captain Charles E. Travis for Company H at Evansville, Indiana; Captain Albert G. Brackett for Company I at Logansport, Indiana and Rock Island, Illinois; and 2nd Lieutenant William H. Lowe for Company K at Cincinnati, Ohio. Captain William R. Bradfute, recruiting for Company G, filled his company with enlistees from the Cavalry Depot, surplus recruits from the other companies, and a few that he recruited himself from various parts of the country.[7]

When Johnston arrived at Louisville on May 28, he sent Lee with a small staff to Jefferson Barracks, near St. Louis, Missouri, where the companies were to be organized and trained. When Lee arrived at Jefferson Barracks in mid-June he found that he was in temporary command as the ranking officer. Although the duties of post commander took some of his time, he devoted most of his energy to clothing and drilling the new recruits of the 2nd Cavalry as they straggled in. Lee was particularly provoked when clothing requisitions went unfilled for weeks. He wrote Mrs. Lee on July 1,

> Yesterday at muster, I found one of the late arrivals in a dirty, tattered shirt and pants, with a white hat and shoes, with other garments to match. I asked him why he did not put on clean clothes. He said he had none, I asked him if he could not wash and mend these. He had nothing else to put on. I told him immediately after muster to go down to the river, wash his clothes, and sit on the bank and watch the passing steamboats until they dried, and then mend them. This morning at inspection he looked as proud as possible, stood in the position of a soldier with his little fingers on the seam of his pants, his beaver cocked back, and his toes sticking through his shoes, but his skin and solitary two garments clean. He grinned very happily at my compliment.[8]

Johnston, in the meantime, spent more than a month in Louisville

---

[7] **Price,** p. 29. The Mounted Recruiting Service Depot was located at Carlisle Barracks, Pennsylvania.
[8] Freeman, p. 361.

attending to regimental business and visiting his Kentucky relatives.[9]

On July 9, 1855, Colonel Johnston and Major William J. Hardee of the 2nd Cavalry and two senior officers from the 1st Cavalry Regiment were appointed as members of a Cavalry Equipment Board which convened at Washington. The Board was specifically charged with adopting the uniform and equipment to be used by the two new cavalry regiments. After meeting for several weeks, the Board submitted a report of its recommendations to the Secretary of War who had the results published to the Army as General Orders No. 13, Adjutant General's Office, Washington, D.C., August 15, 1855. By this order, three squadrons (six companies) of the 2nd Cavalry would be armed with the Springfield Rifle Carbine, one squadron (two companies) would be armed with the Removeable Stock Carbine, the barrel of which was to be ten or twelve inches long, "as may be found best by experiment," and the remaining squadron (two companies) would be armed with the breech-loading Perry Carbine. Colt Navy revolvers and dragoon sabers were authorized for each man. One squadron was to be issued gutta-percha or leather scabbards instead of the usual metal scabbards and one squadron was to be issued gutta-percha pistol cases and cartridge boxes instead of the usual leather ones.[10] The saber belt with shoulder strap and carbine sling were to be of black leather instead of the previously used cotton webbing. Four squadrons were to be furnished with the Grimsley saddle and equipment used by the other mounted regiments and one squadron was to be supplied with a modified Campbell saddle and equipment, featuring brass mountings and wooden stirrups.[11]

As stated in General Orders No. 13, the uniform would

---

[9] **Roland,** p. 171.
[10] Webster defines "gutta-percha" as a "rubber like gum produced from the latex of various SE Asia trees."
[11] There was some question about the merits of the Grimsley saddle. Captain Earl Van Dorn remarked, "In every scout or march . . . in which the Grimsley saddle was used, I never failed to have sore backed horses (withers generally) in proportion to distance I have marched over, or the kind of weather that I had to encounter." Colonel Albert Sidney Johnston, on the other hand, praised the Grimsley, blaming the sore backs of the horses on "the ignorance of the soldiers of the proper method of adjustment" of the saddle. **Merrill,** p. 82.

consist of gray trousers, a short blue tunic with yellow trim,[12] brass shoulder scales and a black slouch hat with the brim pinned up on the right side with an eagle [Australian style], and with black ostrich plumes on the left side slanted back from the crown. Three black plumes denoted a field grade officer, two a company grade officer and one an enlisted man. The number of the regiment was pinned to the front of the hat for the officers and the letters of the company for the enlisted men. The hat was commonly referred to as either a "Hardee Hat," or a "Jeff Davis Hat" and was named for the man who designed it and the man who approved it, Major William J. Hardee and Secretary of War Jefferson Davis. A gutta-percha talma or cloak having large, loose sleeves and extending to the knees was adopted for inclement weather, and a woolen great coat was issued for cold weather.[13]

Not all members of the 2nd Cavalry were happy with what the Cavalry Equipment Board approved. Albert B. Brackett, commander of Company I, was one of these. In his book, *History of the United States Cavalry,* Brackett commented on the uniform and equipment of the 2nd Cavalry as follows,

> The cavalry got — God knows where — the "cavalry hat," familiar to the theatre-goers as that worn by Fra Diavalo [a theatrical personality of the day]. If the whole earth had been ransacked, it is difficult to tell where a more ungainly piece of furniture could have been found. It is now [1864] used by the whole army, being somewhat more unwieldy than the original pattern. It seems to me that soldiers take delight in seeing into what ludicrous shapes they can get these hats, with a tassel hanging in front, on one side, in behind, and a black ostrich feather, which, after one or two wettings, has a most bedraggled and wilted appearance.[14]

Brackett also questioned the advisability of arming the new cavalry regiments with the Navy Colt revolver and the saber. The Mounted Rifles Regiment had been armed with the Army Colt which had done good service; the commander of Company I questioned the changing of a side arm that had proven itself. "The

---

[12] The Dragoons wore orange trim and the Mounted Rifles green trim on their uniforms. When the mounted units were all combined into Cavalry in August, 1861, yellow trim was adopted for the mounted arm.
[13] Price, p. 29: War Department, Adjutant-General's Office, General Orders No. 13, Washington, D. C., August 15, 1855. (See Eliza Johnson, p. 470).
[14] Albert G. Brackett. History of the United States Cavalry. New York: Argonaut Press, Ltd., 1965, (re-print), pp. 160-61. Hereafter cited as Brackett.

saber" Brackett wrote, "in Indian fighting is simply a nuisance; they jingle abominably, and are of no earthly use. If a soldier gets close enough to an Indian to use a saber, it is about an even thing as to which goes under first." Of course, Brackett was right on both counts. Adding a new revolver to the ordnance inventory complicated the supply problem and created a new cost factor, and one could perhaps count on one hand the number of Indians killed with the saber during the last half of the 19th century. Arming troopers with the saber was a custom that the cavalry did not discard until the early 1930's.

In early August, Major Hardee, Captain O'Hara and Lieutenant Field were appointed as a board to purchase horses for the Regiment. To make sure that the 2nd Cavalry had the best horses obtainable and to further add to its image as an elite organization, the Board was not restricted to a maximum amount that could be paid for each animal. The three purchasing officers traveled throughout Ohio, Indiana and Kentucky during August and early September to buy the best blood obtainable. Some 850 horses were purchased at an average cost of $150 per horse, an unusually high amount for that time. Consequently, very serviceable mounts were secured, so durable in fact that a large number of the horses survived the brutal five years of field service in Texas and were still with the Regiment when Twiggs surrendered his department to the Texas-Confederates in February, 1861.[15]

Davis not only wanted the 2nd Cavalry to have the best men, the best equipment and the best horses, but he also wanted "his" regiment to have the best appearance.[16] The Secretary of War had decided that each of the ten companies of the Regiment would

---

[15] Price, pp. 30-31. Captain Richard W. Johnson, commander of Company G in 1861, stated that his company had been furnished 85 horses in 1855 and that in the Spring of 1861 forty-four of them were "still serviceable after six years of constant service."

[16] Davis, probably as a result of his West Point training, was always a stickler for appearance, reasoning that appearance helped to promote unit pride. His 1st Mississippi Volunteer Rifle Regiment of the Mexican War wore the most colorful uniforms and was the best equipped regiment in the U.S. Army. The men wore white duck trousers, red long sleeved shirts and black broad brimmed hats and were equipped with the latest model firearm of the day, the "Mississippi Rifle," carried Bowie knives, smoked cheroots and many of the enlisted men were attended by personal body servants. All of the officers and most of the enlisted men were sons of wealthy Mississippi planters. Clement Eaton. **Jefferson Davis,** New York: The Free Press, 1977, pp. 59-60; Hudson Strode. **Jefferson Davis, Patriot,** 1808-1861. New York: Harcourt Brace & Co., 1955, p. 161.

ride horses of the same color. Thus, Hardee, O'Hara and Field were instructed to purchase only gray, sorrel, bay, brown and roan colored horses. The horses were assigned as follows: Company A, grays;[17] Companies B and E, sorrels; Companies C, D, F, and I, bays; Company G and H, browns; and Company K, roans. Neither white nor black horses were purchased as these colors would not blend into the landscape and thus could be sighted more easily by the Indians. These distinctive colors were maintained while the Regiment was stationed in Texas.[18]

The ten companies, as noted previously, were assigned letters, A through K. The letter "J" was purposely omitted, for in the era of handwritten orders and reports, the letters "I" and "J" were easily confused. This alphabetical designation system, of dropping the "J," still exists in today's army. In the old mounted service those troopers who were temporarily without horses were laughingly referred to as being members of "J Company." Each company of the mounted arm carried a pennant called a guidon. It was swallow-tailed in design, the top half of the guidon was red with the company letters in white, while the bottom half was white with the regimental numbers in red.

In early September, headquarters of the 2nd Cavalry was transferred from Louisville to Jefferson Barracks, and at this time the officers who were on recruiting service were ordered to report to their new duty station to be with their companies. Few military posts have played as important a role in United States History as has Jefferson Barracks. The post, named for President Thomas Jefferson, was established during October, 1826, a few months after his death. It was located just south of St. Louis, some twenty miles from the mouth of the Missouri River. The installation first served as the site from which troops could be conveniently distributed to outlying posts throughout the Mississippi Valley. Later, when the 2nd Cavalry was stationed there, it was one of the major military installations in the United States devoted to recruiting and training.[19]

---

[17] Inasmuch as the men of Company A were recruited from Mobile, Alabama and vicinity and rode gray horses, they were known as the "Mobile Grays." Van Dorn's company was the only company in the Regiment to have a distinctive nickname.

[18] Price, p. 31.

[19] Richard E. Mueller, "Jefferson Barracks: The Early Years." **Missouri Historical Review**, Vol. LXVII, No. 1, October, 1972, pp. 1, 13-14. Cited hereafter as **Mueller**. At various times after the Civil War the Barracks

Neither Johnston nor Lee were at Jefferson Barracks when the headquarters contingent arrived. The two senior officers had been assigned to duty on September 24 as members of a General Court-Martial Board being convened at Fort Leavenworth, Kansas Territory.[20] This was not a War Department blunder, assigning the two ranking officers of a new regiment on detached duty at the same time. Based on past experience it would have taken several months to recruit the 750 men needed to fill the regiment, however, with a new regulation in effect increasing the pay, and the prospect of adventure on the frontier with a select cavalry regiment, recruiting progressed rapidly, and by mid-September the regiment was filled.[21]

In the absence of Johnston and Lee, Major Hardee, the next senior officer, was recalled from his assignment of purchasing horses, and assumed temporary command of the Regiment. Hardee, author of the army manual on "Tactics," saw to it that much time was spent in the drilling of the officers and the men. Perhaps it was fortunate that Hardee was in command, for he was a fine drill master and disciplinarian and this was needed to mold a new regiment of raw recruits into shape rapidly for field service. Richard W. Johnson, 1st lieutenant of Company G, wrote that Major Hardee,

> was thorough in his knowledge of the tactics, and seemed to take great delight in teaching others. A position under him was no sinecure, for when the officers were not drilling their own troops he had officer's drill. Between drilling their companies, reciting tactical lessons, or being drilled in the manual of the sabre and carbine, there was no leisure time for anyone from reveille to tattoo.[22]

Lieutenant Johnson, who had been appointed the Regimental Quartermaster when he reported to Colonel Johnston at Louisville on June 12, 1855, assumed the additional duty of Depot Quartermaster when he reached Jefferson Barracks in early September.[23] One of his duties in the latter capacity was to

---

served as an engineer depot, an ordnance depot and a cavalry recruiting depot. The installation was declared surplus in 1946, and is no longer an active army post.

[20] **Johnston**, p. 186; **Freeman**, p. 362.
[21] **Johnston**, p. 186.
[22] **Johnson**, p. 98.
[23] **Ibid.**, pp. 92-3; **Powell**, p. 401.

receive and receipt for the horses shipped to the Regiment by members of the Purchasing Board until the mounts were assigned to companies. Many of the new recruits in the Regiment were Irishmen, the migration of this nationality to America being particularly heavy in the two decades just prior to the Civil War. Johnson riding out to the picket line one day to look over a shipment of horses that had just arrived, noticed two Irish recruits trying to mount one of the new horses. The Lieutenant halted to watch the strange procedure. It appeared that the horse was wild and would not stand long enough to be mounted. The two soldiers covered the horses head with a blanket, tried to mount him and failed. "One of the men" wrote Johnson, "stepped up on the body [trunk] of a large tree, which had been felled, and instructed the other to back the horse up to him; then he would place his hands on the croup [rump] and spring into position. This was successful. The man who held the horse said, "By the Holy Moses, I never saw a man get on the horse that way befoour!" The other replied, "Go way, you fool, I did not get on him 'befoour;' I got on him behind! And so he did."[24]

Colonel Johnston, as could be expected, was bored with court-martial duty and irritated at being absent from his regiment. He wrote to his son on September 29 from Fort Leavenworth,

> I am much annoyed at being absent from my regiment at a time when the presence of every officer is peculiarly needed. It is really bringing form out of chaos to organize a regiment of raw recruits and prepare them for a long march. They have suffered some from cholera and other diseases, which has caused a considerable number to desert. I do not expect desertion to cease while the regiment remains at Jefferson Barracks.[25]

Hardee, anticipating Johnston's anxiety and recognizing the importance of a commander being with a new regiment, had written Johnston three days previously, on September 26, "I need not say that your ... presence [at Jefferson Barracks] is indispensible."[26]

By late September the War Department deemed the Regiment to be fully organized and the officers and men well enough trained in their duties to move into the field. The movement

---

[24] Johnson, p. 96.
[25] Johnston, p. 186. Reference footnote No. 28.
[26] Roland, p. 172.

order, General Orders No. 5, issued from the Headquarters of the Army, New York,[27] dated September 27, 1855, and signed by General Scott, ordered the 2nd Cavalry to Texas. The order in part read,

> The following movement of troops will immediately be made:
>
> 1. The Second Regiment of Cavalry at Jefferson Barracks will proceed, by easy marches across the country, to Fort Belknap, Texas, to be there disposed of by the Commanding General of the Department of Texas, who will make timely arrangements for stationing the regiment on its arrival within his command. The Commanding General of the Department of the West will give the necessary orders for the march of the regiment to Fort Belknap.

Even though the Regiment had been recruited up to an acceptable strength, the horses had been procured and the officers and enlisted men had been properly trained for field service, it would be almost a month before the 2nd Cavalry left Jefferson Barracks. The delay in leaving was caused by several things, the late arrival of arms and accouterments, the lack of wagons and teams, and the fact that the regimental commander was still on duty at Fort Leavenworth. Unfortunately, prolonged garrison duty led to boredom and restlessness, and this resulted in numerous disciplinary problems, the most serious of which was desertion.

During the five months that the Regiment was forming at Jefferson Barracks, 329 men deserted.[28] This great number of desertions was due to a combination of factors. Many of the new privates were recently arrived immigrants from Ireland and

---

[27] Generals Zachary Taylor and Winfield Scott were unfriendly military rivals during the Mexican War. When Taylor was elected President in 1848, Scott commanding general of the army moved Army Headquarters from Washington, D. C. to New York City. When Taylor died in 1850 and Fillmore became President, Scott moved the headquarters back to Washington. When Pierce, no friend of Scott's, was elected President in 1852, Scott moved the headquarters back to New York City. He kept the headquarters in New York City until he retired in 1861, at which time the Army Headquarters returned to Washington, D. C. permanently. Winfield Scott. Memoirs of Lt.-Gen. Winfield Scott, LLD. N.Y., Sheldon & Co., 1864, pp. 586-94.

[28] "Annual Returns of the Alterations and Casualties Incident to the Second Regiment of the U.S. Cavalry, During the Year 1855." Microfilm Copy No. 744, Roll No. 51. National Archives, Washington, D. C. Hereafter cited as "Annual Returns," with the year following.

Germany.[29] Recruited in the East, many of these young, unattached male immigrants were headed for the West and only desired free board and transportation to St. Louis, "the gateway to the West." Once at Jefferson Barracks, only a state away from the frontier, they deserted. Too, discipline was rigid in the pre-Civil War regular army, too strict perhaps for the ordinary American youth of the day. The cholera epidemic probably hastened the departure of a few, and, no doubt, when it was learned that the Regiment was to be assigned to the Texas frontier with its primitive living conditions and Indian problems, many of the recruits had second thoughts about service in the army.

To add to the morale problem, the command was stricken by sickness, in particular ague (a fever of malarial character attended by paroxysms which occur at regular intervals) and cholera. The latter, the dreaded killer of the 19th century, had appeared at Jefferson Barracks on two previous occasions, during 1834 and 1849. In 1849, the epidemic had claimed the lives of two senior officers, Generals Richard B. Mason and William J. Worth.[30] Twenty-two members of the 2nd Cavalry died of cholera during the 1855 epidemic.[31]

Colonel Johnston was relieved of his court-martial duties in early October and joined his Regiment a few days later. As soon as he arrived at Jefferson Barracks he began a system of rigid discipline. His wife, Eliza, who had arrived at the post in mid-October from Kentucky, was a witness to her husband's disciplinary practices. The day after her arrival she saw the "drumming out of the service" of six members of the Regiment. Eliza noted in her diary that the sight both "shocked and distressed" her. First the soldiers had been whipped, then their heads were shaved and finally the six unfortunate men were marched around the garrison to the tune of "Poor Old Soldier." Mrs. Johnston ended her diary entry for the day with the comment, "surely, surely some less degrading mode of punishment can be substituted."[32]

---

[29] During the decade of the 1850's, some 250,000 immigrants arrived in the United States per year. Dexter Perkins & Glyndon Van Deusen. The United States of America: A History, New York: The MacMillan Company, 1962, Vol. I, p. 425.
[30] Roland, p. 172; Mueller, pp. 21, 26.
[31] "Annual Returns," 1855.
[32] Eliza Johnston, p. 467.

If Eliza Johnston was appalled by the punishment meted out by her husband for the major military crime of desertion, she would have been even more distressed had she been at the post when Colonel Stephen W. Kearny commanded Jefferson Barracks in the early 1840's. "Habitual drunkeness" appeared to be the most serious infraction of Army Regulations by Kearny's standards. On one occasion he ordered a noted tipler "to be confined in charge of the guard for nine calendar months: the first and every alternate month afterwards in a cell, on bread and water, the remainder of the time at hard labor with a ball and chain attached to his leg; and to forfeit his pay for the entire period."[33] On another occasion for a like offense, the offender was "to be confined at hard labor in charge of the guard for two years; wearing on his neck an iron yoke with three prongs, six inches long, the whole weighing twelve pounds, and to forfeit his pay for the same period . . . .[34]

Johnston was no doubt pleased with the destination of his Regiment for he would be returning to Texas, his adopted state. While it had been rumored for several months that the Regiment would be going there, the publication of the order confirmed the fact. Johnston, since his days as paymaster for the U. S. Army on the Texas frontier had complained of the Federal government's laxity in protecting the settlers from Indian depredations.[35] Now he would be in charge of defending the frontier.

By October 15, the 2nd Cavalry was ready to move to Texas. However, it lacked one of the basic essentials for a 600 mile march, supply wagons and teams. Such a need had been anticipated by Major Hardee, who had been trying to procure transportation since first being assigned to Jefferson Barracks in August. Although Hardee's days were spent on the parade ground drilling troops, his evenings were spent writing letters to the War Department requisitioning wagons and mules that would be needed for the move to the frontier.[36] His efforts, however, were in vain for when the movement order for the Regiment was received, there were few wagons and mules on hand.

---

[33] Mueller, p. 25.
[34] Ibid.
[35] Roland, p. 173.
[36] Nathaniel Cheairs Hughes, Jr. **General William J. Hardee.** Baton Rouge: Louisiana State University Press, 1965, pp. 53-54. Hereafter cited as Hughes.

Following the receipt of General Orders No. 5, Regimental Quartermaster Lieutenant Richard Johnson immediately made out a requisition for the transportation of the Regiment. Now that the move to Texas was official, the War Department would have to take immediate action. It was Johnson's belief that each company would have to take the authorized supply of clothing, and camp and garrison equipment so he made out his requisitions accordingly. Johnson estimated that it would require 129 six-mule teams for the use of the Regiment and one ambulance to transport any sick that they might have on the march. Colonel Johnston approved the requisition and it was forwarded to the War Department for final approval. Secretary Davis, however, considered Johnson's request excessive and reduced the number of wagons and teams by an even one hundred, approving just twenty-nine.[37]

Davis, in greatly reducing the amount of transportation, no doubt considered the fact that 129 wagons would appreciably slow down the march of the Regiment, and, too, such a large number of wagons and teams would create a surplus of transportation once the 2nd Cavalry reached its destination. The Secretary, for the sake of economy and expediency, ordered that all company property, the surplus baggage of the officers and the company laundresses be sent by water to Indianola, Texas, and then overland to the various duty stations of the Regiment. First Lieutenant Joseph H. McArthur of Company H was assigned the duty of commanding the water contingent.[38]

By late October the twenty-nine wagons with mules and harness were supplied, and the necessary teamsters detached from the various companies. With everything now ready for the move, Colonel Johnston issued orders for the Regiment to ride from Jefferson Barracks on Saturday morning, October 27, 1855.[39]

[37] Johnson, p. 99. Johnson, reflecting on the march to Texas, with rain a constant companion, was happy that his requisition for wagons had been drastically reduced. He estimated that with 129 wagons it would have taken twice as long to make the trip. Ibid., p. 100.

[38] Ibid. Joseph H. McArthur was graduated from West Point with the Class of 1849, and was assigned to the 2nd Infantry. He transferred to the 5th Infantry in 1851, serving with the regiment in Texas until being assigned to the 2nd Cavalry, March 3, 1855. McArthur participated in several campaigns against the Indians in Texas and was promoted to captain in June, 1860. He remained in the Federal army during the Civil War, rose to the rank of major and was retired for disability in November, 1863. Price, pp. 340-43.

[39] Eliza Johnston, p. 467.

CHAPTER FOUR

FROM MISSOURI TO TEXAS

When I recall the hardships, vexations and
annoyances which I had to endure and overcome, I
pity a quartermaster who has to conduct a large
train through a country so much of which is underlaid
with quicksand.[1]

It was an imposing sight, a sight that would have thrilled the likes of film directors John Ford, Raoul Walsh and Howard Hawks to see the 2nd Cavalry ride from Jefferson Barracks on the morning of October 27, 1855. Trumpets sounded "Boots and Saddles" at 4 A.M. and at 6 A.M. the long column — some 700 men, 750 horses, 29 wagons and 5 ambulances — commenced its march.[2] After clearing the post, the column turned west and headed for Fort Belknap, the initial destination of the Regiment in Texas.

The march to Texas, some 650 miles in distance and two months in estimated time, would be in a southwesterly direction through Missouri and over the Ozarks via the towns of Manchester, Waynesville, Lebanon, Springfield, Mt. Vernon, Jollification and Neosho. Then across the northwest tip of Arkansas through Maysville into Indian Territory (present state of Oklahoma) and through Tahlequah, Fort Gibson, Mico, Perryville and Fort Washita. Finally the column would cross the Red River into Texas at Preston and ride through Gainesville and Buffalo Springs to Fort Belknap.[3] The first ten days of the march, some 50 miles, just past Waynesville, Missouri followed the Pacific Railroad Survey conducted by the War Department a few years earlier.[4]

---

[1] Johnson, p. 101. First Lieutenant Richard W. Johnson was the Regimental Quartermaster for the 2nd Cavalry during the Regiment's trek to Texas.
[2] "Returns of the Second Regiment of Cavalry for the month of October, 1855." Microfilm copy No. 744, Roll No. 51. National Archives, Washington, D. C. Hereafter cited as "Returns" with the month and year following.
[3] Eliza Johnston, pp. 468-85.
[4] Ibid., p. 471.

Colonel Johnston and his family did not accompany the 2nd Texas when it left Jefferson Barracks. Eliza, his wife, was ill with malaria and suffered a chill every other day; Saturday, October 27 was her "chill day."[5] With Lieutenant-Colonel Lee still on court-martial duty,[6] Major Hardee led the column when it left for Texas; Johnston and his family joined the Regiment on the evening of the second day (October 29).[7]

A strict order of march was maintained during the journey to Texas. The pioneers, who were responsible for clearing and preparing the route of march, led the column, next came the ambulances transporting the wives and children of those officers who were accompanied by their families. Following the ambulances were the ten companies of troopers in alphabetical order with Captain Earl Van Dorn's "Mobile Grays" leading. Captain Charles J. Whiting's Company K, astride its matched roans, was the last company in the column. It was followed by the supply wagons, and at the end of the column rode the rear guard.[8] Normally when on the march, "Boots and Saddles" was sounded at 4 A.M., breakfast eaten at 5 A.M., and the column started by 6 A.M. There was no stop to prepare lunch; short rest breaks were taken at the commander's discretion; the Regiment bivouacked before dark and supper was eaten "about 6 P.M."[9]

Four officers: Colonel Johnston, Captains James Oakes and Innis Palmer, and 1st Lieutenant Richard Johnson brought their families, slaves and hired servants with them. The four officers had purchased, for the journey of their families to Texas, specially constructed carriage-ambulances. These vehicles were so built that "the seats and their backs, when laid down, formed a good bed upon which to sleep, if the non-arrival of the wagons with the tents made it necessary."[10] The carriage-ambulances were built with springs, so were much easier riding than the ordinary wagons

[5] Ibid., p. 467.
[6] Lee was plagued with court-martial duty during the fall of 1855 and the winter of 1855-56. Following his court-martial duty at Fort Leavenworth he, in turn, was assigned to same duty at Fort Riley (Kansas Territory), Carlisle Barracks, (Pennsylvania) and West Point. He did not join the Regiment until late March, 1856. Freeman, pp. 362-63.
[7] Eliza Johnston, p. 468.
[8] Ibid. The usual procedure for a Regiment on a cross-country march was to either rotate companies on rear guard detail or assign men from certain companies as a permanent rear guard.
[9] Ibid., pp. 468-69.
[10] Johnson, p. 100; Roland, p. 173.

of the day. In the line of march these "family vehicles", as noted previously, were placed immediately behind the pioneers. Here they were arranged according to the rank of the husband in keeping with military protocol, a tradition or custom which oftentimes is much more important to the wife than to the officer.[11]

The Regiment averaged about thirteen miles a day on the march, on several days it made as little as nine miles, but on numerous occasions, particularly when it reached the more level terrain of the Indian Territory, it marched as much as twenty miles a day,[12] a good distance for a regiment of cavalry burdened with twenty-nine wagons. The mules were young and many were unbroken, thus the progress of the wagons was unusually slow. Also, the terrain was mountainous in areas, and the fall and early winter rains bogged down the column on several occasions. "Even so," Quartermaster Johnson reported, "that with but one exception — one day when the teams were completely bogged down in mud, [he] succeeded in getting the wagons to camp sometime during the night."[13] Too, as the column neared its destination in Texas it was slowed by bitter cold weather.

During the sixty days from Jefferson Barracks, Missouri, to Fort Belknap, Texas, there were nine days that the Regiment did not march. Mud stopped the column on November 2 and again on the 16th; on November 18 the Regiment remained in camp "to give the soldiers an opportunity to wash their clothes;"[14] three days, November 29 to December 1, were spent at Fort Gibson and one day, December 3, at Fort Washita; and on both December 23 and the 25th, a Texas norther froze the column in its tracks.[15]

Dry food for the two months' journey was carried in the wagons. Fresh meat was provided by a St. Louis butchering firm under contract to the government. According to Mrs. Johnston, "a few hours before the regiment [left] its night bivouack the butcher [went] ahead with the forage master and Quartermaster, [to] purchase forage, select the camp and have the beef ready by the time that the troops [arrived]"[16] Fresh food was plentiful

---

[11] Eliza Johnston, p. 468.
[12] Eliza Johnston, pp. 471-85.
[13] Johnson, p. 100.
[14] Eliza Johnston, p. 474.
[15] Ibid., pp. 469-85.
[16] Ibid., p. 468.

along the way. Turkeys, chickens, rabbits, butter, eggs, milk, fruits and vegetables could be purchased almost daily during the march through Missouri and the northern part of the Indian Territory. Mrs. Johnston recorded only one instance where a person refused to sell her food. As the column was approaching the town of Jollification, Missouri, so named because of the distillery located there, a farmer on the outskirts of town refused to sell Mrs. Johnston milk "at any price" for her sick daughter.[17] As the column moved deep into Indian Territory fresh food became less plentiful due both to the weather and the lack of farms. On several occasions officers of the Regiment presented Mrs. Johnston with venison and once a partridge.[18] To supplement the food purchased from the local farmers, there were patches of wild berries and nuts along the route of march and near their campsites. On November 19 when the Regiment was camped close to Mt. Vernon in Southwestern Missouri, Mrs. Johnston noted that "within 50 feet around my tent were Grapes, Raspberries, Gooseberries, Blackberries, Walnuts and Hazlenuts."[19] Food was not a problem during the march of the 2nd Cavalry to Texas.[20]

The trek from Missouri to Texas was, in fact, without serious trouble. There were no Indian attacks, buffalo stampedes or extensive prairie fires. However, several unfortunate incidents did occur. Four members of the command died or were killed enroute to or while the Regiment was encamped at Fort Belknap. On the third day out (October 29), a trooper, drunk in the saddle fell from his horse, struck his head on the ground, subsequently died, and was buried alongside the road.[21] A few days later (November 3), a soldier sick with cholera was kicked by a horse and died soon

[17] Ibid., p. 475. Chickens were purchased for from 10¢ to 12-1/2¢ each and a bushel of apples cost 40¢. Ibid., pp. 471, 474.
[18] Ibid., pp. 472, 476.
[19] Ibid., p. 475.
[20] On November 9, Mrs. Johnston wrote in her diary that "we fare quite sumptuously." For dinner that evening the Colonel and his family sat down to a meal consisting of: homemade rolls, venison, eggs, cornbread, fresh butter, potatoes, apples and dried peaches. Ibid., p. 472.
[21] Ibid., p. 468. Johnston had obtained permission from the War Department to allow the sutlers to sell whiskey to the troops during the march to Texas. He hoped that this would prevent the soldiers from buying "bad" whiskey from citizens along the way. The Commander also thought that with spirituous liquor readily available it "would dull the keen sense of desire that otherwise would arise among the soldiers." Roland, p. 177. The soundness of Johnston's theory of having whiskey readily available, is questionable. Of the four deaths recorded on the march, two were charged to whiskey.

thereafter. He was buried in the woods near the route of march in a coffin built by the Regimental carpenter.[22] No other fatality was recorded in the Regiment until December 16, the day after the column crossed into Texas. On this day Captain Van Dorn, commander of Company A, reported to Colonel Johnston that "one drunken soldier had murdered another" in his company.[23] On December 28, while the Regiment was in camp near Fort Belknap, a corporal died who had been sick during the entire journey.[24] A total of four deaths during a two month period, under semi-campaign conditions, and for that time was probably not excessive.

Johnston was beset with the typical problems faced by a military commander. On November 10, while the Regiment was near Lebanon, Missouri, several men of Company F deserted. Lieutenant Nathan G. "Shanks" Evans of that Company was sent in search of them, and although he returned without the men, he managed to bring one of their mounts back.[25]

Several of the soldiers regarded the ride through Missouri as a license for larceny. The State was dotted with well stocked farms, and unauthorized foraging commonly known in military parlance as "moonlight requisitioning" created another of Johnston's headaches. The Regiment had just cleared Jefferson Barracks when the first instance of stealing was reported. A farmer in the vicinity of Manchester reported to the commander that eight of his turkeys had disappeared when the column went by his farm. Johnston ordered the camp searched that night, and three of the birds were recovered. The culprits, probably teamsters, caught with the gobblers were punished by being made to walk instead of ride and to pay for the poultry.[26] Some two weeks later, a farmer living near Springfield, Missouri, complained to Johnston that one of his hogs had been pilfered by a soldier. The Colonel ordered a search of the camp that night, but the hog was not found,[27] probably having been reduced to chops, loins, hams, etc., and scattered among the men long before the inspection. Poultry and pigs, since time immemorial, have been the primary targets of the

[22] Ibid., p. 471.
[23] Ibid., p. 482.
[24] Ibid., p. 485.
[25] Ibid., p. 473.
[26] Ibid., p. 469.
[27] Ibid., p. 474.

moonlight requisitioner, and undoubtedly many a farmer living on or near the route of march did not discover his loss until the column had long passed by and it was thus too late to protest.

However, food was not the only target for the pilferer. On November 16, a soldier, probably a recruit picked up in a city, picked the watch from the pocket of a citizen who was cheering the column as it went by. A complaint to the commander by the victim triggered a search of the ranks. The thief was apprehended with the stolen goods on his person, placed under arrest, and sentenced "to walk on foot in chains."[28]

The contract butchers that the army hired to provide beef for the Regiment while enroute to Texas gave Johnston trouble. On several occasions the butchers had to be reprimanded. As noted previously, it was the practice during the march for the families of the officers to purchase fresh dairy products and fruits and vegetables from citizens along the route. The butchers, who usually preceded the column buying beef, noting this practice of local purchasing by the women, decided to play the role of the middle man and cut themselves in on a lucrative business. They would purchase all the products available from the farmers and then retail the eatables, at a handsome profit, to the officers wives. The outraged ladies reported the practice to Johnston, who cautioned the butchers, with the result that poultry and produce became much cheaper.[29] On December 4, Mrs. Johnston wrote in her diary, "The officers continually have difficulties with our beef contractor,"[30] and one of the butchers was discharged by the commander for "buying corn from the men" on the day that the Regiment left Fort Belknap (December 31).[31] The contract expired, much to Johnston's relief, when the Regiment established its Texas headquarters at Fort Mason in mid-January, 1856.

Other incidents and problems on the march included a siege of distemper among the horses, causing several of the animals to be abandoned. According to Mrs. Johnston, practically all of the horses had a light case of the affliction, and it was thought that they had caught the disease from the horses of the 1st Cavalry

---

[28] Ibid., p. 474. Mrs. Johnston did not record in her diary how long the man had to "walk on foot in chains;" however, the Regiment was still some 350 miles from Fort Belknap.
[29] Ibid., p. 474.
[30] Ibid., p. 479.
[31] Ibid., p. 486.

while both regiments were at Jefferson Barracks.[32] Lieutenant Kenner Garrard of Company K was bitten by a poisonous snake the first day of the march and left in the hands of a local physician. He did not rejoin the column until six days later.[33] On November 11, near Lebanon, Missouri, just after the Regiment went into bivouac for the night, a prairie fire encircled the campsite. The entire regiment turned out with blankets and successfully smothered the flames.[34]

The weather during the 650 mile march was mostly unfavorable. It rained almost daily for the first month,[35] the wagons being completely mired down and unable to move on two occasions. On both November 2 and the 16th, it rained in torrents and the Regiment lay in camp all day. On November 2, Mrs. Johnston reported in her diary that the mud around the campfires was "over shoe tops" and the horses "had to be moved two or three times in the day to get them out of the mud nearly up to their knees."[36] During the march through the Indian Territory, November 23 to December 15, the weather was mild and precipitation at a minimum. The good weather continued for the first few days in Texas; however, for the last week in December and during the month of January, 1856, the cavalrymen would be exposed to one of the coldest spells on record in the Lone Star State.

After the column rode diagonally across Missouri and nipped the northwest corner of Arkansas, it entered the Indian Territory. This was perhaps the most interesting phase of the march.[37] The Indian Territory was the home of the Five Civilized Tribes who had been moved under protest from the Gulf States east of the Mississippi to this specially designated area. President Andrew Jackson had ordered the move in defiance of the Supreme Court. The migration, or forced removal, commenced in the mid 1830's and continued into the 1840's and involved the Cherokees, Creeks,

---

[32] Ibid., p. 470.
[33] Ibid.
[34] Ibid., p. 473.
[35] Johnson, p. 101.
[36] Eliza Johnston, pp. 470-71.
[37] Brackett, p. 169. Albert Brackett, the captain of Company I, described the Cherokee lands as "wide, undulating prairies . . . with groves of timber of the most magnificent proportions, and the blue outlines of the mountains far away in the distance. The streams of water were pure and sweet." Brackett also noted that "Each day gangs of wolves were seen trotting along parallel with the column, and herds of deer galloped off on the right and left." Ibid.

Choctaws, Chickasaws and some Seminoles. The Indian Territory became the State of Oklahoma in 1907.

The long blue column passed through Talequah, the capitol of the Cherokee Nation on November 17. The commander's wife wrote in her diary on this date about the well-built homes of the community, the attractive public buildings and the Cherokee Male Academy that was located there.[38] Captain Brackett, commander of Company I, estimated that some 20,000 Cherokees lived in the Territory.[39] After transversing the Cherokee Country, the Regiment entered the land of the Creek Nation on December 3.[40] As the column passed through this area, Brackett noted that "many a grim old warrior watched its [the Regiment's] course as it passed along on its journey."[41] Brackett estimated the Creeks to number about 16,000.[42] On the following day the cavalrymen camped near the Indian village of Mico, where there were a few Florida Seminoles.[43] On December 7, Johnston's command camped near Perryville in the Choctaw Nation.[44] The Choctaws living in the Indian Territory numbered about 27,000.[45] The nation of the Chickasaws, which adjoins that of the Choctaws, was the only member of the Five Civilized Tribes whose land the 2nd Cavalry did not ride through. Brackett thought that the Chickasaw Nation would probably number some 5,500.[46]

While marching through the Indian Territory the Regiment stopped at two Federal posts that had been established to protect the peaceful resident Indians from the marauding Plains Indians. The column arrived at Fort Gibson on November 28, and Fort Washita, December 12. The Regiment remained at Fort Gibson four days, camped just outside of the post which Eliza Johnston described as "quite a neat village-like garrison."[47] Apparently the area around Fort Gibson was well stocked with food and game for Mrs. Johnston added not only butter and turkey to her larder but

---

[38] Eliza Johnston, p. 477.
[39] Brackett, p. 169.
[40] Eliza Johnston, p. 478.
[41] Brackett, p. 169. The Creeks were outstanding warriors. They were finally beaten badly by General Andrew Jackson at the Battle of Horseshoe Bend during the war of 1812.
[42] Ibid., p. 170.
[43] Ibid.
[44] Eliza Johnston, p. 480.
[45] Brackett, p. 170.
[46] Ibid. Brackett's estimates appear unusually high.
[47] Eliza Johnston, p. 477.

also partridge and venison.[48]

On December 12, ten days after leaving Fort Gibson, the Regiment arrived at Fort Washita, where Captain Braxton Bragg's 3rd Artillery was stationed. As the cavalrymen rode into the post they were greeted with a thirty-gun salute.[49] The arrival of the 2nd Cavalry, to bolster frontier defenses, was a cause for celebration at the fort and the post sutler, Samuel Humes, "had a bountiful repast in readiness for the officers of the Regiment."[50] Also invited to the banquet were the officers of the garrison and several other officers who were at the Fort on court-martial duty. After the feast, the some fifty officers present indulged in a little elbow bending. Lieutenant Richard Johnson, one of the participants, wrote, "when the champagne began to flow a more jolly set of fellows I do not remember to have ever seen." Johnson was quick to remark, however, "I do not wish to be misunderstood as saying that there was an excessive use of champagne, for such was not the case, but sparkling wine always develops wit and good humor among gentlemen."[51]

During a party composed primarily of artillery and cavalry officers, the subject of horses was bound to come up. Lieutenant "Shanks" Evans of the 2nd Cavalry, owner of a fast Kentucky thoroughbred Glencoe colt named, "Bumble-Bee," challenged all comers to a race the following day. Evans' fellow officers in the 2nd Cavalry knew, several of them by experience, that he had the fastest horse in the Regiment, so the only challenge came from Lieutenant O. D. Greene of the 3rd Artillery. The artillery horses were all light draft horses, and although Greene was game, the race the next day was no contest as "Bumble-Bee" chalked up another of his many victories while with the Regiment.[52]

The Regiment left Fort Washita on Friday, December 14, and on the following day crossed the Red River into Texas at Preston.[53] As the vehicle carrying the Johnston family reached the south side of the river, daughter Maggie, exclaimed, "This is my country, hurrah for Texas."[54] The Lone Star State, however,

---

[48] Ibid.
[49] Ibid., p. 481.
[50] Johnson, p. 103.
[51] Ibid.
[52] Ibid.
[53] Eliza Johnston, p. 482. Preston was located north of Sherman, Texas, on the Red River. It is now covered by Lake Texoma.
[54] Ibid.

seemed anything but hospitable to the men who had come to protect her frontier. A blue norther swept down on the command the evening of December 22 when it was camped near Buffalo Springs (Clay County). Lieutenant Johnson vividly described how suddenly the norther hit,

> On the evening of December 23 [sic.] we encamped on a beautiful prairie. The air was as soft and balmy as spring. Our tent was pitched to the north to catch any cooling breezes coming from that quarter. During the night a norther came upon us, and it was the severest one I had ever witnessed.[55]

The temperature by the morning of December 23 had dropped to four degrees below zero, water froze in the tents, the meat was frozen so hard it could not be cut with an axe, and ice froze to six inches deep on a nearby stream.[56] The wind blew with hurricane force, pelting the shivering soldiers and animals with hail, sleet and snow. The weather was so cold and miserable that "several horses were frozen to death at the picket lines,"[57] the women and children stayed in bed until noon, and the Regiment was unable to march.[58] Captain E. Kirby Smith, commander of Company B wrote, "In the whole course of my military experience I have never seen men suffer more."[59] For the balance of December and for the month of January, 1856, the thermometer remained "uniformly below zero."[60]

On Christmas Day, 1855, the Regiment was within thirty-five miles of Fort Belknap. It was too cold to march, so Christmas was spent in camp and the cavalrymen made the best of the intolerable weather. The spirituous celebration consisted of egg nog (with frozen eggs) and apple brandy for the officers and a dram of whiskey for each of the enlisted men. During the day, a courier arrived from Fort Belknap with information concerning the dispersion of the Regiment. Johnston was to leave four companies

---

[55] Johnson, p. 104.
[56] Ibid., Eliza Johnston, p. 483; Price, p. 34.
[57] Price, p. 34.
[58] Eliza Johnston, p. 483; Johnson, p. 104. The surgeon at Fort Belknap informed Mrs. Johnston that the night the norther struck the temperature in the barracks at the fort was recorded at two below zero. Eliza Johnston, p. 485.
[59] Joseph H. Parks. General Edmond Kirby Smith, CSA. Baton Rouge: Louisiana State University Press, 1962, p. 88. Hereafter cited as Parks.
[60] Price, pp. 34-35.

at Belknap and take the remaining six companies to Fort Mason (Mason County),[61] a post that had been abandoned several months previously. That evening, after tattoo, the buglers from the Regimental Band serenaded the Johnstons with music and Swiss yodeling. For their musical efforts the bandsmen were awarded with "warm rolls and ham" and whiskey.[62]

Following the Christmas interlude, the column continued toward Fort Belknap, reaching the post on December 27,[63] just two months to the day since the Regiment had left Jefferson Barracks. The 2nd Cavalry remained at Belknap for several days, and camped "in the brush" one mile from the fort.[64] The Johnstons were offered accommodations on the post but refused, wishing to remain with the Regiment.[65] It sleeted and snowed the entire time that "Jeff Davis's Own" was bivouacked near Belknap. The men were without sufficient fuel, the temperature remained at zero or slightly below, and the suffering was great.[66]

The 2nd Cavalry left Fort Belknap in two contingents, one on the last day of 1855 and the other the first day of the new year. On December 31, 1855, Major Hardee and Companies A, E, F & K, left the post for the Clear Fork of the Brazos River, some forty miles southwest of Belknap. Their mission was to construct and garrison a station near the Indian Reservation there to protect the peaceful Indians from the warlike Northern and Middle Comanches.[67] Hardee arrived at his destination on January 3, and during the succeeding weeks built Camp Cooper on the Clear Fork about one mile above the Reservation.[68]

On January 1, 1856, Colonel Johnston, with the Head-

[61] Eliza Johnston, p. 484.
[62] Ibid., p. 485.
[63] Ibid.
[64] Ibid.; Johnston, p. 105.
[65] Albert S. Johnston was dedicated to his men and his regiment. Lieutenant Richard W. Johnson wrote, Johnston "was one of the most unselfish men I ever knew, and one of the most just and considerate to those under his command. The officers of the regiment not only respected but loved him. His desire to make the Second Cavalry the finest regiment in the army was seconded by every officer of whatever rank under him." Johnson, pp. 105.
[66] Eliza Johnston, pp. 485-86; Johnson, p. 105.
[67] Eliza Johnston, p. 486. As the four companies rode out they were given a farewell salute by Johnston and the remaining six companies. Ibid.
[68] Price, p. 41. The Camp was named for Colonel Samuel Cooper, the Adjutant-General of the United States Army. As noted previously in the text, Cooper, along with Davis, helped select the officers for the 2nd Cavalry.

quarters and Band and the remaining six companies of the Regiment, B, C, D, G, H, & I, left Belknap for Fort Mason, some 150 miles south near the Llano River. During the march south, Johnston's command passed through the Peters Colony,[69] and crossed the Clear Fork of the Brazos, the Pecan, the Colorado and the San Saba Rivers. The weather was cold and miserable during most of the march south, it was so severe in fact, that a number of horses died during the march from exposure.[70] Mrs. Johnston reported that on January 8, it was only "9 degrees above zero" and observed that the "hot coffee at her side froze before it could be drunk."[71] Too, she noted that several streams were frozen over and the column crossed on the ice. At one small stream, however, near the juncture of the Fort Gates, Austin, and Fort Mason roads (in present Callahan County) the men had fun fishing through the ice. The Colonel's wife reported that the "creek was filled with fish of all sizes from 2-1/2 feet down" and the result was a "fine fish fry" that night for the men and officers.[72] Wild game abounded; the officers killed several turkeys, and geese and several herds of deer were sighted and chased. On January 13, two men killed, near camp, a panther which charged them with "distended jaws and full of fight."[73] As the column approached Fort Mason, Indians were reported nearby; Captain Bradfute and a detail of men were sent out on a scout, but nothing developed. With mild weather prevailing at last, the column marched twenty miles on January 14, reaching Fort Mason that evening.[74]

---

[69] The W. S. Peters Colony was one of the two large "colonies" settled under the Texas Land Law of 1841, and supplementary acts, which restored the practice of making large grants of land to "empresarios" on the stipulation that they settle the area with a specified number of people. Walter Prescott Webb (ed.). **The Handbook of Texas**, Austin: Texas State Historical Association, 1952, 2 vols., I, pp. 366-67. Hereafter cited as **Handbook.**

[70] Price, p. 42.

[71] Eliza Johnston, p. 487.

[72] Ibid.

[73] Price, p. 42.

[74] Eliza Johnston, pp. 489-90. Captain William R. Bradfute was appointed a captain in the 2nd Cavalry from civilian life on March 3, 1855. He was a veteran of the Mexican War. Bradfute commanded Company G and participated in several campaigns against the Indians while in Texas. In July, 1858, Bradfute shot and killed a private in Company K who refused to obey a lawful order and who struck the Captain in the face. Although exonerated by a military court of inquiry, he was turned over to civil authorities on orders from President Buchanan and placed under arrest. Bradfute was released on bail and was never brought to trial. He entered the Confederate service during the Civil War and rose to the rank of colonel. Price, pp. 323-24.

The 2nd U.S. Cavalry had now garrisoned its first two posts in Texas, Camp Cooper and Fort Mason. These posts would be the first of many along the perimeter of settlement that the Regiment would occupy as it prepared to defend the frontier against the Apache, the Comanche and the Kiowa.

CHAPTER FIVE

THE TEXAS FRONTIER, 1855

O, pray for the soldier you kind-hearted stranger;
He has roamed the prairie for many a year.
He has kept the Comanche away from your ranches,
And followed them far over the Texas frontier.
                                                    — Author unknown

To understand the multiple problems of frontier defense that faced the 2nd Cavalry in Texas it is necessary to review the actions and policies pursued by the Federal government, the State government and the frontier citizens, beginning with the annexation of Texas on December 29, 1845. Texas, upon joining the Union, ceded to the Federal government all of the state's material means of defense. Thus the United States, after Texas was annexed, assumed full responsibility for the protection of the state against foreign invasion from without and Indians from within. However, little could be done by the Federal government in the way of frontier defense the first two years after annexation, for the war with Mexico required the commitment of the nation's total regular military force. Hence, the burden of frontier defense was thrown back into the lap of Texas during the years 1846 and 1847.

In 1848 Texas was made part of the 8th U. S. Military District, renamed the Department of Texas in the re-organization of 1853. Federal headquarters in the state was established at San Antonio, the site of a depot and small garrison, when Texas was admitted to the Union. Theoretically, the commander of the San Antonio garrison was in command of the Texas frontier.[1] Due to the exigencies of the war the command of the San Antonio post shifted constantly, each new commander had his own ideas of how best to cope with the frontier problem. Thus no consistent policy was followed.

On June 28, 1846, Colonel William S. Harney, commander of the San Antonio post at the time, requested that Lieutenant-

---

[1] W. C. Holden. "Frontier Defense, 1846-1860." **West Texas Historical Association Yearbook**, Vol. VI (June, 1930), p. 35. Hereafter cited as **Holden.**

Governor Albert C. Horton, the acting governor,[2] furnish five companies of state mounted Rangers for a term of six months. The Rangers were to be mustered into the service of the United States and placed at strategic points along the frontier. Each man was to furnish his own arms, horse and equipment. Horton recruited the necessary companies and stationed them at Castroville, San Antonio, Bryant Station on Little River (Milam County), Torrey's Trading House on the Brazos (McLennan County), and on the West Fork of the Trinity (Tarrant County).[3] Harney left San Antonio shortly after the Rangers were on station. Following his departure there began a long dispute between Acting Governor Horton and Harney's various successors in regard to the mustering of the state troops into Federal service. In the meantime the men had received no pay and their exact status was in doubt. Horton ordered the men to remain at their posts and promised that he would requisition the State for funds to defray their expenses until they were mustered into United States service. Lieutenant-Colonel Thomas J. Fauntleroy, Harney's immediate successor, was not in favor of his predecessor's frontier defense plan and so was deaf to the pleas of Horton to bring the state Rangers into the Federal service. Horton wrote to both the Secretary of War and to President Polk requesting Federal funds for the Texans. Only when the Acting Governor wrote to the Texas Congressmen in Washington, however, did he get action, but then only was permitted to Federalize three of the companies, the three companies on the least exposed southern end of the line.[4]

James P. Henderson returned in November, 1846, from service with General Zachary Taylor's Army in Mexico and assumed his function as governor. Henderson pursued the matter of getting the remaining two companies mustered into Federal service. This problem was temporarily forgotten when it was rumored in early January, 1847, that some 10,000 warlike Indians had invaded Texas from the north. Henderson, reacting to this rumor, asked the Secretary of War for permission to let Colonel John "Coffee Jack" Hays raise a regiment of mounted troops for the frontier. To strengthen his written request, the Governor sent

---

[2] Horton served as acting governor from May 19, to about November 1, 1846, while Governor James Pinckney Henderson was on leave of absence commanding the 2nd Texas Regiment in Mexico. **Handbook**, I, p. 796.
[3] Holden, p. 36.
[4] Ibid., p. 37.

the colorful Ranger colonel to Washington to plead for urgent action. Hays had little trouble in convincing the Secretary and President of the need, and an order was issued March 20, 1847, to raise the frontier regiment.[5] Henderson lost little time in raising the mounted regiment. However, before Hays had returned to Texas, the War Department had decided that the war in Mexico was more important than frontier defense and ordered Hays and his new regiment to join General Taylor in Mexico. This left the Texas frontier in the condition that it was before, with five understrength companies of state soldiers to guard a 1,000 mile front.

Petitions from frontier settlements continued to pour into Austin asking for additional protection, or just protection, as the Indian raids mounted in ferocity and frequency. Such raids were particularly numerous between San Antonio and Corpus Christi during the summer of 1847. On July 16, 1847, the Secretary of War authorized the governor "to raise such forces as he deemed necessary for the protection of the frontier."[6] Four more companies for frontier duty were raised by the state under this authorization. Two of these were posted between San Antonio and Corpus Christi, the greatest area of Indian penetration. By the fall of 1847, the first line of frontier defense in Texas since its annexation had been established. It consisted of nine mounted state Ranger companies in Federal service scattered from the Trinity River in Tarrant County on the north to Corpus Christi in the south via Fredericksburg and San Antonio.

After the war with Mexico when the United States began to withdraw troops from that country, the Federal government began to honor its commitment to Texas by placing seven companies of Regulars on the frontier. General Daniel E. Twiggs, commander of the 8th U. S. Military District, with headquarters at San Antonio, on November 7, 1848, ordered four companies of the 2nd Dragoons to take positions at the following locations: one at Conner's Station on Richland Creek, east of the Brazos in present Hill County; another at Ross's Station on the Bosque, west of the Brazos in present McLennan County; a third company at McCulloch's Station, six miles east of the Colorado; and the fourth company of the Dragoons on the Medina River, ten or fifteen

---

[5] Ibid., p. 38.
[6] Ibid., p. 40.

miles above Castroville. To augment the four companies of Dragoons, three companies of the 1st United States Infantry Regiment were also assigned to duty in Texas; one company was ordered to Fredericksburg and two to Austin.[7] According to an article appearing in the Corpus Christi *Star* of December 16, 1848, the Indians were to be kept west and north of a line connecting the above points of troop concentrations. As soon as these Regular mounted and foot companies reached their stations the state Ranger force was mustered out of Federal service.

Twiggs' defensive alignment had several basic weaknesses. It left unguarded both the critical northern and southern ends of the defense line, some 120 miles on the north from Hill County to the Red River and about the same distance between San Antonio and Corpus Christi in the south. Both of these areas had been prime targets for Indian raiding parties. Too, infantry was next to useless against the Comanches and the Kiowas, some of the best light horse cavalry in the world. The foot soldiers at Fredericksburg and Austin, as one historian wrote, "were not effective outside gunshot of their posts."[8]

This system of defense for Texas was most ineffective, and to compound the problem the United States had agreed by terms of the Treaty of Guadalupe Hidalgo that ended the Mexican War to keep the Plains Indians from raiding south of the Rio Grande.[9] For many years the Comanches, Kiowas and Apaches had crossed into Mexico, marauding through the countryside kidnapping, killing, looting and running off horses and cattle. There is some evidence that the Kiowas had ridden as far south as the Yucatan Peninsula on their raids.[10] While such deep penetrations were uncommon, routine raids by the Plains Indians into the northern states of Mexico were a common occurrence.

---

[7] Ibid., p. 41.

[8] Ibid.

[9] The 11th article of the Treaty of Guadalupe Hidalgo stated that the United States was "bound to protect the Mexican frontier from Indians on the border." 31st Congress, 2nd Session, Senate Doc. No. 1, p. 28. However, in 1853, upon the purchase of the Gadsen Strip, the United States annulled the provision in the Treaty of Guadalupe Hidalgo which made the United States responsible for controlling Indian raids into Mexico. Rebecca Brooks Gruver. **An American History.** Reading (Mass): Addison-Wesley, 1976, p. 465. Robert M. Utley. **Frontiersmen in Blue: The U.S. Army and the Indian, 1848-1865.** New York: MacMillan Publishers, 1967, p. 64. Hereafter cited as **Utley.**

[10] Harold B. Simpson. "The Kiowas." **Indian Tribes of Texas.** Waco: Texian Press, 1971, pp. 112-13.

It was essential that if the United States Government was to adequately protect the frontier of Texas and keep the warlike Indians from raiding into Mexico it had to employ more troops and erect a closer knit line of forts. The first steps toward accomplishing these aims were taken by District Commander, General George M. Brooke, in 1849. During this year nine forts were built and twenty-one additional Regular Army companies were posted to Texas to augment the seven already there.[11] The nine forts were erected on a line from the West Fork of the Trinity on the north to Eagle Pass on the Rio Grande in the south. The northernmost of these was Fort Worth, on the West Fork of the Trinity (Tarrant County). Then followed south in order: Fort Graham on the left bank of the Brazos (Hill County); Fort Gates on the Leon River (Coryell County); Fort Groghan, fifteen miles east of the Colorado River and four miles above McCulloch's Station on Hamilton Creek (Burnet County); Fort Martin Scott, two miles east of Fredericksburg (Gillespie County); Fort Lincoln, on the Seco, two miles north of D'Hanis (Medina County); Fort Inge on the Leon River near Uvalde (Uvalde County); Fort McIntosh near Laredo (Webb County); and Fort Duncan at Eagle Pass on the Rio Grande (Maverick County).[12] This line of forts built in 1849 was generally referred to as the "inner line."

These posts were well located and strategically placed and might have provided the protection needed had they been adequately garrisoned and manned by mounted rather than by foot soldiers. Several of the forts had only one understrength company, numbering in some cases but fifty men, and of this number sickness and special details limited the number available for field duty to barely a dozen.[13] If these had been horse soldiers, even as small as the number was, it would have constituted some measure of defense. Unfortunately, of the twenty-eight companies assigned to Texas,[14] twenty were

---

[11] Lena Clara Koch. "The Federal Indian Policy in Texas, 1845-1860." SWHQ, Vol. XXIX, No. 1 (July, 1925), p. 19. Hereafter cited as Koch, followed by the volume and number.
[12] Other Federal forts were established earlier along the Rio Grande: Forts Polk and Brown (1846) near the mouth of the river in Cameron County; Ringgold Barracks (1848) near Rio Grande City (Starr County); and Fort Bliss (1848) near El Paso (El Paso County).
[13] Holden, p. 42.
[14] Koch, Vol. XXIX, No. 1 (July, 1925), p. 19. During the period from 1848 to 1855, prior to the assignment of the 2nd Cavalry to Texas, Federal troops assigned to duty in the state from time to time were companies of

infantry. To make matters worse a large portion of the soldiers were raw recruits who had little or no experience in Indian fighting. Foot soldiers were of little use on the frontier and as the *Texas State Gazette* (Austin) of October 27, 1849 pointed out, "The idea of repelling mounted Indians, the most expert horsemen in the world, with a force of foot soldiers is here looked upon as exceedingly ridiculous." In 1853, a critic of the Federal government's Indian policy addressing the Texas House of Representatives remarked, "Can your honorable body conceive of anything more absurd than starting in pursuit of the flying Comanche in a wagon drawn by mules?"[15]

The Indians, realizing that the infantry could not cope with their fast hit and run tactics, stepped up the number of their raids in late 1849. Soon the frontier settlers were clamoring for more protection and threatening to organize themselves and take retaliatory measures. In response to this public pressure and at the request of General George M. Brooke, 8th Military District Commander, Governor George T. Wood called up three companies of Rangers which were mustered into the United States service for six months.[16] This augmentation did little to stem the raids, which, in some cases, were conducted within sight of cities like Austin, San Antonio, and Corpus Christi.[17] The term of service of the three Ranger companies was extended for six more months and a fourth and later a fifth company of Rangers was called up in an attempt to turn back the raiders.

General Brooke having little or no success operating on the defense in protecting the frontier, decided to go on the offense and strike into Indian country in an effort to stop the "deplorable barbarites and activities . . . and serious depredation upon property."[18] To carry out the aggressive new policy Brevet

---

the 1st, 5th, 7th and 8th Infantry Regiments, 4th Artillery Regiment, the 2nd Dragoons and the Mounted Rifles. **Ibid.**, p. 21.

[15] **Ibid.**, pp. 20-21. When Frederick Lan Olmstead made a trip through Texas in 1857 he ridiculed the Federal frontier defense arrangements by writing that, "keeping a bulldog to chase mosquitoes would be no greater nonsense than the stationing of six-pounders, bayonets, and dragoons for the pursuit of these red wolves." Quoted in **Roland**, pp. 172-73.

[16] **Holden**, p. 43

[17] Within a twelve month span of time, mid-1849 to mid-1850, it was conservatively estimated that 204 persons had been killed, wounded or carried off in captivity and over $100,000 worth of horses and cattle had been driven off by the Indians. **Senate Journal**, Texas Legislature, 3rd Session, pp. 434-38; **Utley**, p. 72.

[18] **Holden**, p. 44; **Utley**, p. 72.

Lieutenant Colonel William J. Hardee, in the summer of 1850, led a force comprised of the 2nd Dragoons, several companies of mounted infantry from Forts McIntosh, Inge, Merrill and Lincoln, and three Ranger companies on an expedition north into Comanche and Kiowa territory. After several weeks of "fruitless marching, scouting and searching operations" that netted little, the expedition was abandoned. Again the army turned to a static frontier defense anchored on the inner line of forts. To compound Brooke's problems, in the spring of 1850 parties of Delawares, Shawnees, Caddoes, Iones, Anadarkos, Kichies, Wichitas and Kickapoos moved down into Texas from the Indian Territory and permanently settled in the State. Although members of these tribes made an occasional foray past the barrier of forts, it was the Apaches, Comanches and Kiowas who were the primary offenders in Texas.

Even though the frontier was being raided constantly, settlements moved steadily westward and several of the forts that were established in 1849 were now far behind the frontier and were abandoned and new ones built. During 1851, and 1852, the "middle line" of forts was established to protect the fast moving frontier.[19] There were seven forts in this line. Forts Belknap (Young County), Mason (Mason County) and Phantom Hill (Jones County) were established in 1851, and Forts Terrett (Sutton County), McKavett (Menard County), Clark (Kenney County) and Chadbourne (Coke County) in 1852. These forts were built along the western limit of reliable water flow in the rivers starting in the Staked Plains and Edwards Plateau.

General Persifor F. Smith replaced Brooke as the commander of the 8th U. S. Military District in 1851, and soon after his appointment and upon his request, five companies of the Mounted Rifles Regiment were assigned to the District. This augmentation of forces along with the establishment of the new forts brought some measure of tranquility to the State in 1852 and 1853.[20] There were few depredations during these years and most of these were committed by Indians from Mexico. To prevent raids from the south, the garrisons of the forts along the Rio Grande — Brown, Ringgold, McIntosh and Duncan — were considerably

[19] It was estimated that from 1848 to 1852 the western frontier of Texas had advanced almost 150 miles. **Holden**, p. 48.
[20] **Ibid.**, p. 48.

strengthened. This augmentation brought the number of Federal troops assigned to Texas in mid-1853 to 3,265, the largest number up to that time.[21] However this number was less than adequate, for according to Indian Agent, Major Robert S. Neighbors, the military forces in Texas during the 1850's had to deal with some 25,000 Indians in 16 tribes.[22]

The year of 1853 also brought a change of administrations in Washington. Franklin Pierce became President of the United States in March, 1853, and Jefferson Davis, the Secretary of War. The previous Secretary of War, C. M. Conrad, had shown little concern for Texas and her frontier problems and had regarded the Indian menace as primarily a state matter and responsibility. Davis wisely initiated a policy of conciliation and understanding with Texas Governor Peter H. Bell, and the attempt to solve the frontier problem for the next few years was characterized by complete cooperation between the Federal and State governments.

After two years of comparative peace along the frontier, depredations increased alarmingly in 1854. The Indians, after carefully studying the defenses, conducted their raids through areas defended by infantry, where retaliation and interception was least likely to occur. They carefully avoided the regions protected by the Dragoons and Mounted Rifles. Too, the Federal government, relying on the continuance of the good behavior displayed by the Indians during 1852 and 1853, had removed several companies from the frontier forts to other posts in the state. After this re-assignment, only four companies of infantry and two of dragoons were in position to defend the 250 miles of country between the Colorado and Red Rivers.[23] To make matters worse, several of the posts in this area were seriously undermanned, Fort Chadbourne, in present Coke County, being a case in point. Company C, 2nd Dragoons stationed at Chadbourne in the spring of 1854 had only an average of twenty men present for duty and they were commanded by the Post Surgeon.[24] Considering all six companies along the 250 mile front between the Colorado and Red Rivers it is doubtful if more than 200 soldiers were available

[21] Ibid., p. 49.
[22] Utley, p. 71.
[23] Holden, p. 49.
[24] "Post Returns", Fort Chadbourne, March, April, 1854. Microfilm Copy No. 617, Roll No. 195. National Archives. Assistant Surgeon Ebenezer Swift commanded the Post and Company C, March and April, 1854. Ibid.

for field duty at any one time. In fact the paucity of Federal troops along the frontier was so apparent that it caused one Texas frontiersman to quip that it had begun to look as if "the Federal government would have to do something to protect the army from the Indians."[25]

General Smith, sensitive to the situation, did as several of his predecessors had done. In May he asked Governor Elisha M. Pease for mounted Rangers to augment the Federal defense force and to participate in a summer campaign against the raiders. Pease was slow to respond and it was not until October, 1854, that the six companies of requested Rangers were organized and on station,[26] and it was not until December that they were mustered into the service of the United States, far too late for Smith's planned summer campaign.[27] Too, the term of service was for three months instead of the twelve that Smith had requested.

The presence of the six state Ranger companies augmenting the Regular forces on the frontier caused a noticeable cessation of raids during the winter and spring of 1855. This lull was not to last long. In March, the Ranger companies were discharged and trouble in Kansas Territory in mid-summer of 1855 caused the reassignment of many of the Federal mounted troops from Texas to that area. Again the frontier was left in a state of partial defense and, as could be expected, the Indians exploited the situation, penetrating the defense line with impunity. In an attempt to stop the depredations, citizens of several of the frontier counties formed voluntary military units and Governor Pease, deluged with petitions for protection, called out a company of mounted state troops. While these efforts helped to curtail depredations, they were at best a stop gap measure. To remedy a situation that had festered since the Mexican War, more mounted Regular units had to be committed to Texas. This step was taken in the late summer of 1855 when the newly formed 2nd Cavalry Regiment was ordered to duty on the Texas frontier.

The 2nd Cavalry would not only be concerned with frontier defense in the Lone Star State but Johnston's command would

---

[25] Robert Simpson Neighbors to Governor Elisha Marshall Pease, April 10, 1854, as quoted in **Holden**, p. 50. Pease was elected Governor of Texas in 1853 and served two terms, until 1857.

[26] Two companies of the mounted Rangers were stationed at Fort Worth (Tarrant County) and four at Fredericksburg (Gillespie County).

[27] **Holden**, p. 50.

also be directly involved in the Texas Indian Reservation program, a joint Federal-State venture. During September, 1853, Secretary of War Jefferson Davis had proposed to Governor Bell that a reservation system be established for handling the Texas Indians.[28] Nothing came of the Secretary's suggestion until February 6, 1854 when the Texas Legislature passed an act that provided for Indian reservations and authorized the Federal government to select and survey 12 leagues of land for this purpose. The act specified that,

> the land was not to be located over 20 miles south or east of the most northern line of military posts of the United States from the Red River to the Pecos. As soon as the land was surveyed and marked, the Federal government was to settle thereon Indians belonging to Texas, and to have control of them, and establish such agencies and military posts as were necessary.[29]

The act further stated that the land would revert to the State when it was no longer used for the Indians.

The land for the reservations was surveyed by Captain R. B. Marcy of the United States Army and Major R. S. Neighbors, Indian Agent of Texas. Great care was exercised in selecting the land, the Indians being consulted as to their preferences of location. Two reservations were established, the larger one, known as the "Brazos Agency" or the "Lower Reserve" was comprised of eight leagues or 37,152 acres. This agency was located on the main fork of the Brazos River, some 15 miles south of Fort Belknap in present Young County. The main building of the reservation was located three miles east of the present town of Graham.[30] The second reservation, known as the "Comanche Reserve," or the "Upper Reserve," was established on the Clear Fork of the Brazos, about 45 miles west of the Brazos Agency. It consisted of the remaining 4 leagues, or 18,576 acres.[31] There was a delay of over a year in getting the Texas Indians settled. It took almost a year to survey the land. By the summer of 1855, most of the peaceful

---

[28] Ibid., p. 48. As early as February 16, 1852, the Texas Legislature had approved a resolution authorizing the Governor to conduct negotiations with the Federal government concerning the allocation of state land for the use of Texas Indians. Koch, Vol. XXIX, No. 2 (Oct., 1925), p. 98.
[29] Koch, Vol. XXIX, No. 2 (Oct., 1825), p. 99.
[30] Ibid., pp. 99-100.
[31] Handbook, Vol. I, p. 210.

Indians in the State had been moved on the Brazos Reservation, the principal buildings were being erected, supplies had been contracted for and were being received, and much of the land was broken up for planting. The settlement of the Comanche Reserve was several months behind that of the Lower Reservation. The Federal government not only controlled the reservations but it also controlled a ten-mile surrounding area to prevent the sale of liquor to the Indians.[32]

The Brazos Agency was the more successful of the two reservations. It was settled by the so-called civilized tribes, the Caddoes, Wacoes, Tawakonies, Anadarkoes, Tonkawas, Keechies, and Delawares. The majority of the Indians living on the reservation were Caddoes, the others were remnants of tribes. G. W. Hill was the first agent but was only on duty for a few months, and was succeeded by Captain Shapley P. Ross on September 1, 1855.[33] The agents, with the help of the Indians, organized and maintained a reservation police force. The Federal government stationed two companies of the 2nd Dragoons and two companies of the 7th Infantry at Fort Belknap within a short distance of the Reservation. The purpose of having this relatively large concentration of troops at Belknap was to protect the peaceful Indians living on the Agency as well as the frontier settlers from the warlike tribes raiding south of the Red River. Supplies for the Indians cost the Federal government $80,000 annually and contracts were made with local ranchers to furnish the reservation, on the average, 34 head of cattle weekly.[34] As the Indian population on the agency increased, these costs went up correspondingly.[35] Many of the braves on the Brazos Agency were enlisted by both Federal and State troop commanders as scouts against the warring tribes; as many as 100 were employed as scouts and trackers at one time.[36]

The Comanche Reserve was never completely settled. It was specifically established for the Penateka or Southern Comanche, but this tribe was much harder to control than the more peaceful

[32] Ibid.
[33] Koch, Vol. XXIX, No. 2 (Oct., 1925), pp. 101-103.
[34] Handbook, Vol. I, p. 210.
[35] Each year the number of Indians on the Brazos Agency increased by several hundred. In September, 1855, there were 794 on the reservation by the same month in 1858, the population had increased to 1,112. Koch, Vol. XXIX, No. 2 (Oct., 1925), p. 100.
[36] Handbook, Vol. I, p. 210.

tribes of the Lower Reserve, and the reservation never had living on it more than 600 Indians. A number of reasons caused the Upper Reserve to be less successful than the one on the Brazos. The Comanches were not interested in farming;[37] the Penateka band was seriously divided between Chiefs Sanaco and Katumse, the former quitting the Reservation with several hundred warriors; the tendency of the Southern Comanche was to wander off the reservation on hunting and even raiding parties; inadequate protection was given the Agency by Federal troops; and the great hatred of the white settlers for the Comanche and their desire to rid the state of them remained unchanged.

One important cause for the late settlement of the Comanche Reservation was the fact that there was no resident agent on the reservation for several months. George Howard, who was the agent for the Comanches before settlement while they were located near Fort Clark (Kinney County), did not accompany them to the reservation. John R. Baylor was the first resident agent, but he disagreed with Indian Superintendent Robert Neighbors and was dismissed after eighteen months. Baylor was succeeded by Colonel M. Leeper in late 1857.[38] The Federal government established Camp Cooper and garrisoned it with both cavalry and infantry companies to protect the Comanche Agency and the nearby settlers from raids by the hostile Northern and Middle Comanches, the Kiowas and the Kickapoos.

Four companies of the 2nd Cavalry, as stated in the previous chapter, were assigned to both build and then to garrison Camp Cooper, thus the Regiment was directly involved in the Comanche Reserve program. Later, when the reservation program was abandoned and the Indians were moved from Texas to the Indian Territory north of the Red River, units of the 2nd Cavalry provided the escort for the exodus.

When Johnston's Regiment took station in Texas, early in 1856, there were eight active Federal forts on or near the frontier. These were Forts Bliss, Inge, Belknap, McKavett, Clark,

---

[37] It was estimated that the Indians living on the Brazos Agency put over 600 acres in cultivation, raising corn, wheat, vegetables, and melons, and were considered to be excellent farmers. **Handbook**, Vol. I, p. 210. On the other hand, the Comanches cultivated only 96 acres of their reservation. **Koch,** Vol. XXIX, No. 2 (Oct., 1925), p. 107.
[38] **Koch,** Vol. XXIX, No. 2 (Oct., 1925), pp. 104-107, 119.

Chadbourne, Davis and Lancaster.[39] All others had been temporarily or permanently abandoned as the frontier moved west. During the Regiment's tenure in Texas seven new camps or forts would be established, namely Camps Cooper (Throckmorton County), Colorado (Coleman County), and Verde (Kerr County) in 1856, Camp Hudson (Val Verde County) in 1857, Camp Wood (Real County) and Fort Quitman (Hudspeth County) in 1858, and Fort Stockton (Pecos County) in 1859;[40] Fort Mason (Mason County) would be re-activated in 1856. In fact, Colonel Johnston's command, as noted previously, was directly involved in the establishment of one of these, Camp Cooper, and in the re-opening of another, Fort Mason. Companies of the 2nd Cavalry would garrison, at one time or another during the Regiment's five years in Texas, the majority of these outposts.

Most of the camps and forts on the Texas frontier were laid out in a similar manner, a series of crude buildings clustered around a parade ground. The forts were not palisaded as most of the western forts were in the post-Civil War era. Officers quarters, normally small, uncomfortable cottages, lined one side of the parade ground and poorly built enlisted mens barracks lined the opposite side. Mess huts were either in the rear of or at one end of the row of barracks. On the third side of the parade ground was the administrative building and headquarters, flanked by the Quartermaster's warehouse. The fourth side of the square was normally open, but on some posts the guard house was located there. The post hospital, sutler's store, mortuary, and magazine were scattered around the perimeter of the fort, as were the stables, wagon sheds, and the huts for the laundresses. Depending on the geographic location, buildings were constructed of adobe, wood, brick and stone or a combination of several of these materials. Most of the quarters, of officers as well as enlisted men, were badly heated and poorly ventilated. Fleas, bedbugs, mice, snakes, and other vermin and rodents, and the sun, rain, wind and snow were impossible to keep out of the crudely constructed

---

[39] Fort Davis (Jeff Davis County) had been built in 1854 and Fort Lancaster (Crockett County) in 1855, both had been established to guard the San Antonio-El Paso Road.

[40] Barrett, pp. 129-139. Camps Hudson and Wood and Forts Quitman and Stockton had been established to guard the San Antonio-El Paso Road. Camp Verde was built for the U.S. Army camel experiment and Camp Colorado to guard the Colorado River settlements.

buildings. Some posts, the older ones in particular, were better built than others, but troopers of the 2nd Cavalry moving from outpost to outpost as they did and campaigning much of the time, lived under primitive conditions on most occasions.

A trooper on the Texas frontier had to endure the rigors of hard marches over impossible terrain, suffer from intensive cold and heat, pocketed meager pay and risked his life daily, with disease counting for as many deaths as the Indians.

CHAPTER SIX

1856 – FIRST BLOOD FOR THE REGIMENT

*The troops were exposed to wet and cold
weather, and for more than seven days
subsisted upon two day's allowance of
bread and coffee, such game as they could
kill, and the flesh of horses they were
obliged to abandon.[1]*

Unfortunately for Colonel Johnston and his command
nothing was ready for them on their arrival at Fort Mason. The
Fort was in a bad state of repair, having been abandoned some two
years previously. The last command to garrison the post, Company
A, 2nd Dragoons, had been reassigned to Fort McKavett in
January, 1854.[2] With the soldiers gone the local settlers had
stripped many of the buildings of doors, windows and siding in
what appeared to have been a community effort of "moonlight
requisitioning." Except for a few officers quarters and storeroom
buildings nothing else was standing, consequently a tent city
sprang up near spring fed Comanche Creek north of the fort. Not
only was the shelter inadequate but the Department Commander,
General Persifor F. Smith, had not provided provisions and stores
for the incoming command. The only bread that the officers and
men could obtain was made of corn crushed in a mortar.[3]
Provisions and stores were not available in quantity or quality
until the regimental wagons were sent to San Antonio some 110
miles south. In due time, after weather delays, they returned fully
loaded along with the wagon-train carrying the regimental and
company property that had been sent from Jefferson Barracks via

---

[1] Price in describing the return of Captain James Oakes' command to Fort
Mason after their fight with the Waco Indians, March 22, 1856, p. 44.
[2] Harold B. Simpson, "Fort Mason," pp. 151, 153-54. **Frontier Forts of
Texas,** Waco: Texian Press, 1966. Hereafter cited as **Simpson,** "Fort Mason".
Fort Mason was occupied temporarily from March to May, 1855, when
2nd Lieutenant Charles E. Norris and a small detachment from Companies
A & G, 2nd Dragoons, garrisoned the post when Comanche raids were
reported in the area. Ibid., pp. 151-52.
[3] **Johnson,** pp. 106. Regimental Quartermaster Johnson called this lack of
prepositioned provisions and stores "culpable neglect [that] should have
secured the punishment by court-martial of the guilty party." **Ibid.**

water to Indianola, Texas.

Only two buildings of the old officers' quarters were fit to use. Each consisted of two rooms with a covered way or "dog trot" between them. Colonel and Mrs. Johnston kindly shared their quarters with Lieutenant Johnson, the Regimental Quartermaster, and his family. Johnson's "family" was rather large, consisting of his wife and two children and a maid who was raising a soldier's child.[4] The other two officers who had brought their families, Captains Oakes and Palmer, occupied the other usable frontier duplex. Although cramped living conditions posed a problem for the Johnson family a more serious situation arose a few days after occupancy. Johnson reported the problem and how he solved it in his *Reminiscences,*

> The passageway [dog trot] between [Colonel Johnston's] apartment and mine was used in common, as we entered our respective rooms from it. It occurred to him that if the passageway was closed in it would give him another room, and he directed me to have it done. It did not occur to him then, and probably never did, that the closing up of the passageway would compel me to egress and ingress through a window. I soon had this [the window], however, converted into a door, and enclosed the back porch for a dining room. The front room was used for a bedchamber, parlor, and library all combined, and while the accommodations were decidely limited, yet they were so far superior to anything we had had since leaving Jefferson Barracks that we felt quite comfortable indeed.[5]

The other officers and men set up camp just north of the fort near Comanche Creek, the only available water supply in the area. The officers were provided with hospital and wall tents while the men lived in makeshift "barracks" of Sibley tents and adobe mud. The Sibley tents "were raised five feet from the ground and supported on posts, the intervals between which were closed with adobe mud."[6] The fact that the last half of January remained

---

4 Eliza Johnston, p. 490.
5 Johnson, pp. 106-07.
6 Price, p. 42. The Sibley tent, invented by Major H. H. Sibley of the 2nd Dragoons, was conical in shape and had a smoke flap at the top opening that acted as a directional draft control . . . . The tent was supported at the top by a single pole, the bottom of the pole sat in a socket held stationary by a metal tripod. The edges of the tent were fastened to the ground by wooden tent pins, which held it in circular form. Randy Steffen. **The Horse Soldier, 1776-1943**, Norman, Okla.: University of Oklahoma Press, 1978. 4 Vols.. Vol. II, pp. 48-49.

uniformly cold added to the discomfort of the troops in their makeshift housing. One norther followed another through the area, causing the death of three men by exposure. The weather was often too miserable to drill and too cold for the Colonel to hold school for the officers.[7] Within a few months, however, the members of the 2nd Cavalry would witness the other uncomfortable extreme in Texas weather.

Major Hardee and the four companies of the 2nd Cavalry that were in the process of establishing Camp Cooper on the Clear Fork of the Brazos fared even worse than Johnston's six companies. For almost two months, Hardee had inadequate food and supplies, improper shelter and unusable mounts.[8] All of the officers and men lived in tents and suffered correspondingly as the frigid northers swept through. If anything, the weather at Camp Cooper, some 150 miles north of Fort Mason, was more frigid than that endured by Johnston's command. There was no material available near Hardee's post to erect stables for the horses, and the unfortunate beasts had to be picketed in the open in the shelter of creek banks and hills. The animals suffered severely, frequently being covered with frozen sleet.[9] Having been exposed to the frigid weather during the winter, many of the horses died from the staggers when warm weather came.[10] Regardless of the inclement weather and physical discomfiture, the soldiers were encouraged to hunt and ride in the vicinity of the camp. Such activity would not only provide recreation for the men and food for the camp, but, according to the biographer of the command, would "assist in educating [the soldiers] to ride, shoot, and acquire a knowledge of the adjacent country."[11] The companies at Camp Cooper spent the remainder of the winter under these less than comfortable circumstances.

With the assignment of the 2nd Cavalry to Texas, the War Department changed its strategy in regard to frontier warfare. No

---

[7] **Eliza Johnston,** p. 491. A norther that struck the latter part of January caused the death of 113 oxen near Fredericksburg belonging to a train that was bringing provisions to Fort Mason. **Ibid.**
[8] **Hughes,** p. 54.
[9] **Price,** p. 42.
[10] Staggers or "blind staggers," as it is sometimes called, is a nervous disorder caused by a congestion of the brain. It is often fatal. **Cavalry ROTC Manual.** Harrisburg (Pa.): The Military Service Publishing Co., 1935, 6th Edition, p. 343.
[11] **Price,** p. 42.

longer would the military garrisons merely maintain a defensive patrol cordon as had been the case since the Mexican War. With the posting of the 2nd Cavalry along the frontier, the War Department advocated a policy of offense. Patrol, pursue and punish was the tactic to be used to carry out the new offensive strategy. Orders passed down to the company commanders encouraged them to keep as many patrols in the field as possible, to find the Indian trails, to follow them relentlessly and to bring the red marauders to battle.

On Washington's birthday, 1856, the Regiment drew its first blood in Texas. Captain James Oakes, with a detachment from Company C, left Fort Mason on February 14, just a month to the day after the Regiment had arrived at the post. Oakes was in pursuit of a band of Waco (Huaco) Indians reported to have been lifting scalps and stealing horses in present Kimble County. A frenzied settler had ridden in with the news. On the third day out, Oakes picked up the Indian's trail and followed it for six days. Finally the horse soldiers caught up with the Wacos and brought them to battle just west of old Fort Terrett (present Sutton County) on February 22. The Indians were routed, several being killed and wounded. Two men of Company C, Sergeant Samual Reis and Private John Kuhn, were severely wounded, and arrows passed through the clothing of several others. The cavalrymen were exposed to cold, wet weather and ran out of food on the way back to the Fort. Several of the beautiful bay horses of Company C had to be killed and eaten. Oakes and his detachment were commended by Army Headquarters for "their gallant conduct ... under circumstances of great hardship and privation ...."[12] Trophies were brought back from the battle, and Mrs. Johnston received "two arrows stained with the blood of a brave warrior."[13] Thus did the 2nd Cavalry draw their first blood in Texas.

---

[12] General Orders, No. 14, Army Headquarters, November 13, 1857. Captain James Oakes who led the detachment was graduated from West Point with the Class of 1846 and was initially assigned to the 2nd Dragoons. He served with the 2nd Dragoons in the Mexican War where he was brevetted twice for bravery, and in Texas following the war where he saw action in several engagements with the Indians and was wounded twice. Oakes was assigned to the 2nd Cavalry upon its establishment in March, 1955, and fought with the Regiment in Texas. He remained with the Federal Army during the Civil War and rose to the rank of colonel. Oakes remained in the Regular Army (6th Cavalry Regiment) after the war. Price, pp. 280-82.
[13] Eliza Johnston, p. 492.

The next contact with the frontier raiders followed shortly. Captain Albert Brackett, while out on a routine scout with a detachment from Company I, on March 8, 1856, surprised a party of Lipan Apaches near the Guadalupe River. The Indians were returning from a raid along the Cibolo, not far from San Antonio. They had killed two settlers, looted cabins and driven off live stock. First Sergeant Henry Gordon of Company C discovered the Apaches, about 25 in number, camped in a dense cedar brake not far from the Guadalupe. Inasmuch as the cedar was too dense and the ground too rocky for horses, the troopers charged on foot firing their carbines as they advanced. The Indians were completely surprised and after slight resistance fled through the cedar brake and rocks leaving their ponies and plunder behind. Papers and clothing found at the abandoned camp proved they had done the killing and looting along the Cibolo. The total loss of the Apaches was not known, but three warriors were killed. Brackett's men suffered no casualties. The Department commander complimented the command upon "its brilliant success" and cited 1st Sergeant Henry Gordon, Sergeant Thomas E. Maley and Corporal John E. Weige for their "gallant conduct."[14]

Scouting expeditions were not the only affairs that enlivened the days of the 2nd Cavalry at Fort Mason. A sensational court-martial and a hushed up scandal had the post buzzing during the spring of 1856. The former concerned the son of a famous Texas hero, and the latter one of the most promising young officers of the Regiment.

The most publicized court-martial in the history of the 2nd Cavalry, and one of the most famous ever held in Texas, concerned Captain Charles Edward Travis, commander of Company H. The trial was held at Fort Mason, as most of the witnesses, both for the prosecution and defense, were stationed at

---

[14] **Price,** pp. 44, 663; **Eliza Johnston,** pp. 492, 500. Captain Albert Brackett, the detachment commander, served in the Mexican War as an officer with a company of Indiana volunteers. He was appointed a captain in the 2nd Cavalry from civilian life when the Regiment was organized. He saw much action in Texas with the Regiment and was commended for his actions several times by both the Department and the Army commanders. Brackett remained with the Federal Army during the Civil War and saw extensive action in both the Western and Trans-Mississippi theaters of war. He was promoted to brevet colonel at the end of the conflict. During the latter part of the Civil War Brackett wrote **A History of the U.S. Cavalry, 1793-1863.** Following the war he served at various posts in the West and commanded the 3rd U.S. Cavalry Regiment. **Price,** pp. 326-330.

the Fort. The court-martial convened on March 15, 1856, with Lieutenant-Colonel Henry Bainbridge, 1st Infantry Regiment, as President. Other members of the court were from the Mounted Rifles and both the 1st and 7th Infantry Regiments.[15] The trial revived memories of one of the great episodes in Texas history — the Battle of the Alamo. Charles E. Travis was the only son of Colonel William Barret Travis, commander at the ill-fated mission, who like the rest of his command had died on March 6, 1836, fighting for Texas independence.[16] On March 3, 1836, Colonel Travis had written to a friend; "Take care of my little boy. Should I perish he will have nothing but the proud recollection that he is the son of a man who died for his country."[17] The court-martial created a great sensation throughout Texas and was closely followed by the leading journals of the State.

Charles Travis had been appointed to the 2nd Cavalry from civilian life upon the activation of the Regiment in the spring of 1855. At the time of his appointment, March 3, 1855, he was the captain of Company E, Texas Rangers, stationed at Fort Clark. Travis reported to Regimental Headquarters at Louisville, Kentucky in early May, was assigned as commander of Company H and was then detailed to recruiting service at Evansville, Indiana on May 29. He continued on this duty until August 6, when he joined his company at Jefferson Barracks. Charges were preferred against Travis by 2nd Lieutenant Robert C. Wood, Jr. while the Regiment was still at Jefferson Barracks. Wood accused the Captain of slander and of circulating a gambling debt charge against him. Other charges were made against Travis on the march to Texas, which caused Colonel Johnston to relieve him of command of his company and put him "under arrest in quarters" on December 10, 1855.[18]

The formal charge against Travis was, "Conduct unbecoming an officer and gentleman." Specifically Travis was accused of (1)

---

[15] Record Group 153, Records of the Office of the Judge Advocate General, H H 626, "Proceedings of the Court in the case of Captain Charles E. Travis, 2nd Cavalry." National Archives, Washington, D.C. Hereafter cited as **Record Group 153.**

[16] Charles Travis was born in Alabama in 1829. He later lived in New Orleans with his mother and step-father, and upon their deaths in 1848, he moved to Brenham, Texas, to live with his sister, Mrs. John Grissett. A practicing attorney, he represented Caldwell and Hays Counties in the Texas Legislature, 1852-54. **Handbook**, Vol. II, p. 795.

[17] **Price**, p. 325.

[18] **Price**, p. 325; **Record Group 153; Eliza Johnston**, pp. 479-80.

cheating at cards at Jefferson Barracks on October 1, 1855; (2) unauthorized absence from Camp, November 16, 1855; and (3) creating and circulating false and slanderous imputations against 2nd Lieutenant Robert C. Wood, Jr. Travis pleaded "not guilty" to the charge and three specifications. He employed H. M. Lewis as his counsel, but being an attorney himself, he acted as his own counsel during most of the trial. Captain Eugene E. McLean, Quartermaster Department, was appointed Judge Advocate of the court. Many of Travis' fellow officers, including Colonel Albert Sidney Johnston, and five of the ten company commanders served as witnesses for the prosecution and condemned the Captain's actions. The testimony of the Regimental Commander was particularly damaging, for Johnston testified that Travis had lied to him on several occasions.[19]

The court-martial dragged on for almost a month and was finally adjourned on April 11, 1856. The verdict was "guilty" of the charge and the first specification and "guilty" on the second and third specifications with certain deletions. Travis was sentenced "to be dismissed from the service of the United States." The decision of the Court was upheld by President Pierce, and Travis was dropped from the rolls of the Army as of May 1, 1856.[20] Many officers of the Regiment thought that the sentence was too severe.[21] Perhaps if Travis had been a graduate of the United States Military Academy the verdict might have been different, but there is no doubt after reviewing the testimony that the Texan was indiscreet, untruthful, and guilty of poor judgement.

A bitter Charles Travis went to Austin, after his dismissal, to enlist the help of the Texas Legislature in clearing his name. He found a sympathetic audience, a joint committee of legislators examined the testimony of the military trial and recommended that he be publicly vindicated. This vindication came on August 30, 1856, in the form of a joint resolution by the Texas Legislature which expressed the opinion that "the sentence was not sustained by the testimony, and requested that President Pierce re-examine the proceedings, and, if possible, to reverse the

---

[19] **Record Group 153.**
[20] General Orders No. 6, Adjutant General's Office, Washington, D.C., May 9, 1856.
[21] **Price,** p. 325.

findings and reinstate him."[22] The President refused to heed the joint resolution, and the findings stood. Travis attempted then by "ill-advised means" to make several officers who had been active in his prosecution amend their testimony as given at the trial. Unfavorable newspaper comments concerning his tactics precluded any further efforts to clear his name. Travis returned to his sister's home in Washington County, where he died of consumption in 1860.[23]

Although Fort Mason was far from the bright lights of the city and the avenues of sin and debauchery, at least one major scandal was hushed around the post during the spring of 1856. This "skeleton in the closet" was never made a matter of official record, as far as can be determined, but Mrs. Albert Sidney (Eliza) Johnston made it a matter of unofficial record by referring to it from time to time in her diary. No doubt it was the major subject of gossip among the officers' wives and helped to enliven their drab days at the post.

The scandal revolved around one of the most dashing and debonair officers of the 2nd Cavalry, 1st Lieutenant Charley Field.[24] Charles William Field was a native of Kentucky, a West Point graduate and was known as the *beau sabreur* of the Regiment. According to Eliza Johnston's cook, the handsome lieutenant had enticed a St. Louis woman away from her husband while the 2nd Cavalry was forming at Jefferson Barracks. In order that she could accompany him to Texas, Field arranged to have her employed as a laundress with the Regiment. A baby born to the laundress several weeks after the Regiment arrived at Fort Mason looked surprisingly like the sandy haired, blue eyed lieutenant — so said the women of the post. Mrs. Johnston noticed, much to her disgust that shortly after the baby was born the two "lived openly as man and wife." Captain Oakes' wife kept the commander's wife informed daily of the more romantic details of the illicit love affair. The prolonged affair finally caused Eliza

[22] Ibid., p. 326.
[23] Ibid., p. 326. Handbook, II, p. 795. Eliza Johnston had little regard for Charles Travis. In her diary she referred to him as a "mean fellow [whom] no one respects or believes a word [that] he says . . . ." **Eliza Johnston, p. 480.**
[24] Field was born in Kentucky and was graduated from West Point with the Class of 1849. He served with the 2nd Dragoons in New Mexico, Texas and Kansas before being assigned to the 2nd Cavalry in the spring of 1855. **Price, p. 343.**

Johnston to record in her diary, "Oh! You immoral men, what should be your fate for all of the sorrow you cause in the world."[25]

As a matter of fact, Charley Field's fate was not too bad. His subsequent career was most successful. During the Civil War he rose to the rank of major general in the Confederate Army. He was wounded severely at 2nd Manassas (Bull Run) but recovered sufficiently to lead Hood's Division the last year and half of the war. Field's combat record was outstanding, and at Appomattox it was said that his "was the only organized and effective Confederate division" left in the Army of Northern Virginia. Following the war the ex-Confederate general was hired by the Khedive of Egypt to help train his army. In 1878, Field returned to the United States where he served as doorkeeper of the National House of Representatives. He died in Washington, D.C. in 1892 at the age of 64. Although Charley Field's private life cannot be condoned, his public life was exemplary.[26]

On March 31, Colonel Johnston was ordered to San Antonio to replace General Persifor E. Smith and take command of the Department of Texas. Less than a year previously he had been a major and paymaster for the forts in Central Texas; now he was the Department Commander. Johnston also continued as commander of the 2nd Cavalry, and thus the Regimental Headquarters was transferred from Fort Mason to San Antonio. He remained the department commander until he was relieved by General David E. Twiggs on May 18, 1857. Colonel Johnston, however, would retain command of the Regiment until July 28, 1857, when he was placed in command of the Utah Expedition during the Mormon trouble.[27] The Texan was greatly loved and respected by his officers and men, and much of the success that the Regiment enjoyed while stationed in Texas prior to the Civil War was due to

[25] Eliza Johnston, p. 493. Following this diary remark, Mrs. Johnston commented, "I never can talk to the man [Field] with pleasure or patience again and yet he is considered a gentleman and a fine officer." Ibid. To rid the Regiment of the scandal, in early June, 1856, Johnston had Field assigned to recruiting service with duty station at West Point. "Post Returns," Ft. Mason, June, 1856. Microfilm Copy No. M 617, Roll No. 759, National Archives, Washington, D.C. Hereafter cited as "Post Returns" with name of Post, dates and roll number.
[26] Warner, pp. 87-88; Douglas Southall Freeman. Lee's Lieutenants, 3 Vols., New York: Charles Scribner's Sons, 1944, Vol. 3, pp. 112, 768. Hereafter cited as Freeman, Lee's Lieutenants; Price, pp. 344-45.
[27] Price, pp. 186-87; Eliza Johnston, pp. 494-95.

his dedication and diligence. Lieutenant Richard Johnson, who served as Johnston's quartermaster and who lived next to him at Fort Mason, knew him as well as any officer in the Regiment. Johnson wrote, "He was one of the most unselfish men I ever knew, and one of the most just and considerate to those under his command .... His desire to make the 2nd Cavalry the finest regiment in the army was seconded by every officer of whatever rank under his command."[28]

Even though the Regimental Headquarters had moved to San Antonio with Colonel Johnston, the bulk of the 2nd Cavalry remained at Fort Mason, and scouting expeditions continued to leave the post weekly. Captain Oakes, who had drawn first blood for the Regiment in February, had another brush with the Indians on May 1. Oakes, accompanied by 1st Lieutenant William B. Royall, two noncommissioned officers and thirty-one troopers of Company C, rode west from Fort Mason on April 21 in search of Comanche trails. The men rode 450 miles through desolate, waterless country, routed a party of Comanches near the headwaters of the Concho River, killing one warrior and wounding several others. Oakes and his command returned to Fort Mason on May 11 after an absence of twenty-two days. The detachment from Company C was cited in General Orders for "gallant conduct ... under circumstances of great hardship and privation . . . ." and Sergeant Alex. Mck. Craig, and Privates James Montgomery, John M. Plample and William C. Smith were specifically cited as "distinguishing themselves" in the engagement against the Indians.[29]

One of the most ambitious attempts to bring the red

[28] **Johnson**, pp. 107-08.

[29] **Price**, pp. 45, 663; "**Post Returns**," Fort Mason, May, 1856. Lieutenant Royall, who accompanied Captain Oakes on this foray was a veteran of the Mexican War, serving as a lieutenant with a Missouri volunteer cavalry company. His record in the war was outstanding. Following the war, Royall returned to civilian life. He was given a commission in the 2nd Cavalry when that Regiment was organized in March, 1855. Lieutenant Royall, while with the 2nd Cavalry, engaged in several fights with Indians and spent much time recruiting for the Regiment in the East. When the Regiment left Texas in March, 1861, he commanded Company C. Royall remained with the Federal Cavalry during the Civil War. In hand to hand fighting during the War he received six saber cuts which disabled him for field service for the rest of the conflict. Following the Civil War, Royall served at various posts in the West mostly in an administrative capacity. He fought under General Crook during the Sioux Campaign of 1876, and was commander of the 4th Cavalry when he retired in the mid-1880's. **Price**, pp. 292-98.

marauders to battle occurred during the summer of 1856, when four companies of the 2nd Cavalry combined their efforts to seek out the raiders. Companies A and F left Camp Cooper under Lieutenant Colonel Robert E. Lee on July 11, and Companies B and G rode from Fort Mason on June 12, the four companies uniting at Fort Chadbourne on June 18. It was reported by scouts that a large party of Comanches under Chief Sanaco had gathered near the headwaters of the Brazos not far from Chadbourne. Lieutenant Colonel Lee was in command of the expedition. Lee, who had not marched with the Regiment to Texas, finally rejoined it at Fort Mason on March 11, after court-martial duty at Fort Leavenworth and Riley (Kansas Territory), Carlisle Barracks in Pennsylvania, and West Point. Johnston assigned Lee to command Camp Cooper on March 27, and the Virginian relieved Major Hardee there on April 9.[30]

On June 18, Lee, with four companies of cavalry, supply wagons, guides and Indian interpreter Jim Shaw, rode northwest from Chadbourne toward the headwaters of the nearer branches of the Brazos and Colorado Rivers (present Fisher County). After a week of slow travel and no signs of fresh Indian trails, Lee sent the wagons back along with several sick men and lame horses, and proceeded westward with no tents and with but seven days rations for the remaining men and horses. After another two days of riding, the column struck the trail of a small party of Comanches. Lee sent Captain Van Dorn and two companies west to follow the trail, while he took the other two companies north to find the main stream of the Brazos, thinking that the Indians would be heading for water. He found the main course of the Brazos, scouted the area for several days but saw no fresh Indian trails, and so turned back south to rendezvous with the other column. Van Dorn had had better luck: he had finally caught up with the small party that he was trailing on July 1, after a 200 mile ride. Two of the four warriors in the party were killed, and all of their property and thirteen horses and mules were taken. A squaw with the party was captured and later was returned to her father.[31]

---

[30] **Price**, p. 45; "**Post Returns**", Camp Cooper, June, 1856, Microfilm No. 253. Soon after leaving Camp Cooper, Hardee was assigned as commandant of the Corps of Cadets at West Point. **Hughes**, p. 55. Lee had written his daughter from Camp Cooper that he had to live in a tent, had seven hens to furnish him eggs and a rattlesnake for a pet. Freeman, **Lee**, I, pp. 364-65.

[31] Freeman, **Lee**, I. pp. 366-67: **Price**, p. 45: "Regimental Returns." Second

The expedition into the Comanche Country had netted little for the many days of hard riding in the hot sun. The companies returned to their stations on July 23 after an absence of forty days. The distance covered by all of the units was 1,600 miles, and they traversed some thirty-two present Texas counties. Lee was to write after the expedition that the "weather was intensely hot, and as we had no tents we had the full benefit of the sun . . . the water was scarce and bad, salt, bitter and brackish."[32] Headquarters of the Army in General Orders No. 14, dated November 13, 1857, noted the long ride into Comanche Country, citing the "gallant conduct of the troops under circumstances of great hardship and privation."

One of the few sporting events and recreational activities enjoyed by the troops at Fort Mason in the summer of 1856 was horse racing. Several of the officers had thoroughbred mounts and on the slightest provocation would stage races for visiting officers attending court-martial sessions or inspecting the post. These races were referred to as "The Fort Mason Derby." The two fastest horses proved to be "Bumble-Bee" owned by Lieutenant Nathan G. Evans and "Gray-Eagle" owned by Lieutenant Walter H. Jenifer. However, Captain Innis N. Palmer's chestnut mare and Lieutenant Charles W. Field's bay filly were good enough to provide exciting competition for the Evans and Palmer horses. Ladies attending the Derby bet gloves and handkerchiefs and the officers baskets of champagne "and here and there, a pay account." The course normally run was 1,000 yards, but occasionally a mile course was laid out. The best jockey proved to be Lieutenant Van Camp who "had an easy and graceful seat" and "had never lost a basket of champagne on the slowest horse." Other jockeys with winning records were Lieutenants Jenifer, Wood and Field, all were light in weight and skilled at riding.[33]

During the summer of 1856 the Regiment of Mounted Rifles was reassigned from Texas to New Mexico. This necessitated the

Regiment of Cavalry, July, 1856, Microfilm Copy No. 744, Roll No. 54. Hereafter cited as "Regimental Returns" followed by date. Col. M. L. Crimmins, "Robert E. Lee in Texas: Letters and Diary." WTHA, Vol. VIII (June, 1932), p. 6. Hereafter cited as Crimmins, "Lee in Texas." R. C. Crane, "Robert E. Lee's Expedition in the Upper Brazos and Colorado Country," WTHA, Vol. XIII, Oct., 1937, pp. 54-58. Hereafter cited as Crane, "Robert E. Lee's Expedition."

[32] Crimmins, "Lee in Texas," p. 6; Crane, "Robert E. Lee's Expedition," p. 61.

[33] Price, pp. 45-59.

redistribution of the companies of the 2nd Cavalry to other posts along the frontier vacated by the Rifles. The first squadron, Companies A and F, under Captain Van Dorn, was to move from Camp Cooper and establish a new camp where the direct road from Fort Mason to Fort Belknap crossed the Colorado River in present Coleman County. This post, established in early August, was called Camp Colorado and would act as a buffer zone between Camp Cooper and Fort Mason. Too, this would give more flexibility to the central defense area and protect the exposed settlers along the Llano and Colorado River valleys. The second squadron, Companies B and G, commanded by Captain E. K. Smith, was to remain at Fort Mason. The third squadron, Companies C and I, was divided; Company C (Captain James Oakes) remained temporarily at Fort Mason but would soon move to Fort Clark (present Kinney County), while Company I (Captain Albert Brackett) was to establish a new post where the El Paso Road crossed the Sabinal, to be called Camp Sabinal. The fourth squadron, Companies D and K, was divided, Company D (Captain Innis Palmer) was to take station at Camp Verde (present Kerr County), and Company K (Captain Charles Whiting) was to garrison Fort Inge (present Uvalde County). The fifth squadron, Companies E and H, was also divided, Company E (Captain George Stoneman, Jr.) remained at Camp Cooper, and Company H (Captain Nathan Evans) was ordered to join the first squadron at the new camp on the Colorado. [34] The Regimental Band remained at Fort Mason. Following this redistribution, the companies of the Regiment were widely scattered along the frontier; they would not come together again until the winter of 1861-62, during the Civil War.

In the midst of these company reassignments, Colonel J. K. Mansfield, on an inspection tour of the Department of Texas, visited Fort Mason. He remained at the Fort from July 17 to the 19 and his observations give a good picture of the post and the companies of the 2nd Cavalry stationed there in mid-1856. Major George H. Thomas was in command of the post. There were still three companies of the Regiment at the Fort, Companies B, C, and G, commanded respectively by Captains E. K. Smith, James Oakes and W. R. Bradfute. Most of the officers and men of Companies B

---

[34] "Regimental Returns," July, August and September, 1856; **Price,** pp. 49-50.

and G were with Colonel Lee's Expedition. Only Captain Oakes' Company was in garrison during Mansfield's inspection, and it had but two officers, fifty-five men and forty-two horses present for duty.[35]

Colonel Mansfield noted that the cavalrymen did not score as high with the "new rifled Musketoon" as did the infantry companies, and that Post Quartermaster Lieutenant R. W. Johnson had hired a "citizen saddler at 40 dollars [per month] and a ration, 2 citizen guides at 40 dollars and a ration and forage. — And as extra duty men, 10 teamsters, 2 clerks, 2 herdsmen, 2 ostlers, and [for transportation] 17 wagons, 2 ambulances, 175 mules, 6 horses." The Inspector reported that the rent for the post was $50 per month, paid to sutlers Howard and Lane who owned the land, and that he [Mansfield] ordered to be dropped [condemned] from the supply records "2 bridles, 21 valises, 17 holsters, 3 lariats and straps, 3 horse brushes, 2 curry combs and 50 nose bags."[36] Mansfield further stated that bacon was locally purchased for 14¢ a pound and fresh beef at 6¢ per pound, and that the nearest sutler, the beef contractor, lived nine miles away. "There are no Indians about here," wrote Mansfield, "except marauding parties, principally heretofore Comanches, and they sometimes come to destroy property without capturing it, as arrows have been fired through calves while in an enclosure. But they have latterly [sic] been hunted so severely," he added, "that those not on the reservation, have gone west and north."[37]

Several important engagements with the Indians, principally Comanches, took place soon after the companies reached their new stations. Captain Oakes, Lieutenant Witherell and thirty men of Company C, accompanied by small detachments of the 1st Infantry and 1st Artillery Regiments left Fort Clark on August 20 for the Pecos River to scout for Comanches. No other Federal troops had ever moved through this area (present Val Verde County). On August 30, Oakes and his command performed a feat not again performed while the 2nd Cavalry was in Texas. They

---

[35] "Colonel J. K. F. Mansfield's Inspection Report of Texas," SWHQ, Vol. XLII (April, 1939), No. 4, pp. 357-359.
[36] Ibid., pp. 359-60. Howard and Lane who operated the sutler's store (post exchange) at Fort Mason must have done well financially. Not only did they collect a monthly rent for the land but sold liquor at the post by "sufferance." In relation to the latter, they must have garnered a good share of the monthly payroll.
[37] Ibid., pp. 360-61.

surprised and fought three separate bands of Indians in one day. The encounters took place on August 30, 1856, near the junctions of the Pecos and Rio Grande Rivers. During the three engagements eight warriors were killed or wounded and their animals and other property captured or destroyed. For these engagements, Oakes' command was cited in General Orders from Army Headquarters for "gallant conduct . . . under circumstances of great hardship and privation . . . ."[38] The detachment was absent 20 days from Fort Clark.[39]

After Company I (Captain Albert Brackett) arrived at Camp Sabinal in late July, it was constantly out on scout between the Hondo and Nueces Rivers. There were few settlers in this country and those that were there were of the hardiest type, as this area was far beyond the "settled frontier." The civilian guides employed by Brackett at Sabinal were Westfall and Robinson, who were not only expert trackers but experienced Indian fighters as well. Both had been shot several times in encounters with roving Comanche bands the year before. Even though detachments of Brackett's company were out on patrol almost daily, they did not encounter a single war party.[40] Company I left Camp Sabinal on September 3 for Fort Clark and was replaced at Sabinal by Company K (Captain Charles Whiting).[41]

November and December, 1856, were busy months for the Regiment, and the companies at Fort Mason provided their share of this increased activity. It was not uncommon for several patrols to leave a fort during a month or even a week, but an unusual occurrence took place at Fort Mason in mid-November, two scouting parties left the post the same day, November 17, and both actively engaged bands of Comanches. Lieutenant Walter Jenifer, with a small detachment from Company B, left the Fort early on the morning of the 17th; and Captain William Bradfute, with a detail from Company G, left that same afternoon. Jenifer, two days out, on November 19, surprised a small Comanche war party on the Llano River, just south of Fort Mason. In an old fashioned cavalry charge with bugles blowing and sabers drawn, the Lieutenant and his command bore down on the camp of the

---

[38] **Price**, pp. 50-51.
[39] "Regimental Returns," September, 1856.
[40] **Price**, pp. 51-52.
[41] "Regimental Returns," September, 1856.

startled warriors. Scattering in all directions, the Indians fled into the cane brake and thick undergrowth, leaving no bodies but plenty of equipment and other property for Company B to take back to Mason.[42]

A few days after Jenifer's affair — on November 26, Captain Bradfute's patrol had a sharp encounter with a party of marauding Comanches near the headwaters of the Middle or Main Concho. Four Indians were killed, about the same number were wounded, and one was captured. Bradfute also captured their horses and mules and much camp equipment was seized. One soldier, Private John Curtis, was severely wounded. The detachment from Company G returned to Fort Mason in early December after a march of 500 miles.[43]

Lieutenant James Bonaparte Witherell with detail from Company C and accompanied by Lieutenants Wesley Owens of Company C and E. W. H. Read of the 8th Infantry,[44] left Fort Clark on patrol December 18. After riding in bad weather for three days, Witherell surprised a party of Mescalero Apaches on December 21 camping on the east bank of the Rio Grande. The cavalrymen charged the Indians, who were posted in a dense stand of chaparral, and drove them across the river into Mexico. Two of the Apaches were killed, two were wounded and all of their property, including horses and guns, were taken. Lieutenant Read, the volunteer from the 8th Infantry, "was distinguished in this combat for conspicuous gallantry" and the entire command commended for "gallant conduct . . . under circumstances of great hardship and privation . . . ."[45]

A major Indian fight, perhaps the most desperate of the year, terminated the 2nd Cavalry's first year of operation in Texas. Captain Richard W. Johnson,[46] with a detachment of 25 men

---

[42] **Price**, p. 53.

[43] "Regimental Returns," December, 1856; **Price**, p. 153.

[44] Both Owens and Read were volunteers. Read was enroute to his duty station, but, being unable to secure an escort, reported for duty with Company C of the 2nd Cavalry at Fort Clark. He remained with the Company from December 16, 1856, to January 7, 1857. **Price**, p. 54.

[45] "Regimental Returns," December, 1856; **Price, pp. 54, 663.**

[46] When Captain Theodore O'Hara resigned on December 1, Johnson was promoted to Captain and took command of Company F. Johnson had not enjoyed his year as the Post Quartermaster. He wrote, after being promoted to Captain, "I had reached that rank which would ever exempt me from duty with mules, broken harness, and the accumulated trash and rubbish which drift into the storehouses in charge of a Post Quarter-

from Company F, left Camp Colorado on Decmeber 18 with rations for twenty days. Johnson was accompanied by 2nd Lieutenant A. Parker Porter, newly assigned to Company A (Captain Van Dorn) from West Point. Johnson had been given a map sketched by Van Dorn of the country that he had planned to scout, and the commander of Company A had also given Johnston his personal notes of the area made during an earlier expedition. At one point on the map, near the headwaters of the Concho, Van Dorn had printed, "BIG INDIAN FIGHT." After four days march in "cold weather with short fuel," Johnson's command on December 22 came upon a large Comanche camp in a thicket near the headwaters of the Concho. It was part of Chief Sanaco's band.[47] By coincidence Johnson found the Indian camp to be at the spot that Van Dorn had marked on the map.

The conflict was sharp. After cutting off the horses and mules from the surprised Comanches, Johnson divided his command into two groups. He commanded one and Porter the other. The Indians, assaulted from two sides, retreated from the thicket into a dense chaparral, here the Comanches stopped and put up a stubborn fight. The cavalrymen dismounted, charged the position and finally drove the Indians through the chaparral and beyond, killing three and badly wounding several others who were carried off. The troops "rescued" a Mexican captive, who had been with the Indians since early life. However, he refused Johnson's offer to return him to his people. First Sergeant Thomas Gardner termed the Mexican, "a naturalized Comanche," and wanted to kill him but Captain Johnson refused the request, and "the captive lived to

---

master." **Johnson,** p. 109. Richard W. Johnson was graduated from West Point with the Class of 1849. He served with the 1st U.S. Infantry in Texas in the early 1850's prior to being transferred to the 2nd Cavalry in March, 1855. Johnson distinguished himself in combat with the Indians on several occasions while he served with the Regiment in Texas. He remained in the Federal Army during the Civil War and rose to the rank of major-general. Johnson retired at this rank in 1867 for disability from wounds received in battle. He had a distinguished post war career as an author and educator. Johnson's two best known works were **A Soldiers Reminiscences** and his biography of General George H. Thomas. **Price,** pp. 336-37; **Warner, Gray.** pp. 253-54.

[47] Chief Sanaco and his 800 followers had originally settled on the Comanche Reservation in Texas in September, 1855, but three months later fled from the encampment on the Clear Fork of the Brazos and tried to get the other Comanches to follow suit. Sanaco remained off the reservation permanently and raided the frontier thereafter. **Koch, SWHQ,** Vol. XXIX, pp. 104-05.

eat roast beef in the guardhouse at Camp Colorado."[48] Thirty-four horses were captured, as well as all of the Indian's camp equippage. Company F had two men killed in the attack, Bugler Ryan Campino and Private Timothy Lamb. Both were shot through the heart with arrows. These were the first members of the 2nd Cavalry killed in combat in Texas. Two of the Company were wounded, 1st Sgt. Gardner and Private Jim McKim. The detachment was commended in General Orders from Army Headquarters for "gallant conduct . . . under circumstances of great hardship and privation."[49]

The Regiment was actively employed during 1856 on a frontier line that extended from the Red River in North Texas to Fort McIntosh on the Rio Grande. Most of that time the men were fighting and living under field conditions. The companies were successful in every combat with the Indians, killing and wounding many, and capturing numerous horses and mules and seizing much camp equippage and other property. Thirty major and minor expeditions were made during this first year in Texas, which served to train the men in field service against a worthy foe. The word spread rapidly among the marauding tribes that an aggressive search and fight campaign was now being waged by the horse soldiers. The daring Indian raids of 1855 and early 1856 through the line of forts would almost cease by 1857. After 1856 the cavalry detachments had to patrol farther and farther west in search of their quarry. A scouting expedition which lasted a month and covered 600 miles would not be uncommon.

---

[48] **Price,** p. 54; **Johnson** pp. 109-110. Johnson in his **Reminiscences,** wrote of 1st Sgt. Gardner, he was "a splendid old soldier . . . but occasionally he would indulge his appetite in drink." **Johnson,** p. 110.
[49] **Price,** p. 663.

CHAPTER SEVEN

1857 – HOOD'S DEVIL'S RIVER FIGHT

Then, the war drums broke the silence,
And re-echoed from its crest;
   Now, the gentle zephyr ripples
The Llano's placid breast.
   And at eve its shining waters
Flowing onward to the sea,
   Bring in fancy, ghostly shadows
Of the gallant Hood and Lee.
   It was here the dark marauders
Played havoc in their day;
   While undaunted the 2nd Cavalry,
Kept the savage hordes at bay.
                    – Author Unknown

The stable of Company G, 2nd U.S. Cavalry, at Fort Mason, Texas, was alive with activity in the early morning hours of July 5, 1857, as twenty-five troopers of Captain Bradfute's Company, swearing and sweating, hurriedly saddled their brown mounts.[1] Joseph P. Henley, 1st Sergeant of Company G, passed from man to man helping to adjust equipment, inspecting saddle bags — mess kit and personal belongings in one; hardtack, bacon and coffee in the other — and passing out ammunition, 25 rounds to a man. Pack mules would carry reserve ammunition, extra food and forage, enough for a month's campaigning.[2]

With the call, "Boots and Saddles," each horse soldier who had finished checking his weapons (saber, carbine and pistol) and adjusting his saddle and equipment led his horse out to the parade ground on the sloping crown of Post Hill. After the last cavalryman had left the stable, Sergeant Henley, leading both his horse and that of the detachment commander, made his way up the rocky slope, past the officers quarters and joined his men on the parade ground. Here the Sergeant formed his detail and

---

[1] J. B. Hood. **Advance and Retreat.** New Orleans: G. T. Beauregard, 1880, p. 8. Hereafter cited as **Hood.**
[2] **Ibid.**

awaited the appearance of the leader of the scouting expedition.[3]

The wait was short. From the direction of Post Headquarters, strode the tall, lean, tawny-bearded lieutenant, West Point graduate and man of action — John Bell Hood. With the grace of a born Kentucky horseman, Hood swung easily into the saddle, wheeled his big brown mare around, and faced his command. Crisp, clear orders rang out — "Stand to horse;" "Prepare to mount;" "Mount, ho" — and the twenty-five horse soldiers settled into their saddles and brought their mounts into line.

Hood, putting the troopers at ease, briefed the command on the orders that he had received from Major George H. Thomas, the Post Commander. The detachment, Hood said, was to ride west from Fort Mason along the North Llano to a point some 15 miles the other side of old Fort Terrett.[4] The purpose of the expedition, he added, was "to examine and explore" an Indian trail, running north and south, that had been reported by Lieutenant John T. Shaaff, out on a scout, a few days before.[5] The Lieutenant, asked for questions; receiving none, he brought the command to attention and then gave the orders: "Prepare to move out;" "Column of twos by the right flank, ho." The column led by Hood moved off the parade ground, down the eastern slope of Post Hill to the Fredericksburg Road and turned south toward the Llano.[6] At the head of the column, accompanying the Lieutenant, was John McLoughlin, famous Delaware scout and tracker of the 2nd Cavalry.[7]

The detachment soon struck the Llano and turned west

---

[3] Simpson, p. 135. Henley, who was born in Ireland, enlisted in the 2nd Cavalry in 1855, and as a non-commissioned officer was involved in several engagements while the Regiment was in Texas. He left Texas with the 2nd Cavalry in March, 1861, and remained in the Federal Army during the Civil War. Henley was the 1st Sergeant of the Regiment when he was commissioned a 2nd Lieutenant in April, 1863. Promoted later to captain and a company commander, Henley fought at Gettysburg and other engagements in the East. He was killed in action at the battle of Trevillian Station, Virginia, June 12, 1864. **Price**, pp. 505-06.

[4] Fort Terrett in present Sutton County was established February 5, 1852 and abandoned on February 26, 1854. Robert W. Frazer. **Forts of the West** Norman: University of Oklahoma Press, 1965, pp. 163-64. Hereafter cited as **Frazer**.

[5] "Report of Lieutenant John B. Hood" included in the Report of the Secretary of War, 1857. Sen. Exec. Doc's. 35th Cong., 1st Session, No. 11, p. 131. Hereafter cited as **Hood's Report**.

[6] Simpson, p. 136.

[7] H. G. Rost. "Desperate Fight on Devil's River," **Frontier Times**, Vol. 21, p. 142. Hereafter cited as **Rost**.

toward Indian country. After three days ride, the column came to the crumbling ruins of Fort Terrett, abandoned to the elements several years previously. Hood decided to camp here for the night, and Private Dick Hopkins, the designated "huntsman" for the detachment, was sent out on a quest for wild game to supplement their hard tack and bacon. Hopkins cornered a bear in a cave not far from camp and came back for help to dispatch the animal. Sergeant Deaton, who led the volunteers, succeeded only in wounding the bear, and in the ensuing flight from the cave with the enraged brute at his heels, Deaton rolled down a hill dislocating his knee cap. Fortunately a shot from another member of the party felled the animal, and the detachment feasted on bear meat for supper that night and breakfast the following morning. Deaton was too badly injured to continue on the patrol, so was sent back to Fort Mason accompanied by Corporal Henry Jones.[8] This reduction in the size of the detachment would almost prove fatal.

Not finding the trail reported by Shaaff, Hood, bent on action, continued on in a northwesterly direction toward the headwaters of the Middle Concho and the bleak country beyond. The detachment passed several old trails, but saw nothing worth pursuing and continued on westward through wasteland dotted occasionally with cactus and sagebrush. John McLoughlin, the Indian scout, dependenable when sober and always daring, ranged far in front of the column, seeking a fresh pony trail or other signs of recent Indian activity.

Hood's persistence finally paid off. After 12 days out from Fort Mason, while exploring several creeks that emptied into the Middle Concho, McLoughlin discovered a recent Indian trail near the mouth of Kiowa Creek. The trail, from all indications, appeared to be but two or three days old, and there were from 15 to 20 ponies in the party. The raiders were moving south toward Mexico via the headwaters of the Devil's River. Hood, without hesitation, after hearing the scout cry, "Comanche," McLoughlin's signal for a fresh trail, directed the column south and took up the chase on July 17. With the trail three days old, and a land barren of food, forage and water ahead, overtaking the marauders before they reached Mexico would be a difficult task. Fatigue and

---

[8] Ibid., p. 142.

privation would be the daily routine for both men and animals.[9]

The detachment, rode south several miles, then turned east to a water hole, "two miles south of the head of Lipan Creek." The war party had stopped here and then had headed due south. Hood continued the chase, following a line of water holes that were from 35 to 50 miles apart, a course that marked one of the main Comanche trails into Mexico. The dogged cavalrymen rode rapidly south under a brutal July sun. Unfortunately, few of the water holes yielded palatable water. The smell was so bad at several of the watering places that the men had to hold their breath as they drank from the stagnant pools. At the scum-covered, brackish ponds the soldiers filled their canteens and the sleeves of all waterproof coats; they could take no chances: even if the water was bad, each water hole might be the last.

For four days Hood led his command, their blue uniforms grey from alkali dust, in a relentless forced march across the barren plains of southwest Texas. A private riding with the detachment, wrote, ". . . we pushed on out to the dry plains, and soon the cry for water was heard among the men. It was the hottest weather I ever experienced and our horses suffered beyond measure . . . ."[10] Each day the Indian trail became more distinct. While this encouraged the troopers to greater effort, the pace was telling on the horses, several of which began to show great fatigue and leg weariness. An ominous sign appeared on the morning of July 20, when the command came to a waterhole a few miles above the head of Devil's River — a second party of Indians had joined the first group. Evidence at a campsite near the stagnant body of water indicated that not fewer than 50 marauders had camped there. Wisps of smoke still rose from the embers; the quarry was near.

The increase in the size of the Comanche force, the jaded condition of the army mounts, and the extreme thirst and hunger of the soldiers caused the young West Pointer to reassess the situation. His command would be outnumbered at least two to one, and while the Indians, who had been traveling at a much less punishing pace, would be fresh and alert, his animals and men were much fatigued. Fortunately the horse soldiers were well

[9] **Hood's Report**, p. 131.
[10] **Rost**, p. 142.

armed. Each private carried a Springfield rifle carbine and a Navy Colt six-shooter revolver. The noncommissioned officers carried the same arms as the privates and in addition a heavy dragoon saber. Hood himself was a veritable mounted arsenal. He carried, besides a dragoon saber and two Navy Colt revolvers, a double-barreled shotgun loaded with heavy buckshot. The consensus (no doubt dominated by the aggressive lieutenant) was to continue the pursuit and bring the "Terrors of the Plains," as the Comanches were often called, to combat as soon as possible.

The detachment from Fort Mason pressed on during the afternoon of July 20, expecting any moment to sight the war party. The cavalrymen crossed the bluffs near Devil's River and followed south some three miles east of the river. "Late in the afternoon," Hood wrote, "from the extreme thirst of my men, I left the trail to go to the river and camp. About one mile from the trail," he added, "I discovered some two miles and a half from me, on a ridge, some horses and a large white flag waving."[11] The Lieutenant was not certain whether the group he sighted was the Comanches he sought or a band of friendly Tonkawas on their way to Mexico under safe passage orders from Army Head-quarters. According to information that he received prior to leaving Fort Mason, the Tonkawas were to display a white flag for identification if they were intercepted by a military force. Hood, aware that the flag and the small group of Indians clustered around it could be bait for a trap, cautiously approached the ridge and its occupants.

The terrain in the area was rough and partially covered with a growth of Spanish bayonet that offered excellent concealment. When the detachment was a hundred yards or so from the Indians, the Lieutenant halted his men and warned them not to fire until he gave the order. Leaving six men with leg weary mounts and Scout McLoughlin to guard the pack mules and supplies, Hood formed the remaining 17 troopers into line and, taking position to the front and right of his command, gave the order to advance. The Lieutenant was taking no chances; his shotgun, double-cocked, was lying across the pommel of his saddle.[12] As the cavalrymen drew near to the cluster of Indians, a half dozen or so of them, bearing the white flag, left the hill and walked towar⁻˙

---

[11] **Hood's Report**, p. 131.
[12] **Rost**, p. 142; **Hood**, p. 11; **Hood's Report**, p. 132.

Hood, apparently in a show of friendship. However, when the warriors were within "some 30 paces" of the advancing horse soldiers they threw the flag to the ground, brandished their concealed weapons and rushed toward Hood and his men.[13] As the warriors threw down the flag (which apparently was the signal for the attack), some thirty others on foot arose from the Spanish bayonet and about twelve on horseback rode from behind the ridge toward the cavalrymen. Simultaneously with this assault, the squaws fired a large heap of dried grass, weeds and leaves directly in front of the troopers. The dense smoke and crackling fire greatly effected the soldier's horses, causing several of them to plunge and rear. With hideous yells, some 50 warriors, vividly painted, stripped to the waist, and with horns or feathers on their heads, advanced on the troopers from both flanks.[14]

The cavalrymen answered the challenge of battle with a shout of their own and engaged the warriors in hand-to-hand fighting. All of the Indians carried tough buffalo-hide shields, and while those on foot were armed with either guns or bows and arrows, those mounted carried flint-tipped lances — deadly in the hands of expert horsemen like the Comanches.[15] Outflanked by a force at least three times his number and hemmed in by a wall of fire and smoke to his front, all that Hood could hope for was that superior marksmanship and discipline would prove to be the decisive elements in the fight.

Lieutenant Hood, who was well in advance of his men, was the first target. Two warriors rushed at him, one from each side, and attempted to drag him from the saddle. Two quick blasts from his shotgun at point blank range all but decapitated his attackers and frustrated a quick attempt by the Comanches to down the leader of the horse soldiers. Hood then drew his revolver and led his men into the midst of the advancing Indians driving them back toward the fire. The handful of troopers, like their leader, fought fiercely in their attempt to whittle down the odds against them. After firing their carbines, the soldiers drew their revolvers and, firing at close range, did fearful execution. The melee continued unabated for some time; the fighting was primarily hand-to-hand, and no quarter was asked or given. Sergeant Henley killed a chief

---

[13] **Hood's Report,** p. 132.
[14] **Ibid.; Hood,** p. 12; "General John B. Hood's Victory," **Frontier Times,** Vol. IV, No. 7 (April, 1927), p. 16.
[15] **Hood's Report,** p. 132.

decked out in a war bonnet by parrying his lance thrust and then cleaving his skull open with a saber stroke. Several cavalry mounts were beaten about the face and neck with the buffalo hide shields in an attempt to unhorse the rider.[16]

Herman G. Rost, a veteran of the Mexican War, and a member of Hood's command, wrote, concerning the severity of the action,

> In the heat of the hand-to-hand encounter, an Indian seized my horse by the bridle reins, another seized me by the right leg, and yet another had me by the left leg, trying to pull me off. I still held my gun, although it was empty, when an Indian from behind rushed forward and seized it and wrenched it from my hands . . . . When I drew my pistol, I shot the Indian that was pulling my left leg and he fell over . . . . When I shot the Indian on my left I turned to attend the Indian on the right, but just at that moment one of the boys shot him . . . .[17]

Rost, along with his surviving comrades, was later cited in Army Orders for "gallant conduct" during the engagement.[18]

Hood kept rallying his men as the fighting waged back and forth, with first one side and then the other gaining temporary advantage of the smoky field.[19] As the Indians discharged their rifles, they passed them back to their squaws, who handed back a second rifle while they reloaded the first one. Thus the Comanches were able to deliver a punishing sustained fire. The soldiers, after expending the full loads of their Navy Colts, following Hood's orders, fell back about 50 yards and dismounted to reload their weapons.[20] The restlessness of the horses and the "deadly fire of the Indians" would not permit the troopers to reload while

---

[16] **Hood's Report**, p. 132. Hood stated in his autobiography that he "felt most grateful that [his] horses were so broken down as, but for these conditions," he wrote, "they would, doubtless, when beaten over the head with shields, have become totally unmanageable and caused the massacre of my entire command." Hood, p. 13.

[17] Rost, p. 143. The hand to hand combat at Devil's River caused Hood thereafter to arm half of his command with sabers and the other half with pistols, in addition to their carbines. **Price**, p. 60.

[18] **Price**, p. 664.

[19] Rost wrote, that Hood's "stentorian voice of cheer and command was heard above the unearthly din" and that he could "never forget the coolness and bravery of Lieutenant Hood . . . ." **Rost**, p. 143.

[20] It was Hood's contention that if each of his men had had two six-shooters he could have killed or wounded all of the Indians. **Hood's Report**, p. 132.

mounted.[21] Just before falling back with his men to reload, Lieutenant Hood was painfully wounded. An arrow pierced both his left hand and the reins, pinning his hand to the bridle. After breaking the arrow head off, Hood withdrew the shaft from the wound. A handkerchief, wound tightly around his hand, staunched the bleeding.[22]

As the cavalrymen were in the process of reloading their arms, a terrible wailing and howling arose from beyond the smouldering brush. This sound, although bloodcurdling, was reassuring to the soldiers, for it meant that the Indians would not renew their attack. It was the sound of sorrow uttered by the squaws as the dead and wounded were being gathered up. Another attack by the Comanches while the men were dismounted and loading would have wiped out the detachment from Company G, for Hood had but a half dozen men and mounts left that were suitable for combat. The Lieutenant attributed the survival of his command against such great odds to two things, one, that the "Indians did not have the self-possession to cut our bridle reins, which act would have proved fatal to us," and, two, that "we were mounted and above their level seems to have rendered their aim very imperfect."[23]

The Indians, after picking up their dead, and with nightfall approaching, disappeared through the underbrush toward the Rio Grande. The detachment from Fort Mason, with worn out mounts, short on food and water, and having suffered several casualties, was in no condition to pursue.[24] Hood moved his crippled command to Devil's River, where it bivouacked for the night. At the same time he dispatched a rider to nearby Camp Hudson for supplies and medical aid.[25]

The loss for Company G had been rather severe for a small command; two soldiers had been killed (Privates William Barry and Thomas Ryan), one had ben dangerously wounded, and three

---

[21] **Hood's Report**, p. 132; **Hood**, p. 13.
[22] "Battle With Indians on Devil's River," **Frontier Times**, Vol. III, No. 6 (March, 1926), p. 14.
[23] **Hood**, p. 13, 15.
[24] Trooper Rost reported that the suffering of the command after the battle was "beyond description. Nearly every man was wounded, some severely, and few of our horses escaped the shafts of the enemy. We had not a drop of water and were tortured with thirst." **Rost**, p. 143.
[25] Camp Hudson in present Val Verde County was established on June 7, 1857 on San Pedro Creek near Devil's River. **Handbook**, I, p. 281.

soldiers and Hood had been badly wounded. One horse was killed, three were wounded, and the rest were leg weary. After the engagement Hood had but 11 men left to protect his wounded and his horses.[26]

In his official report of the battle, Lieutenant Hood estimated that his command had killed 8 or 9 Indians and had wounded about double that number.[27] The exact number of Comanche casualties, Hood explained, was difficult to determine due to the nature of the ground cover and the pall of smoke that hung over the battlefield. It was verified later (by Reservation Indians who had been in the engagement) that there had been close to 100 Comanches and Lipan-Apaches in the party that Hood attacked and that the Indians had nineteen warriors killed (including two minor chiefs) and a great number wounded.[28]

A relief column under Lieutenant Theodore Fink from Company G of the 8th U.S. Infantry Regiment stationed at Camp Hudson reached Hood's battered command on July 21, the day following the battle. The wounded, other than Hood, were sent back to Camp Hudson to rest and recuperate. Hood and the remnant of his cavalry detachment, accompanied by a 15 man detail from the 8th Infantry, returned to the scene of the battle to bury the dead and continue the fight if any of the marauders still lurked around. The blood, feathers, torn clothing, spent arrows, and discarded equipment that littered the churned-up ground attested to the severity of the struggle. Private Thomas Ryan's body was found "horribly mutilated," in addition to multiple wounds and marks a rifle ramrod had been thrust lengthwise through his body. Private William Barry's body was not found.[29] The scouts who had been sent forward to pick up the trail soon returned and reported that the Indians had scattered in so many directions that further pursuit was impossible. Using picks and shovels brought from Camp Hudson, the soldiers buried Ryan in the field. A close search for Barry's body proved futile.[30]

Lieutenant Hood and the troopers of his command who were

---

[26] **Hood's Report**, p. 132.
[27] **Ibid.**
[28] **Hood**, pp. 14-15.
[29] **Rost**, p. 143; "Post Returns," Camp Hudson, July, 1857. Microfilm Copy No. M-617, Roll No. 495.
[30] **Hood**, p. 14.

fit to travel rode by easy stages east to Fort Clark, in present Kinney County, arriving there on July 27. Here Hood wrote his report of the Devil's River Fight and forwarded it to the Headquarters of the Texas Military District at San Antonio. After remaining at Fort Clark for a few days to rest the men and the horses, the survivors of the expedition rode northeast to Fort Mason, where they arrived on August 8.[31] Hood's command had been on the mission for almost five weeks and had ridden over 500 miles through dry, desolate country. Except for Van Dorn's two battles north of the Red River in 1858 and 1859, Hood's encounter on the Devil's River in 1857 would be the most severe engagement fought by the 2nd Cavalry while it was in Texas.

The expedition leader and his men were commended for gallantry by both General David E. Twiggs, commander of the Department of Texas, and General Winfield Scott, commanding general of the United States Army. Twiggs, in forwarding Hood's report on to Washington stated in his endorsement, "Lieutenant Hood's affair was a most gallant one, and much credit is due to both the officers [sic] and men." Winfield Scott before passing the report on to the Secretary of War wrote, "This combat was . . . a most gallant one, and I shall take pleasure in taking some further notice of it."[32]

The battlefield aggressiveness and disregard for his personal safety shown by John Bell Hood at Devil's River in 1857 would carry over into the Civil War, where he would first gain fame as commander of the hard-fighting Texas Brigade. Hood would climb rapidly in the Confederate Army, advancing from a 1st lieutenant in April, 1861, to a full general in July, 1864 — the eighth and last Confederate officer to achieve this rank. He rose more rapidly in rank than any officer in the Civil War — North or South. Badly maimed by the loss of an arm at Gettysburg and the amputation

---

[31] "Post Returns," Fort Mason, Texas, July, 1857. Microfilm Copy No. M-617, Roll No. 759.

[32] "Report of the Secretary of War, 1857." Sen. Exex. Doc's., 35th Cong., 1st Session, No. 11, pp. 131-2. Shortly after Hood returned to Fort Mason he was promoted to 1st lieutenant, reassigned to Company K, and placed on duty at Camp Colorado. In 1858 he reestablished Camp Wood and remained here until he was granted a leave of absence in November, 1860. Hood refused an assignment as Chief of Cavalry at West Point and, although still on leave, returned to Camp Wood in February, 1861. He accompanied the Regiment to Indianola when it left Texas in March, 1861, and soon thereafter resigned his commission in the U.S. Army. **Hood**, p. 15.

of a leg at Chickamauga, he nevertheless fought throughout the conflict, aggressive to the end.

By 1857 the Regiment was in excellent condition for field service. A year on the Texas frontier had enabled the cavalrymen to acquire a knowledge of the country, to improve their horsemanship and to gain valuable experience in fighting their wily foe. Too, by this time the Indians had come to realize that they could not successfully engage the mounted troops on equal terms, consequently they began to mass their numbers into larger bands for their depredations along the frontier. Hood's fight on the Devil's River in mid-July was an example of this change in strategy by the Southern Plains Indians. Heretofore no cavalry detachment had fought such a large band of the red marauders.

The year 1857, with fourteen engagements and several long scouting expeditions, was the most active year for the 2nd Cavalry in Texas. Although the Devil's River fight was the most serious of the engagements, several of the others are worth recording in some detail. In early February, Lieutenant Robert C. Wood, Jr.,[33] accompanied by Scout John McLoughlin, and with a detail of 15 men from Company B left Fort Mason on a routine scout. Three days from the Fort, the detachment struck a fresh Comanche trail. Wood and his men followed the trail at an extended pace and overtook the raiders — a party of five braves — near the North Concho on February 12. The troopers fired a volley from their carbines then followed up the fusillade with a saber charge, driving the Indians through the chaparral. The entire party was wiped out, three being killed and two captured along with their horses and other property. Lieutenant Wood, who was slightly wounded, was the only casualty suffered by the cavalry.[34]

Two months later Wood would engage the Indians a second time. With a detachment of 28 men from his company, Lieutenant Wood left Fort Inge in early April, soon picked up a fresh Indian trail northwest of the Fort, and vigorously pursued it. The

---

[33] Wood was appointed to the 2nd Cavalry from Louisiana. He resigned his commission on January 1, 1858, and returned to his home state. During the Civil War he fought with the Confederate States and participated in many campaigns with the Army of Tennessee. At the end of the war he was a colonel of cavalry. Following the Civil War, Wood resided in New Orleans. **Price,** pp. 545-46.

[34] **Price,** p. 57; **Brackett,** pp. 172-73; "Post Returns," Fort Mason, February, 1857.

troopers of Company B, after five days of alternately riding and leading their horses through mountainous country, finally caught up with the marauders on April 19 near the headwaters of the Nueces. Wood defeated the Comanches, inflicting on them "a severe loss" and captured most of their property, including horses, without loss to his detachment.[35]

Due to the few officers present for duty in some of the companies, non-commissioned officers, on many occasions, were detailed to lead scouting expeditions. Such was the case in mid-February, 1857, when a detachment from Company D, stationed at Camp Verde, met a band of Comanches on Kickapoo Creek (present Schleicher County). The cavalry detachment lead by 1st Sergeant Walter McDonald, after pursuing the Indians closely for several days, finally brought them to battle on February 13. After "a severe combat," McDonald and his men drove the Comanches from the field, killing six and capturing their pony herd. Two of the cavalrymen were badly wounded, Private John Martin and Bugler James Tafford. Martin died the following day (February 14) at Fort McKavett. Sergeant McDonald was recognized for his outstanding leadership by being "honorably mentioned" in General Orders from the Army Headquarters.[36] This was the first of two such citations that McDonald would receive while in Texas with the 2nd Cavalry.

During February and March several of the companies changed duty stations. Company F, now commanded by the recently promoted Captain Richard W. Johnson, the former Regimental Quartermaster, on February 22, was moved from Camp Cooper to Fort Mason. On March 4, Company B, commanded by Captain E. Kirby Smith, was reassigned to Fort Inge from Fort Mason. Company K, Charles J. Whiting commanding, moved from Fort Inge to Fort Clark in mid-March, and Captain Albert Brackett's Company, Company I, was transferred from Fort Clark to Fort McIntosh on the Rio Grande. It took Brackett 9 days (March 19 to 27th) to make the 175 mile ride from Clark to McIntosh, encumbered as he was with his baggage and equipment.[37]

One of the most courageous actions performed by a

---

[35] Price, p. 58; "Post Returns," Fort Inge, April, 1857, Microfilm Copy No. M-617, Roll No. 517.
[36] Price, pp. 57, 664; "Regimental Returns," March, 1857.
[37] "Regimental Returns," March, 1857.

detachment of the 2nd Cavalry took place in early April near the headwaters of the Nueces in present Edwards County. Lieutenant Walter H. Jenifer with a sergeant and 12 privates from Company B left Fort Inge on March 23 on a routine scout north along the Nueces.[38] After a search of 13 days in which the detachment traveled about 300 miles, Jenifer discovered a fresh Indian trail on April 4 near the headwaters of the north branch of the Nueces and followed it through hilly, rocky country for the better part of a day. Due to the ruggedness of the terrain, the Lieutenant decided to pursue the Comanches on foot. Leaving five men to guard the horses, Jenifer led the remaining seven men on a fatiguing march of several miles through broken country, finally sighting a camp of some 100 Indians. Instead of quietly withdrawing when faced with such odds, Jenifer continued his approach until he was about 150 yards from the Comanche camp. The troopers were finally discovered and attached by those Indians in camp as well as a returning mounted party coming up on their flank. The cavalrymen, heavily outnumbered and withdrawing slowly, fought a skillful delaying action taking cover behind the rocks as they fell back. After losing three warriors and being repulsed several times, the Comanches broke off the engagement. When night came the Lieutenant and his men withdrew and rejoined the rest of his detachment.[39]

Jenifer, undaunted by his narrow escape, determined to inflict more casualties on the enemy. The next morning the plucky officer returned to the scene of engagement, but the Comanches had disappeared. The detachment from Company B was in the field for 17 days and ran out of rations several days before they returned to Fort Inge. For this action on April 4, Lieutenant Jenifer and his command were cited in General Orders from Army

---

[38] Lieutenant Jenifer had an interesting military career. He served as a lieutenant in both the 2nd and 3rd Dragoons during the Mexican War, resigning his commission at the end of that conflict. He was commissioned a lieutenant in the 2nd Cavalry from civilian life on March 3, 1855. He resigned his commission in the U.S. Army at the start of the Civil War and served the Confederacy with distinction as a cavalry officer. He was promoted to brigadier general at the end of the war but never served in that grade. Following the war he spent 5 years in the Army of the Khedive of Egypt as Inspector-General of Cavalry. Jenifer was an outstanding horseman, and once rode from Fort Mason to Fort McKavett, a distance of 70 miles, in seven hours without changing horses. He was the inventor of the well known Jenifer saddle. Walter H. Jenifer died in 1878 with cancer of the throat. **Price,** pp. 467-68.

[39] **Price,** pp. 57-58; "Regimental Returns," March, April, 1857.

Headquarters for "gallant conduct . . . under circumstances of great hardship and privation [and were] entitled to high approbation."[40]

Three more expeditions by detachments from Company B were made from Fort Inge during May, June and July. Walter H. Jenifer, the intrepid lieutenant assigned to Company B, left the Fort in mid-May with a small detachment on a routine scout. After several days out Jenifer came across a fresh trail near the Nueces River. He pursued the Comanche band for a short time, overtaking it on May 25 near the headwaters of the river. After a token resistance in which they suffered some casualties the Indians scattered. Jenifer's detachment had no losses and captured the ponies and supplies left behind by the fleeing raiders. The detachment returned to Inge on June 8, after three weeks in the field.[41]

Two non-commissioned officers from Company B lead successful scouting expeditions from Fort Inge during the summer of 1857. Lance Corporal John Boyden, commanding a detachment of 10 men, left on a routine scout in mid-June. After a few days of riding northeast from the Fort, Boyden came across a fresh Indian track near the Frio River. Following north he overtook the Comanche raiding party near the headwaters of the Frio on June 30, and immediately engaged the raiders in battle. After a sharp skirmish, the cavalrymen scattered the Indians, causing an undetermined number of casualties and capturing all of their equipment and animals. Boyden's command suffered no casualties.[42] Sergeant William P. Leverett left Inge a few days after Boyden, riding northwest with a detachment of 12 men. The Sergeant and his men trailed a party of marauders north, finally catching up with them on July 2 near the south branch of the Llano. Leverett charged the camp of the Comanches, causing some loss, and drove the survivors across the river, capturing one horse and much of their property.[43] Both Boyden and Leverett were commended in General Orders for their leadership.[44]

There was a change of regimental commanders during the summer of 1857. Albert Sidney Johnston, the popular Texan, who

---

[40] **Price**, pp. 58, 664.
[41] **Ibid.**, p. 58; "Post Returns," Fort Inge, June, 1857.
[42] "Post Returns," Fort Inge, July, 1857.
[43] **Ibid.**
[44] **Price**, p. 664.

had commanded the elite organization since its activation in March, 1855, was reassigned to Army Headquarters in Washington, and was succeeded in command by Lieutenant Colonel Robert E. Lee. Johnston had been selected to lead the largest body of troops ever assembled on the frontier (5,500 men) to the Utah Territory where Brigham Young and his Mormon followers had disputed Federal authority.[45] Lee, whose duty station was Camp Cooper, was sitting on a General Court-martial, at Fort Mason when informed of his new assignment. He immediately left for San Antonio, arriving there on July 28, and assumed command of the Regiment the next day.[46] Lee's tenure as commander of the 2nd Cavalry in 1857 was short, less than three months. On October 21, he received word that his father-in-law, G. W. P. Custis, had died at Arlington, Virginia. Lee was granted a two months leave to go to Virginia to be with his wife, a semi-invalid, and to administer the Custis estate. He left San Antonio on October 24 for Virginia and would not return to Texas again until mid-February, 1860.[47] Upon Lee's departure, Major George H. Thomas was assigned to command the 2nd Cavalry. Thomas would continue as Regimental Commander until November 12, 1860, and would command the unit while it was in Texas longer than any other officer.[48]

Scouting parties involving all companies of the 2nd Cavalry at regular intervals traversed the area some 200 miles west of a line running from Camp Cooper on the north through Fort Mason to Fort McIntosh on the Rio Grande during the summer and fall of this pivotal year. Captain Charles J. Whiting,[49] accompanied by

---

[45] **Herr**, p. 83; **Roland**, p. 184. Fortunately the Utah Expedition turned out to be a bloodless affair, but it did win a star for Johnston and assignment as commander of the Department of Utah. He later commanded the Department of the West, a position from which he resigned in 1861 to join the Confederate States of America as its ranking field general. **Warner**, pp. 159-160.

[46] **Lee**, pp. 377-78.

[47] **Ibid.**, p. 405. Due to his wife's delicate health, involvement with the Custis estate and John Brown's Raid on Harpers Ferry, Lee had his leave extended on several occasions and was on leave or detached duty for over two years.

[48] **Price**, p. 594.

[49] Whiting was graduated from West Point with the Class of 1835, but resigned his commission soon after graduation and entered the civil engineering profession. He was appointed a captain in the 2nd Cavalry when that Regiment was activated in March, 1855. Whiting remained loyal to the Federal government during the Civil War but was dismissed from the army in December, 1863 "for disloyalty and for using contemptuous and disrespectful words against the President of the United States [Lincoln]." He was restored to duty as a major by order of Lincoln's successor,

Lieutenant James P. Major, led a 40 man detachment composed of Companies C and K from Fort Clark on July 21, and picked up the trail of a Comanche party near the headwaters of the Devil's River. The party was thought to have been the same one that had attacked Hood a few days earlier. Whiting, using a camel instead of the customary pack mules, pursued the retreating foe until August 10th when he overtook them in the Wichita Mountains. After a sharp fight, the cavalrymen scattered the Comanches, killing two, wounding several others and capturing all of the horses and mules belonging to the raiders. The detachment returned to Fort Clark on August 29. The captured animals were later sold at auction, and in an unprecedented action, the proceeds, some $400, were equally divided among the men.[50] Whiting and his command were mentioned in General Orders for "gallant conduct . . . under circumstances of great hardship and privation . . ."[51]

Two engagements were recorded for September. Captain Nathan G. Evans,[52] set out on September 10 from Camp Cooper with a detachment of 50 men from Company H. Riding north toward the headwaters of the Washita, Evans surprised a large group of Comanches near the headwaters of the main Brazos on September 24. Before scattering the Indians, the detachment killed two of the party, captured one, and secured all of their horses and camp equipage.[53]

About the same time that Evans led a scouting party from Camp Cooper, Sergeant Charles M. Patrick left Fort McIntosh with a contingent of 12 men from Company I. On September 28, after a search and pursuit of an Indian trail for seven days, Patrick caught up to a hostile band of Comanches near the settlement of Santa Catarina. The raiders fled after the first volley, losing one

---

Andrew Johnson, in May, 1866. Whiting served at various frontier posts in the Southwest during the post-war period, ending his career as the commander of Fort Griffin, Texas, in 1870. **Price,** pp. 333-34.

[50] **Price,** p. 61; "Regimental Returns," August, 1857.

[51] **Price,** p. 664.

[52] Evans, a South Carolinian, was graduated from West Point with the Class of 1848. He was nicknamed "Shanks" by his West Point classmates because of his spindly legs and carried the sobriquet the rest of his life. Evans had a turbulent Civil War career. He was placed under arrest and court-martialed more times than any other Confederate general with the possible exception of Henry H. Sibley. Evans two principal weaknesses and cause for his poor record were his predilection for strong drink and his inclination to be insubordinate. He was said to have been well liked by his fellow officers. **Warner,** p. 84; **Price,** pp. 335-36.

[53] **Price,** p. 61; "Regimental Returns," September, 1857.

killed and four wounded. Ten of their animals were captured by the cavalrymen. Patrick, eager to destroy the entire party, followed the Indians closely for the next two and a half days, covering some 160 miles over rough and mountainous terrain. Finally catching up to the retreating band, Patrick led a charge against the remaining hostiles, driving them into the thicket and down a ravine, where they dispersed in the tall grass. During the charge Patrick's horse fell, and while he survived the concentration of fire directed against him, his horse was killed. For this fine example of leadership, tenacity and courage, Sergeant Patrick and Private John McCarty were given "honorable mention" in General Orders and all members of the command were cited for "gallant conduct . . . under circumstances of great hardship and privation . . . ." Captain Albert Brackett, Commander of Company I, in his official report of the affair that was forwarded to Departmental Headquarters in San Antonio, "highly commended [the detachment] for persistent pursuit, gallant conduct and successful encounter."[54]

Second Lieutenant Cornelius Van Camp, on October 29, lead a detachment from Company D out of Camp Verde, in pursuit of marauding Comanches. The Indians had been terrorizing the settlers along the Guadalupe River Valley. Van Camp overtook the raiding party on October 30 on Verde Creek and after a "hot chase of six miles over a country so broken and rocky that many of his horses were disabled — the sharp rocks tearing the shoes from their hoofs" caught up to the raiders. In a running battle the cavalrymen succeeded in wounding two warriors and capturing most of their property. For this determined pursuit and resulting action, the command was cited in General Orders as "deserving of high praise for gallantry."[55] Van Camp, a young officer of great promise, would be killed in battle the following year.

A detachment composed of men from both Companies C and K and commanded by Lieutenant James B. Witherell[56] rode out

---

[54] Price, pp. 61, 664; "Regimental Returns," September, 1857.
[55] Price, pp. 61, 664.
[56] Witherell was appointed a second lieutenant in the 2nd Cavalry when the Regiment was activated in March, 1855. He had no prior military experience. Witherell was commended for his leadership and bravery several times while the 2nd Cavalry was assigned to the Texas frontier. When the Regiment was preparing to leave the state in March, 1861, he was drowned near the mouth of the Rio Grande while changing ships. Witherell's body was never recovered. **Price**, pp. 478-79.

from Fort Clark on November 4 to pursue a band of Comanches. The Indians had stolen 18 mules from the Overland Mail and Stage Company the day before. Pursuing the raiders for four days and a distance of 90 miles, the detachment overtook and routed them on November 8 some 70 miles northeast of the Nueces River in present Kimble County. During the engagement one warrior was killed, several were wounded, the stolen mules were recovered and most of the raider's property and camp equipage was captured. Lieutenant Witherell and three privates, Louis Gehring (Company C) and Charles Morris and Patrick Connell (Company K) were wounded. The detachment was commended in General Orders as "deserving of high praise for gallantry."[57]

The last conflict for the year 1857, involved a detail from Company I, commanded by Lieutenant Wesley Owens.[58] Owens left Fort McIntosh in early November on a punitive expedition to chastise a group of Lipans and Comanches who had committed depredations within the corporate limits of Laredo. After several days on the trail the cavalrymen caught up with the raiders near Salamonana. Owens pressed the Indians closely, forcing them to abandon most of their "animals, camp equipage and ammunition" and to seek safety on foot in dense chapparal. The troopers followed the raiders into the undergrowth but found it impossible to dislodge them. A few days later, a party of Indians thought to be the same party that had been attacked by Owen's detachment appeared some 16 miles below Laredo and kidnapped a boy. Captain Brackett, leading a second detachment from Fort McIntosh,[59] failed to make contact with the roving band.

In General Orders No. 14 dated November 13, 1857, Winfield Scott, Commanding General of the U.S. Army, commended nine exploits of the 2nd Cavalry for that year. Besides these nine there were five additional skirmishes with the Indians; however, even

---

[57] Price, pp. 62, 664; "Regimental Returns," November, 1857.
[58] Wesley Owens was graduated from the U.S. Military Academy with the Class of 1856. He joined Company I of the 2nd Cavalry at Fort Clark in December, 1856. He participated in several engagements while assigned to the Regiment and was commended on two occasions for his bravery and leadership. He was assigned to the academic staff at West Point in the Fall of 1860, and fought with the Federal Army during the Civil War. Owens rose to the rank of lieutenant colonel and was on duty with the Military Division of the Pacific when he died of tuberculoses in 1868. Price, pp. 361-63.
[59] Price, pp. 62-63.

this battle record of fourteen engagements is no measure of the activity, hardships and the useful results of the Regiment's employment along the frontier. Detachments of the 2nd Cavalry scouted the country continuously. Scores of scouting expeditions left the various posts during the year, and each was a test of endurance and tenacity. The troops were exposed to severe cold in the winter and a merciless sun in the summer; they endured great thirst and were often compelled to subsist on the flesh of broken down horses or, in some cases to go without food for several days. Many of the marches were made through rocky, hill country and dense undergrowth, the country so broken, in fact, that often the horses had to be led. Even under these conditions they made some surprising marches, in some cases as much as 150 miles in less than three days. These expeditions, conducted with energy, judgement and courage, inflicted a serious loss of personnel, equipment and mounts on the marauding foe and made the frontier a safer place to live.

CHAPTER EIGHT

1858 – VAN DORN STRIKES NORTH

*A victory more decisive and complete than
any recorded in the history of our Indian Warfare.
The general commanding the department
[Twiggs] hoped much from this command, and
he is most happy to say that the brilliancy
of its success has been such as to exceed his
most sanguine expectations.*[1]

Clearly one of the things that made the 2nd Cavalry great was the outstanding quality of the officers assigned to the Regiment. Another of the strengths of the 2nd Cavalry, and one that is not so well known, was the high caliber of its non-commissioned officers — the backbone of any military unit, and the unsung heroes of the Indian fighting army. As noted in the previous chapter, the first non-commissioned officer in the Regiment to lead a detachment that engaged the Indians was 1st Sergeant William McDonald of Company D. McDonald had fought a band of Comanches along Kickapoo Creek in mid-February, 1857. Fittingly, a sergeant would also lead the last contingent of the 2nd Cavalry to see action in Texas. First Sergeant John W. Spangler of Company H would engage a Comanche war party along the Pease River in mid-December, 1860.[2] Many of the Regiment's most successful encounters would be led by troopers with two or three stripes on their arms. Of the forty engagements that the 2nd Cavalry had with the Indians in Texas, non-commissioned officers would lead detachments into battle ten times,[3] and many of the casualties suffered by the Regiment would be sergeants and corporals. Three non-commissioned officers would be killed in battle and eight would be wounded. Several sergeants and corporals would be cited in General Orders for "conspicuous gallantry and unflinching courage".[4] First Sergeants Walter McDonald (Company D) and John W. Spangler (Company H) were specifically cited for such

---

[1] From General Orders No. 25, Department of Texas, October 19, 1858 in regard to Van Dorn's victory over the Comanches at Wichita Village, October 1, 1858.
[2] Price, p. 93.
[3] Ibid., pp. 650-51.
[4] Ibid., pp. 663-67.

conduct on two occasions. Spangler was later commissioned a 2nd lieutenant during the Civil War and received a brevet captaincy at Gettysburg "for gallantry and meritorious service."[5] In fact, 13 enlisted men assigned to the Regiment in Texas became commissioned officers during the Civil War.[6]

Not only were the officers and non-commissioned officers of superior caliber, but a great number of the privates, thanks to selective recruiting, appeared to be a good cut above the ordinary soldier of the day. By 1858, the companies had rid themselves of their malcontents either by desertion or by discharge and most of the troopers that remained were inured to prolonged campaigning and were excellent horsemen and aggressive fighters. Time and again, the gallant conduct of private soldiers in action was cited in General Orders and in the commander's battle reports.[7] One company commander in particular was profuse in his praise of the enlisted men that composed his unit. Captain Richard W. Johnson, Commander of Company F, wrote that he did not believe that "a more superior lot of men could have been found in the army" than those constituting his company. "About forty of them", he said, "weighed from one hundred forty to one hundred fifty pounds . . . . Each was an excellent horseman, afraid of nothing, never tired, and always cheerful and always willing to endure fatigue and hardship, if I expected it of them."[8] No doubt the other captains, had they written their *Reminiscences,* would have verified Johnson's observations in relation to their own companies.

Probably no better authority exists concerning the value of the non-commissioned officers in the Indian fighting army of the last century than Colonel M. L. Crimmins. Crimmins, who spent 52 years in the army from 1898 to 1950, was well acquainted with the role of the non-commissioned officers in the cavalry campaigns in the West: he served with many of them in the sunset of their careers and then researched and wrote about them during his last years in the army and in retirement. Colonel Crimmins con-

---

[5] Francis B. Heitman, **Historical Register and Dictionary of the U.S. Army.** 2 vols., Washington: Government Printing Office; 1903. I, p. 909; Col. M. L. Crimmins, "First Sergeant John W. Spangler, Company H, Second United States Cavalry." WTHAYB, Vol. 26, Oct., 1950, p. 75. Cited hereafter as **Crimmins,** "Spangler."
[6] **Price,** p. 618. See Appendix
[7] **Ibid,,**pp. 663-66.
[8] **Johnson,** p. 126.

tributed numerous articles concerned with the horse soldiers, especially those serving in Texas, to the *Southwestern Historical Quarterly,* the *West Texas Historical Association Year Book* and other learned journals devoted to western history.

In an article written principally about the exploits of 1st Sergeant John W. Spangler, Company H, 2nd Cavalry Regiment, Crimmins mentioned the worth of non-commissioned officers, particularly the 1st Sergeants in the Indian fighting regiments of yesteryear. He wrote as follows,

> Much has been written about our officers fighting Indians in Texas, but very little about our non-commissioned officers. Still in the regular army of fifty-two years ago, we looked upon our first sergeants as the backbone of our armed forces. The 1st Sergeant was not only in contact with his company at drills and parades; he was on duty twenty-four hours a day for seven days a week, subject to call any hour of the twenty four, any day in the week every week. He was responsible for the discipline of the company and usually stayed in the Company from his appointment until death or retirement. When war came he was often appointed a captain in the temporary armed forces in the new regiments. He was picked for his job because he was a leader, and could handle men.[9]

It was an old army saying that "a commanding officer was only as good as his sergeants." This statement was far often more correct than wrong.

Non-commissioned officers would play an increasingly important role in the scouting activities of the Regiment during the remaining years that the 2nd Cavalry served in Texas. The first engagement in 1858 was led by a non-commissioned officer, 1st Sergeant Walter McDonald of Company D. McDonald with a detachment of 13 privates left Camp Verde on January 25 to pursue a party of marauding Comanches who had been raiding settlements along San Geronimo Creek in Bandera County. After a close pursuit of four days, the cavalrymen finally overtook and attacked the Comanches on the South Llano River in Kimble County. Following a sharp engagement in which two Indians were killed and three of the troopers wounded, the marauders fled, leaving behind the horses they had stolen in Bandera County. General Orders issued by Headquarters, Department of Texas,

---

[9] Crimmins, "Spangler", p. 68.

named 1st Sergeant McDonald for the second time for "his energy and daring" and stated that his actions are "emminently worthy the emulation of every soldier in the department."[10] The same day that Sergeant McDonald's detachment left Camp Verde a second group left the Camp under Captain Palmer,[11] Commander of Company D. Lieutenant Cornelius Van Camp, Sergeant Alexander, Corporals Chase and Higgins, a bugler, a farrier and 23 privates composed Palmer's command. After searching the area west and north of Camp Verde for several days, Palmer returned to the post in early February without sighting a fresh trail.[12]

Palmer's detachment was the ideal composition for a scouting party — two officers, three non-commissioned officers, a musician (bugler), a blacksmith (farrier) and a sizeable number of troopers — 23. All that Palmer lacked was a doctor. However, only a small percentage of the scores of scouting expeditions sent out by the 2nd Cavalry had such a full complement of leaders and specialists. Most detachments were led by either a single officer or non-commissioned officer and had assigned normally 13 or 14 troopers. If a single officer commanded the detachment, he usually had a sergeant or corporal assigned, the non-commissioned officer performing both the duties of an officers aide and providing liaison with the enlisted men. Many detachments, as already noted, were commanded by a single non-commissioned officer and these were often the most effective.

During February and March of 1858, several citizens of Webb County were seized by Mexican authorities at Guerrero, in the state of Nuevo Leon. The American citizens were impressed into the army of one of the revolutionary factions of Mexico. When this fact became known in Laredo the people of the town held a mass meeting to protest the illegal seizure. Two resolutions were passed at the town meeting — the first being that prompt

[10] Price, pp. 64-65, 665; "Regimental Returns," January, 1858. The three wounded men were: Privates Thomas Hughes, Tony Stracker, and John Denny. "Regimental Returns," February, 1858.
[11] Innis Palmer was graduated from West Point with the Class of 1846 and served in the Mexican War with the Mounted Rifles. He also served in Texas with the Mounted Rifles in the early 1850's, and was appointed a captain in the 2nd Cavalry when the Regiment was organized March 5, 1855. Palmer remained with the Federal Army during the Civil War, and fought with the Army of the Potomac. At the end of the war Palmer was a major general of volunteers. He served with the 2nd Cavalry after the war and retired as a colonel in the Regular Army in 1879. Price, pp. 284-86.
[12] Price, pp. 65-66.

reparations be made to satisfy the honor and dignity of the United States; if this was not done "a Declaration of War was in order". A second resolution proclaimed that the Rio Grande was not a suitable national boundary, that Mexican renegades and hostile Indians cross the river at will and that both civil and military authorities were defied daily.

The ire of the Laredo citizens was somewhat tempered when Captain Albert Brackett, commanding Fort McIntosh, with a detail from Company I marched down the Rio Grande in late March to Redmond's Ranch, across the river from Guerrero, and demanded the release of the men in question. This demand backed by a show of force was complied with by local Mexican authorities and the men were released on March 26. Brackett became a local hero, the town council passing a resolution in his honor, commending him for his aggressiveness and bravery.[13]

Texas temporarily lost the backbone of its frontier defense system in the spring of 1858 when the War Department alerted the 2nd Cavalry for movement to Utah by the way of Fort Leavenworth. Department Commander Twiggs was informed in April that the 2nd Cavalry had been relieved from duty in Texas, and he was instructed to issue orders for the various companies of the Regiment to march immediately from the State. Major Thomas, commander of the Regiment, designated Fort Belknap as the rendezvous point in Texas for the march north to Leavenworth. The companies began to gather near Belknap during June, and by July 8 all of them were in the concentration area and had set up temporary encampments along the Clear Fork of the Brazos and on Caddo and Elm Creeks close by. The Regiment remained in the vicinity of Fort Belknap for most of July awaiting further orders and the arrival of the supply train for the move north.

The Utah disturbance turned out to be less serious than first believed and the order sending the 2nd Cavalry to Fort Leavenworth was revoked on July 31.[14] The encampments were then

[13] Ibid.
[14] Ibid., p. 66: "Regimental Returns," June and July, 1858. The Mormons had disregarded United States authority since they had emigrated to Utah in 1846. In the fall of 1857 a delegation of Federal officials under military escort were sent to Salt Lake City to establish United States jurisdiction there. As noted previously, Albert Sidney Johnston was in command of the expedition bound for Utah. Johnston's force on the approach march to Utah spent a miserable winter at Fort Bridger in the present state of Wyoming. As the United States forces drew near to Salt Lake City in the

broken up and most of the companies were reassigned back to stations on or near the frontier. Companies A and G were assigned to Fort Chadbourne, Company B to Fort Mason, Company C to Fort Clark, Company E to Camp Colorado, Company I to Camp Hudson and Companies D, F, H and K remained at Fort Belknap. The companies of the Regiment would not come together again until the spring of 1861 during the Civil War.

When General Twiggs learned that the 2nd Cavalry was to remain in Texas, he requested permission from the War Department to send an expedition into Indian country to strike the Comanches in their homeland. He desired to abandon the limited offensive scouting system completely and begin a grand offensive campaign against the hostile Southern Plains Indians that would keep them out of Texas forever. To make the move against the Comanche homeland more acceptable to Washington, Twiggs proposed to employ the troops while enroute in laying out a wagon road to the Wichita Mountains "or as near thereto as possible".[15] General Twigg's idea to carry the war north of the Red River was bolstered when the commanding officer of Fort Arbuckle, Captain W. R. Prince, informed Twiggs that large parties of Apaches, Comanches, Kiowas and Cheyennes were camped on the Canadian River near Antelope Hills and were raiding the settlements of the Choctaw Nation. The Fort Arbuckle commander was of the opinion that these raids had been made by the Southern Plains Indians "for the purpose of capturing horses with which to make incursions upon the frontiers of Texas."[16] Other indications were present that a general war with the Comanches, and other tribes that they could induce to join them, would soon break out along the entire frontier. Marauding parties from Mexico were increasing their raids north of the Rio Grande, which could be crossed with ease along most of its course. Hostile Indians visited the Comanche Reservation on the Clear Fork of the Brazos with impunity, causing unrest among the friendly Comanches and inducing many of the younger braves to leave the government compound.

---

spring of 1858, the Mormons evacuated the city and Johnston entered it without a fight. An understanding was soon reached with Brigham Young and his followers. United States authority was recognized and the army was gradually withdrawn.
[15] Price, p. 67.
[16] Ibid.

Twiggs was not the first public official to advocate carrying the war against the Comanche to their homeland north of the Red River. When the Federal Government ordered the 2nd Cavalry from Texas in April, Governor Hardin R. Runnels with the concurrence of the Texas Legislature decided to invade the lair of the marauders along the Canadian River. Runnels promoted senior Ranger Captain John Salmon "Rip" Ford to major,[17] placed him in command of all the Texas Ranger companies; regular and irregular, and ordered him "to seek out and attack the Comanche in his heartland above the Red River and to deal him a blow from which he would be a long time recovering." Ford lead a combined force of some 100 Rangers and about the same number of friendly Reservation Indians against the Comanches during May, 1858. The Reservation Indians were under the immediate command of Captain Shapley P. Ross, agent for the Brazos Indian Reservation. The forces of Ford and Ross joined at Cottonwood Springs (present Spring County) and then proceeded under Ford's command 150 miles north to the Indian Territory. Ford attacked the Indians early on the morning of May 12, in their camp a few miles north of the Canadian River. The Comanche Chief, Iron Jacket, was killed early in the fight but his followers fought bitterly for several hours before being driven from their encampment. It was a complete victory for the Texans. The Rangers had but four casualties, two men killed and two wounded. The Indian loss included 76 braves killed and an unknown number wounded. No casualties were reported for the Reservation Indians; however, it was noted that the Tonkawas, adhering to the old adage that "to the victor belongs the spoils" feasted that night on the severed hands and feet of their hated enemies, the Comanches. Ford had dealt the perennial raiders a severe blow in their own back yard.[18]

Secretary of War John Floyd concurred with Twiggs'

---

[17] Ford was one of the great Texans of the 19th century. He was a doctor, newspaper editor, legislator, Ranger, soldier, statesman and historian. He acquired his famous nickname during the Mexican War when he was Adjutant of "Coffee Jack" Hays' Texas Cavalry Regiment. As Adjutant, Ford had the duty of sending out notices of deaths in the Regiment and always included at the first of the message "Rest in Peace." Later in the war when the Regiment saw more action and the deaths were more numerous, Ford shortened his message to "R.I.P.," hence his nickname. Ford had the distinction of commanding the Confederate force at the last battle of the Civil War at Palmito Ranch, Texas, May 13, 1865. He was colonel of the 2nd Texas Cavalry Regiment. **Handbook,** I, pp. 617-18.

[18] Harold B. Simpson, "John Salmon Ford", **Rangers of Texas,** Waco: Texian Press, 1969, pp. 95-99. Cited hereafter as **Simpson,** "Ford."

suggestion for a major offense against the heartland of the Comanches. Although, Major George H. Thomas, commander of the 2nd Cavalry was the logical choice to lead the expedition, the Department Commander selected Captain Earl Van Dorn, Commander of Company A for the honor. Georgian Twiggs and Mississippian Van Dorn had similar political (secessionist) leanings. In addition, Twiggs had always admired the dash and daring of Van Dorn and had less respect for Thomas, a more stolid, slow moving officer, and although a Virginian, Thomas' position in regard to the secession movement was not known. Too, Twiggs and Thomas had a misunderstanding during the Mexican War which Twiggs had never forgotten.[19] Van Dorn's command consisted of Companies A, F, H, and K of the 2nd Cavalry, a detachment from the 1st Infantry, and some 60 Caddo and Delaware Reservation Indians. The Indians were led by Lawrence Sullivan "Sul" Ross,[20] The 20 year old son of Shapley P. Ross, the Indian Agent, who had accompanied Ford's expedition four months earlier. Van Dorn had a total force of some 300 men. The command was smaller than General Twiggs had intended, but he could not safely spare more. The various units of Van Dorn's force were to leave from Fort Belknap in mid-September and march to Otter Creek in the Choctaw Nation. A supply base from which the cavalry would operate, garrisoned by the detachment from the 1st Infantry, was to be established on Otter Creek.[21]

The expedition left Fort Belknap on September 15 and, marching in a northwesterly direction, arrived at Otter Creek in present Tillman County, Oklahoma, on the 23rd. The supply base was established on the south side of the stream near the present town of Tipton. A stockade was built on the site to protect the animals and supplies during the absence of the cavalry. The hastily erected post was called Camp Radziminski after the popular Polish-born lieutenant of the 2nd Cavalry who had died of tuberculosis earlier in the year. On September 29 information was

---

[19] Hartje, p. 63.
[20] Sul Ross, like Ford, was one of the great Texans of the last century. Ross was a captain in the Texas Rangers and earned the reputation as an outstanding Indian fighter prior to the Civil War. During the war he was promoted to brigadier general and led Ross' Texas Cavalry Brigade in the Army of Tennessee. Following the Civil War Sul Ross was elected governor of Texas (1887-91) and was serving as the President of Texas A&M College when he died in 1898. Handbook, II, pp. 506-07.
[21] Price, pp. 67-68; "Regimental Returns," August and September, 1858.

received through the Delaware scouts that a large village of Comanches was located near Wichita Village on Horse Creek in the Choctaw Nation. The Indian encampment was directly east of Camp Radziminski and the scouts estimated the distance to be about 40 miles.[22]

Van Dorn decided to strike immediately and perhaps surprise the Comanches before their scouts discovered his presence. The extra horses and supplies were quickly moved into the stockade and the cavalry and Ross's Indians moved out that afternoon (September 29) expecting to attack at daybreak the next morning. The Delaware scouts, however, having no way of measuring distance in miles had badly underestimated the mileage to Wichita Village, the 40 miles turned out to be over 90. Dawn came on the 30th, and there was no camp in sight. Van Dorn pushed his command to the limit in his eagerness to reach the Comanche encampment. The troopers and their Indian allies rode hard over rugged terrain all day of the 30th, eating their jerked beef while in the saddle. They had their first rest at sundown when the column was halted so that they could boil coffee and feed their horses. The men had ridden almost 90 miles in 38 hours, being continuously in the saddle the last 16-1/2 hours — they were close to exhaustion.[23]

After dark one of the Caddo scouts came into camp and brought word of the size and location of the Comanche village. Upon receiving this news, Van Dorn decided to move as close as possible to the Indian encampment during the night and then attack at dawn. The commander also learned from his scouts that the camp that had been sighted was that of Buffalo Hump, one of the better known Comanche chiefs, a notorious marauder, and a formidable warrior. Silently the cavalrymen and their Indian allies advanced over the rough and broken ground. The pace was painfully slow due to both the darkness and the condition of the terrain. Just before daylight, the command came upon a rolling prairie bounded on the north by a series of ridges that appeared to be from a half to three-quarters of a mile apart. The column halted, Van Dorn ordered, "Scouts out," the objective was near.

---

[22] Price, pp. 67-68; Col. M. L. Crimmins, "Major Van Dorn in Texas." WTHAB, Vol. XVI, October, 1940, p. 123. Hereafter cited as **Crimmins,** "Van Dorn."
[23] Brackett, p. 192; Johnson, p. 119.

Word was soon sent back that the Comanche camp was in a valley just beyond the ridges.[24]

Van Dorn called the company commanders together and outlined his battle plan. It was explicit. They would charge the village in four columns, each company constituting a column. The men would ride in a column of twos and the columns would be 100 yards apart, thus permitting the commanders to deploy in a company front for the attack. Upon a given signal the columns were to move out at a trot up the slopes of the ridges to their front, and, on gaining the crest, if the encampment was not in sight, they were to resume the advance at the walk, regulating or dressing on the right company. The company commanders, once Buffalo Hump's village was sighted, were to "deploy in company front and charge." The companies were to repeat this "trot-walk" procedure as they approached each ridge until their objective was sighted. Sul Ross and his Reservation Indians were instructed to detach themselves prior to the charge on the village and secure the Comanche pony herd, thus forcing the Indians to fight on foot.[25]

The tired command negotiated four ridges before the sun appeared on the horizon. Through the haze and mist that hung over the creek valley below the fourth ridge, the troopers in the advance sighted the camp of the Comanches. It stretched several hundred yards along the banks of Horse Creek and was located only a short distance from Wichita Village, a large Kiowa settlement. Buffalo Hump's camp was favorably situated for defensive purposes, the lodges being located adjacent to a series of rough and broken ravines. All was quiet in the camp. Not even a yapping dog was heard. The surprise was complete. Ross and the friendly Indians immediately moved out to complete their mission of capturing the ponies. The buglers, on Van Dorn's command, sounded the charge and some 225 troopers cheering and yelling, their sabers glistening in the early morning sun, splashed through the shallow stream and charged the village.[26]

The Comanches were dazed by the suddeness of the attack. Many of the Indians hid themselves in the lodges and tepees, others rushed out to do battle just as they were aroused and were barely dressed. A few had found time to put on war paint.

---

[24] Hartje, p. 65; Price, p. 69.
[25] Price, p. 69; Hartje, p. 66.
[26] Price, p. 69.

Although the presence of a large force of cavalry in the vicinity had been reported to Buffalo Hump the preceding day, the Chief, thinking that they were friendly soldiers sent from Fort Arbuckle to negotiate a treaty, neglected to put out the usual camp guards.[27] This failure would cost him dearly. After recovering from the initial shock of the surprise attack the Indians, deprived of their ponies, fought stubbornly on foot among the lodges in the village. The cheers of the troopers and the war cries of the Comanches were intermingled as the fighting progressed through the village and finally to the ravines beyond where Buffalo Hump and his followers put up a stubborn resistance. Despite heavy losses the warriors fought on, being aided in some cases by their women who were observed both loading guns for them and firing guns themselves. Some of the troopers dismounted and fought on foot through the brush while the mounted troopers defended the flanks and attempted to seal off escape routes from the ravines. For two hours the conflict raged, then suddenly the Indian defense gave way and the warriors, desperately trying to cover the flight of their families, fled in all directions down and over the ravines and into the underbrush beyond with the horse soldiers in close pursuit.[28]

Although the main battle of Wichita Village was over, several bands of Indians who had fled the ravines were hunted down and brought to battle. Many warriors were killed and wounded several miles from the encampment. Lieutenant Harrison of Company H, with a small detachment, discovered a party of 18 warriors driving a large herd of horses over a distant hill and immediately gave chase.[29] After a pursuit of some two hours the detachment

[27] **Hartje**, p. 65. Unfortunately, two departments of the government were working at cross purposes. While the Interior Department was attempting to negotiate treaties with the Southern Plains Indians, the War Department was ordering the military forces to attack and punish the Indians. Mildred Mayhall, "The Battles of Wichita Village and Crooked Creek," **True West**, Jan.-Feb., 1972, pp. 14-15. Hereafter cited as **Mayhall**.
[28] **Hartje**, pp. 65-67; **Price**, pp. 69-70; "Regimental Returns," October, 1858.
[29] James E. Harrison had an interesting career prior to his assignment to the 2nd Cavalry. He was a 2nd Lieutenant in the U.S. Revenue Service during the period 1853-1856, but fought in an Indian campaign in the fall of 1855 in the Washington Territory in which he was cited for his coolness and bravery. Harrison was appointed a 2nd lieutenant in the 2nd Cavalry on June 27, 1856. He engaged in numerous Indian campaigns with the 2nd Cavalry and remained with the Federal army during the Civil War. He was promoted to lieutenant-colonel during the war, but his health broke and he was forced to retire. Harrison died of consumption in 1867. **Price**, pp. 358-61.

overtook the fleeing Comanches, killed and wounded several warriors and captured 80 horses. As Harrison approached the battlefield on his return, he found his comrades in a skirmish line preparing to engage his "horse driving detachment", thinking that they were a body of the Comanches returning to renew the conflict.[30]

The Battle of Wichita Village was the most complete victory ever achieved over the Comanches. The tribe never really recovered from Van Dorn's blow. Although the Comanches still conducted raids during the next few years, they had lost much of their influence with the other Southern Plains Indians. The known Indian dead in and around their camp and the nearby ravines was between 70 and 80 warriors and many others were killed during the pursuits that extended miles from the main battle area. Among the killed was sub-chief Arickarosap (White Deer). The wounded, most of whom were carried away or crawled to safety in the underbrush, were estimated at about 100. The encampment, comprised of 120 lodges, was burned; large amounts of dried buffalo meat and pemmican were destroyed, and 300 animals besides those brought in by Lieutenant Harrison, were taken by Sul Ross and his Indians. Many arms, much ammunition and a large quantity of supplies were captured. Unfortunately, Buffalo Hump and about two-thirds of his warriors escaped to fight again, but his tribe had been soundly chastised. The surviving Indians made their way to the Wichita Mountains and into the Kansas frontier, where they remained the following winter.[31] The element of surprise, discipline and superior firepower had broken the back of one of the powerful tribes of the Southern Comanches.

The Cavalry was not without its casualties. Lieutenant Cornelius Van Camp,[32] a young officer of great promise, assigned to Company D, was killed during the latter phase of the battle when an arrow went directly through his heart. He was found after

[30] Price, p. 70.
[31] Ibid.; Hartje, p. 69; Brackett, pp. 192-93; Mayhall, p. 16.
[32] Cornelius Van Camp was graduated from the U.S. Military Academy in 1855, and was assigned as a 2nd lieutenant to the 2nd Cavalry on July 1, 1855. He was an outstanding horseman and was considered the best close-seat rider in the Regiment. On October 30, 1857, when pursuing a party of Comanches his command rode 200 miles in five days. He was assigned as Adjutant and Topographical Officer of the Wichita Expedition. Price, pp. 546-47.

the battle "lying on his back. His saber, fastened to his wrist by the knot, was beside him, while in his left hand was the fatal arrow that he had pulled from his heart in the unconscious moment that preceded death."[33] Three enlisted men were killed, and one was mortally wounded.[34] Nine enlisted men were severely wounded, and several more were slightly wounded.[35] Major Van Dorn was severely wounded twice, one of the wounds being almost fatal. The sutler, Mr. J. F. Ward, was slightly wounded and Sul Ross was severely wounded, both were volunteers with the expedition.[36] Three of the friendly Indians were killed and two were mortally wounded. Twenty horses were killed and wounded.[37] It had been a complete victory but a costly one.

Much of the fighting had been hand-to-hand and involved the officers as well as the enlisted men. Lieutenant Harrison was credited with killing two warriors in hand-to-hand combat and was commended in orders from Army Headquarters for "conspicuous gallantry".[38] First Sergeant John W. Spangler, Company H, was cited in Departmental General Orders "for his cool courage, daring intrepidity, and gallant bearing throughout the whole engagement, together with his skill and fortune in having killed six of the enemy in personal combat . . . ."[39] This would be the first of two commendations that Spangler would receive for his bravery in battle while he was with the 2nd Cavalry in Texas. Lieutenant James P. Major,[40] Company K, killed three warriors, including

---

[33] Ibid., p. 547.

[34] The three enlisted men killed were all in Company H, Privates Peter Morgan, Henry Howard and Jacob Echard. Sergeant James E. Garrison, Company F, was mortally wounded and died on October 5, 1858. "Regimental Returns," October, 1858.

[35] Corporal Joseph P. Taylor, Company A; Privates Emery, McNamara and Franck, Company F; Sergeant Curwin B. McLellan, Corporal Bishop Gordon, Bugler Michael Arbogast and Private Alexander, Company H; and Private Hinckley, Company K were severely wounded. "Regimental Returns," October, 1858.

[36] Crimmins, "Van Dorn," p. 124. Ross, who was badly wounded and on the ground, was saved by Lieutenant James Major. Mohee, a Comanche sub-chief, was in the act of firing at Ross at close range when Major galloped up and killed the Comanche. Mayhall, p. 16.

[37] Price, p. 71; Mayhall, p. 16.

[38] Price, p. 359.

[39] Ibid., p. 665; General Orders No. 26, Headquarters, Department of Texas, November 6, 1858. Spangler remained with the Federal Army during the Civil War and was commissioned a 2nd lieutenant in the 6th U.S. Cavalry Regiment in May, 1861. He was promoted to 1st lieutenant in October, 1861 and to captain in July, 1866. Spangler died of yellow fever in New Orleans, September 17, 1867. Crimmins, "Spangler," p. 75.

[40] James P. Major was graduated from the U.S. Military Academy in 1856

sub-chief Mohee, in personal combat and was commended in orders from Army Headquarters for "conspicuous gallantry." Captain N. G. Evans, commander of Company H, and Lieutenant Charles W. Phifer, of the same company, each killed two Comanches in hand-to-hand combat.[41] Undoubtedly there were other unreported instances where the cavalrymen distinguished themselves in personal combat with a brave and tenacious adversary.

Van Dorn had had a close brush with death. From the beginning he was involved in the fiercest action, spurring his men on by personal example. Late in the battle when the Indians were retreating, Van Dorn, Sul Ross, Lieutenant Van Camp and a private tried to cut off a group of fleeing Comanches. Van Dorn, an outstanding horseman riding a "splendid gray," outdistanced the rest of his party and soon found himself charging alone into the rear of the retreating enemy. Undaunted by his predicament, the fearless Mississippian selected as his target two Indians riding double and fired at them. His shot killed their pony, throwing the two riders to the ground. Van Dorn then attempted to ride down and saber the two warriors who had rolled to their knees and were in position to shoot directly at him as he charged. Both shot arrows at close range and the cavalryman instinctively threw up his arm and took the initial blow of one of the arrows in his arm, the other arrow entered his body. Van Dorn managed to kill one of his two assailants before falling from the saddle; however, had not some of his men arrived on the scene before the Indian could fire again, he would have certainly been killed. Corporal Joseph P. Taylor of Company A is credited with saving his commander's life by diverting attention to himself and away from Van Dorn and

---

and was appointed a 2nd lieutenant in the 2nd Cavalry, December 1, 1856. He engaged in several combats with the Indians while serving with the Regiment in Texas. Major fought in the Confederate Army during the Civil War. He was promoted to brigadier general during the war and served primarily in the Trans-Mississippi Theater. Following the war he moved to Canada but returned to Texas to live. He died at Austin, Texas in May, 1876. Price, pp. 548-49.

[41] Hartje, p. 66; Price, p. 549; Crimmins, "Van Dorn," p. 124; Mayhall, p. 16. Charles W. Phifer was appointed a 2nd lieutenant in the 2nd Cavalry from Mississippi on March 3, 1855. He participated in several engagements with the Indians in Texas and during the Civil War fought with the Confederate Army. During the war he was promoted to colonel and commanded a brigade in the Trans-Mississippi Theater. After the war he lived in Texas. Price, p. 481.

was dangerously wounded in the process.[42] The Expedition Commander himself admitted later in half jest that if his troops had not appeared when they did he "would have been stuck as full of arrows as Gulliver was by the Lilliputians," and his best friends would have had a hard time picking him out "from among a dozen porcupines."[43]

In a letter to his wife shortly after the battle Van Dorn described in some detail his wounds. "My first wound," he wrote, "was in the left arm, the arrow entered just above the wrist, passed between the two bones and stopped near the elbow. The second," he continued, "was in my body; the arrow entered opposite the ninth rib on the right side, passed through the upper portion of the stomach, cut my left lung and passed out on the left side between the sixth and seventh rib."[44] Later in the same letter in picturesque language, the Captain expressed his inward feelings concerning the wounds. He wrote,

> When I pulled the arrows from me the blood followed as if weary of service and impatient to cheat me of life — spilling like red wine from a drunkard's tankard.
>
> It was sublime to stand thus on the brink of the dark abyss, and the contemplation was awful . . . . I had faced death before — I gasped in dreadful agony for several hours, but finally became easy.[45]

The command remained in the vicinity of the battlefield for five days while the wounded healed enough to be moved. All of the dead were buried on the battlefield except Lieutenant Van Camp. His remains were taken back and he was eventually buried at Lancaster, Pennsylvania. Assistant surgeons William A. Carswell of the 2nd Cavalry and John J. Gaenslene from Fort Arbuckle attended the wounded. On October 6th a litter was made for Van Dorn and he was carried by two mules back to Camp Radziminski where the expedition arrived October 10. It is difficult to see why the trip back to the base camp did not kill the badly wounded Captain — a 90 mile ride over rough, roadless country in a crude litter suspended between two mules. Van Dorn requested and

---

[42] Crimmins, "Van Dorn," p. 125; Hartje, p. 67.
[43] Hartje, p. 67.
[44] Van Dorn to his wife, October 12, 1858, quoted in Hartje, p. 67.
[45] Ibid.

received a five week recuperation leave to his home in Mississippi. Here he was welcomed as a conquering hero and feted locally by his fellow Mississippians. He had in the past been presented handsome sabers by his friends and admirers for his outstanding services in the Seminole and Mexican Wars; now he was given a beautiful silver service for his gallantry on the Texas frontier. Other honors came his way: several of the more important newspapers in the state published glowing accounts of his accomplishments in fighting Indians, he was called upon to address public meetings and one of his sisters composed a martial air called the "Wichita March," which she dedicated to him.[46] The march became a special favorite with the members of the 2nd Cavalry. The Captain recovered rapidly in his home environment and was back in Texas again by late November and was leading a scouting party by the end of the year.

Van Dorn's natural aggressiveness and his leadership of the Wichita Expedition earned him the reputation as an outstanding soldier and Indian fighter. He would enhance this reputation the following year in another major strike north of the Red River. The Commander of the Army and the Commander of the Department as well as others were generous with their praises of Van Dorn and his men. General Scott called it "a most decisive and important victory" and singled out the expedition sutler, Mr. J. F. Ward, and Sul Ross who was in charge of the Reservation Indians, as "deserving of the highest praise for their gallantry during the action." Scott also mentioned in General Orders, No. 22 issued by Headquarters, U.S. Army on November 10, 1858, that all of the officers, non-commissioned officers and privates of Companies A, F, H and K were "deserving of the highest meed of commendation that can be bestowed upon them." The Army Commander signaled out Sul Ross for additional praise, stating that the friendly Indians under him "rendered essential services in first stampeding and afterward securing the enemies animals and are deserving of like praise with the regular troops."[47]

General Twiggs in General Orders, No. 25 issued by the Department of Texas and dated October 18, 1858, cited the many officers, non-commissioned officers and privates of the companies

---

[46] "Regimental Returns," October, 1858; **Powell**, p. 235; **Hartje**, p. 68; **Mayhall**, p. 16.
[47] **Johnson**, p. 120.

involved in the battle, as being "entitled to great commendation for their gallantry." Twiggs also stated in General Orders 18 that it was

> A victory more decisive and complete than any recorded in the history of our Indian warfare. The general commanding the department hoped much from this command, and he is most happy to say that the brillancy of its success has been such as to exceed his most sanguine expectations . . . .[48]

Captain Van Dorn in his official report of the engagement was unstinting in his praise for the enlisted men of his command. He wrote,

> I am equally indebted in the same manner to all the soldiers of my command, who, under all the circumstances of the forced march and of the battle, proved themselves to be soldiers worthy of the name. Their gallantry, personal bravery, and intrepidity are the admiration of their officers, but they feel themselves unable to discriminate where all are brave.[49]

Major Hardee, writing from West Point where he was the Commandant of Cadets, voiced his approval of the victory at Wichita Village, calling it the "handsomest affair with the savages" of which he had knowledge.[50] Several of the officers involved in the battle had been personally trained by "Old Reliable" when he was with the 2nd Cavalry, and he was proud of their efforts.[51]

Although the battle of Wichita Village was the high point for the Regiment in 1858, an unfortunate event occurred during the year that virtually ended the career of one of the company commanders. William R. Bradfute, captain of Company G, shot and killed Private William Murray of Company K on July 20 in camp on the Clear Fork of the Brazos. Bradfute had just returned from leave and was commanding a squadron composed of Companies G and K at the time of the fatal shooting. The Captain had given an order to Murray who took exception to Bradfute's tone of voice and struck him "a violent blow on the face with his

---

[48] Price, p. 665.
[49] Ibid.
[50] Hartje, p. 69.
[51] Officers participating in the battle of Wichita Village who had been trained by Hardee were, Captains Evans, Johnson and Whiting and Lieutenant Phifer.

clenched first." Bradfute, staggered by the blow, reacted impulsively by shooting the soldier with his Navy Colt. The Captain immediately proceeded to Fort Belknap and surrendered himself to the Regimental Commander. A "long and searching" Court of Inquiry was held at Regimental Headquarters, and Bradfute was exonerated. He returned to duty with his company at Fort Chadbourne on August 6. The result of the military investigation did not satisfy a group of citizens living near Fort Belknap who instituted proceedings against the Captain. The citizens succeeded in obtaining an order for his arrest and subsequent transfer to the civil authorities for trial from President Buchanan. Consequently Bradfute was relieved of command of Fort Chadbourne and ordered to Fort Belknap where the President's order was carried out on November 25. He was released on bail but was never brought to trial, although he made repeated requests to be tried. At the outbreak of the Civil War, two and one half years later, he was still a civilian prisoner. Bradfute resigned his commission and entered the Confederate service March 21, 1861, and rose to the rank of colonel during the war.[52]

In the waning weeks of 1858 there was no activity along the frontier except for scouting expeditions seeking out the defeated Comanches. Van Dorn's command, now under Captain Charles J. Whiting, rested and refitted at Camp Radziminski until October 28. On this date the four companies (A, F, H & K) left on a reconnaissance of the Antelope Hills area. Whiting set up camp on the False Washita River and using it as a base examined the country contiguous to the North and South Canadian Rivers. After riding several hundred miles and seeing no sign of the Indians, the expedition returned to Camp Radziminski on November 14.[53]

Captain James Oakes with Companies C and D was dispatched in late October to augment Whiting's command. Oakes was charged with attempting to keep Buffalo Hump's band from retreating into New Mexico. Like Whiting's command, the squadron under Oakes after many days on scout failed to pick up a trail.[54] In late November Captain Richard Johnson commanded a detachment from Company F that scouted the area near the

[52] Price, pp. 323-24; "Regimental Returns," July and November, 1858.
[53] Price, p. 71.
[54] Ibid.

mouth of the Salt Fork of the Brazos. Johnson was gone two weeks. The country that he scouted was barren, and he had to abandon several horses that had completely broken down for the lack of forage. Johnson found no fresh trails.[55]

Van Dorn returned from Mississippi in late November and by early December had recovered sufficiently from his Wichita Village wounds to ride again. In mid-December he led three companies (A, H and K) on a scout of the upper Brazos and to explore the country adjacent to the Big Washita. Van Dorn rode some 80 miles to the west and southwest of Camp Radziminski without seeing a fresh sign. He would have ridden further but learned that a scouting expedition from Fort Belknap was in the vicinity and returned to camp.[56]

It was apparent that the Comanches, since Wichita Village, had concealed their whereabouts, and to Van Dorn it appeared that they "had disappeared as a mist,"[57] but must be found and further chastised. However, the command at Camp Radziminski, the 2nd Cavalry's advance base, was not in condition to continue the winter campaign; the unusually long and severe marches had broken down the horses and they would be unfit for field service until spring. Some of the companies had ridden 1,500 miles and none less than 1,200 miles during the campaigns and scouting expeditions in the fall and winter of 1858. Thus the proposed winter operations of 1858-59 had to be abandoned, and the troops were held in readiness for field service early the following spring.

---

[55] Johnson, pp. 120-21.
[56] Price, p. 73; Hartje, p. 69.
[57] Price, p. 73.

—Company of Military Historians

Uniforms, 2nd U.S. Cavalry, 1855-1861.

Musician   *Company Officer*   *Private, fatigue*   *Corporal, full dress*

ALBERT SIDNEY JOHNSTON
Colonel, 2nd U.S. Cavalry
General, Confederate States Army

ROBERT EDWARD LEE
Lt-Colonel, 2nd U.S. Cavalry
General, Confederate States Army

EDMUND KIRBY SMITH
Captain, 2nd U.S. Cavalry
General, Confederate States Army

JOHN BELL HOOD
Lieutenant, 2nd U.S. Cavalry
General, Confederate States Army

WILLIAM J. HARDEE
Major, 2nd U.S. Cavalry
Lt-Gen., Confederate Army

EARL VAN DORN
Capt., 2nd U.S. Cavalry
Maj-Gen., Confederate Army

FITZHUGH LEE
Lieut., 2nd U.S. Cavalry
Maj-Gen., Confederate Army

CHARLES W. FIELD
Lieut., 2nd U.S. Cavalry
Maj.-Gen., Confederate Army

NATHAN G. EVANS
Capt., 2nd U.S. Cavalry
Brig.-Gen., Confederate Army

GEORGE B. COSBY
Lieut., 2nd U.S. Cavalry
Brig.-Gen., Confederate Army

JAMES P. MAJOR
Lieut., 2nd U.S. Cavalry
Brig.-Gen., Confederate Army

GEORGE H. THOMAS
Maj., 2nd U.S. Cavalry
Maj.-Gen., U.S. Army

GEORGE STONEMAN JR.
Capt., 2nd U.S. Cavalry
Maj.-Gen. U.S. Army

KENNER GARRARD
Lieut., 2nd U.S. Cavalry
Maj.-Gen., U.S. Army

RICHARD W. JOHNSON
Capt., 2nd U.S. Cavalry
Maj.-Gen., U.S. Army

INNIS N. PALMER
Capt., 2nd U.S. Cavalry
Brig.-Gen., U.S. Army

DAVID EMMANUEL TWIGGS
Maj.-Gen., Commander, Dept. of Texas, USA
1856-1861
Maj.-Gen., Confederate Army

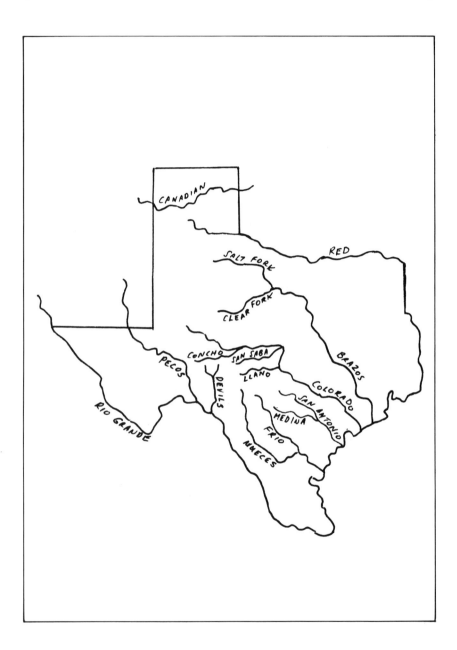

Important Rivers of Central and West Texas

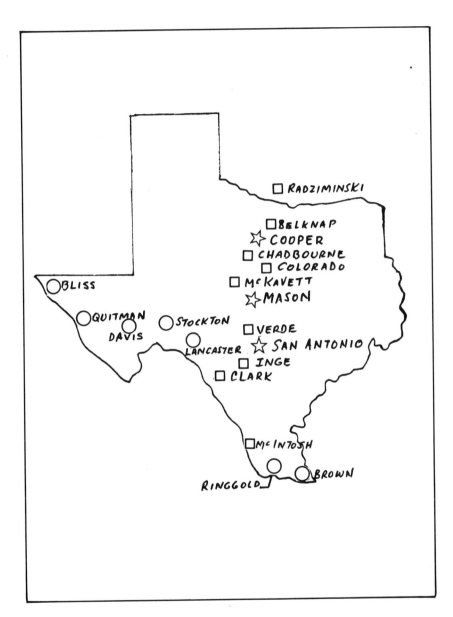

☐ Major posts garrisoned by the 2nd Cavalry, 1855-1861.
☆ Posts that served as Rgmtl. Hdqtrs. for the 2nd Cavalry.
◯ Other important military posts in Texas, 1855-1861.

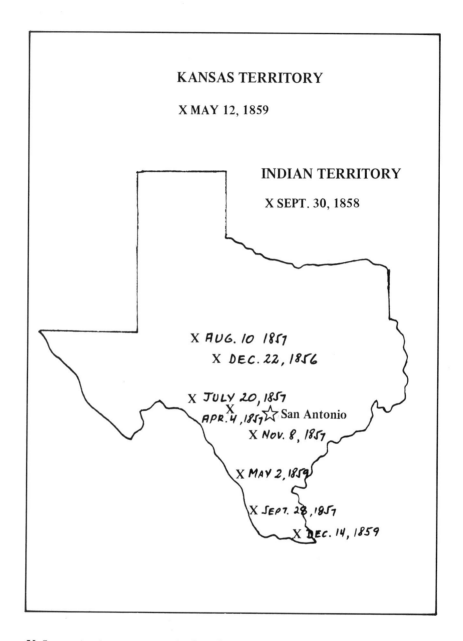

KANSAS TERRITORY

X MAY 12, 1859

INDIAN TERRITORY

X SEPT. 30, 1858

X AUG. 10 1857

X DEC. 22, 1856

X JULY 20, 1857
X
APR. 4, 1857 ☆ San Antonio

X NOV. 8, 1857

X MAY 2, 1859

X SEPT. 28, 1857

X DEC. 14, 1859

X Important engagements fought by the 2nd Cavalry, 1855-1861.
☆ Headquarters, Department of Texas.

CHAPTER NINE

1859 – ACTION ALONG THE RIO GRANDE

The Second Regiment of Cavalry since its organization has been in the saddle and the field, and, by its repeated successes and encounters with hostile Indians, has proven its value and efficiency, and, as a corps, has justly won for itself a lasting and enviable reputation.[1]

The year 1859 saw the 2nd Cavalry engaged with hostile Indians from below the Rio Grande in Old Mexico to above the Arkansas River in the Kansas Territory, a distance of some 1,000 miles. In no other year that the Regiment was stationed in Texas would the companies conduct operations over so great an expanse of the frontier. While very little action occurred during the first few months of the year, by April offensive operations were in full swing. Captain Albert Brackett led an expedition south of the Rio Grande in May, and Captain Earl Van Dorn struck north again into Comanche country during the same month, winning yet another major victory over the Comanches. This year also witnessed the termination of the Texas Indian Reservation program when the residents of both the Brazos Agency and the Comanche Reserve were moved under 2nd Cavalry escort in August to the Indian Territory. During October and November of 1859 Major George H. Thomas led a long reconnaissance mission to the headwaters of the Red and the Canadian Rivers and into New Mexico Territory. A corporal from Company I made a name for himself when the detachment he led routed a Comanche war party near the Guadalupe River. This year of far-flung actions closed with a series of spirited engagements along the Rio Grande when Federal and State forces combined to defeat Juan Cortinas, the self-styled "Robin Hood of the Rio Grande," or, as the Texans called him, "The Rogue of The Rio Grande."

In January, General Twiggs, informed that he could no longer pursue the Indians south of the Rio Grande and fearing new Comanche and Kiowa raids from the north, withdrew the infantry garrisons from the forts along the Mexican border and re-

---

[1] General David Twiggs, Commander of the Department of Texas, in General Orders No. 13, Hdqtrs., Department of Texas, October 28, 1859.

distributed them along the western frontier.[2] In doing this the Commander of the Department of Texas encouraged depradations from the lawless Mexican element along the Rio Grande and from the Indians south of the River. Both parties accepted Twiggs' invitation of providing an unguarded waterway and consequently crossed the Rio Grande at their pleasure.

The first encounter of the year with the Indians involved Company I, stationed at Camp Hudson. Captain Brackett, Lieutenant Wesley Owens and 66 men of the Company left the camp on San Pedro Creek near Devil's River on April 13 on an extended scout toward the Rio Grande. From Camp Hudson Brackett marched to Fort Lancaster on the Pecos River and then continued west along the El Paso Road to Comanche Springs (Fort Stockton).[3] From here the Command followed the Great Comanche Trail to Mexico. This Trail was as wide as a wagon road and literally strewn along much of its length with the bones of mules and horses. It ran through wild and desolate country and was used for many years by the Indians returning from their raids in Mexico. The Trail ran from the vicinity of Presidio on the Rio Grande, crossed the Pecos near Horsehead Crossing, passed near the present town of Big Spring, angled across the Staked Plains, and went as far north as the Arkansas River.[4] The men and horses suffered greatly from thirst as Brackett followed the Great Comanche Trail south. He reached the Rio Grande on April 30 and halted on the American side opposite the Presidio de San Vicente. Here the Company camped among the cottonwoods, concealed from view, awaiting developments.

On May 2, Brackett's Indian scout discovered a party of Comanches, some 10 miles below the camp, apparently on their way to a raid in Mexico. The cavalrymen moved out immediately, struck the Indians before they could organize a proper defense and drove them south across the Rio Grande. Brackett reported that two of the Comanches were killed and several wounded during the running fight. In their flight the Indians lost much of their equippage and practically all of their food supply of dried horsemeat. The engagement was termed the battle of Presidio de

---

[2] Price, pp. 75-76.
[3] Comanche Springs is located at the headwaters of Comanche Creek at the town of Fort Stockton in present Pecos County. Fort Stockton was established March 23, 1859. **Handbook**, I, pp. 385-632.
[4] **Handbook**, I, p. 386; **Price**, p. 77.

San Vicente, and in his report to the Department Commander, Brackett, specifically cited 1st Sergeant Henry Gordon and Privates John McEnery and Joseph Neill for "good conduct".[5] Brackett was perhaps the most taciturn of the company commanders of the 2nd Cavalry, so this was praise indeed for the three enlisted men.

Brackett, following the engagement, found himself short of rations. His Command had been on the march several more days than had been expected, and it had ridden through an area barren of game. He had a choice, they could either subsist on the dried horsemeat taken from the Comanches on their march back to Camp Hudson or he could cross the river and obtain more food, particularly beef, in Mexico. There were no settlements on the American side of the Rio Grande from which to obtain provisions. The Presidio de San Vicente, an old Spanish fort, had been abandoned many years before and was nothing more than crumbling ruins. Upon a close scrutiny and smell of the dried horsemeat taken from the Comanches, it was quickly decided to chance the procurement of rations by marching into the interior of Mexico, even though it was against War Department policy. Too, cavalrymen, faced with an alternative are not prone to subsist on their best friends, the *Equus Caballus,* dried or otherwise.

The Company crossed the Rio Grande on May 3 and after a fatiguing 50 mile march reached San Carlos in the State of Coahuila on May 6.[6] While Brackett's Command was securing rations and resting for its ride back to Texas, a party of distraught Mexicans rode into town and reported that Indians had attacked them on the Monclova Road and stolen their cattle. The Alcalde, other city officials, and the victims of the cattle theft begged Brackett to chastise the thieves. The Captain was of the opinion that the Indians were the same ones that he had driven across the Rio Grande at San Vicente a few days previously and so agreed to attack them if the Mexicans would gather a force to accompany him. The Alcalde soon raised an ill-armed company of volunteers composed of local inhabitants and a group of friendly Seminoles from a nearby village. Brackett led his polygot "army" of Americans, Mexicans and Indians down the Monclova Road toward the raiders. The cavalry was well mounted and armed, but

---

[5] Price, p. 665.
[6] Ibid., pp. 77-78.

the rest of his force rode ponies, burros and mules and carried everything from spears to blunderbusses. The Comanches, not expecting that an organized force might be so close, were totally surprised and quickly put to route and the stolen cattle recovered. Thus, Albert Brackett for the second time in as many years found himself to be a local hero, feted for his audacity and leadership.[7]

After resting a few days at San Carlos and enjoying the accolades of the population, the Company marched to Presidio Del Norte, in the state of Chihuahua. As they approached the town, they noted that the population appeared to be apprehensive and uneasy. The State of Chihuahua, at the time, was in the throes of a revolution, and Brackett and his dusty and bedraggled troops were taken for a revolutionary force, particularly so as they approached the town from the interior of Mexico. Once they were identified, however, the Americans were welcomed and entertained by the city officials, who were much relieved at not being assailed by a hostile army.[8]

The Command recrossed the Rio Grande in mid-May and marched to Fort Davis and then on to Camp Van Camp where it arrived on May 21.[9] The Odyssey was over. Brackett and his men had traveled over 600 miles in a little over a month, during which time they fought Indians both north and south of the Rio Grande, and had traversed two Mexican States, Coahuila and Chihuahua. During the expedition the men suffered much from the want of food and the animals from lack of water and forage.

Brackett was violating United States policy in pursuing Indians into Mexico, and was criticized in some quarters; however, he had his defenders. The San Antonio *Texan* of May 26, 1859, in defense of Brackett's entry into Mexico, reported,

> Information reached our city yesterday that the Indians had been making themselves rather familiar on the Pecos in the vicinity of the Horsehead Crossing,[10] and that a company under the command of

---

[7] Ibid., p. 78.
[8] Ibid.
[9] Camp Van Camp, named for Lieutenant Cornelius Van Camp, killed at the battle of Wichita Village, was established near New Castle in Young County on April 30, 1859. It was abandoned August 28, 1859. **Handbook,** I, p. 285.
[10] Horsehead Crossing was the most used crossing of the Pecos and was located where the river forms the boundary between present Pecos and Crane Counties. The Butterfield stage from St. Louis to San Francisco crossed the Pecos here from 1859 to 1861. The crossing was on the main

Captain Brackett started in pursuit and overtook them in the vicinity of the Rio Grande — which side we did not inquire — and had a combat with them. If Captain Brackett *did* cross the river of which fact we are not informed, he was perfectly justifiable in doing so. There is no law of nature that will permit outlaws to commit outrages upon citizens of one nation and then flee to another, and thus, be screened from their guilt and punishment that should await them. Again, if the conflict began on this side of the river and ended on the other, it was but one conflict and must be located on this side. The facts in the case are simply these: Captain Brackett has done what several other officers could have done long ago, and which had they done it, would long since have cut short these marauders who cross the river take their plunder, and flee into Mexico.[11]

The Department of the Army in General Orders No. 5, dated November 10, 1859, recognized the engagements and march of Brackett by noting the "Gallant acts and soldier-like endurance of hardships highly creditable to the troops" of his command.[12] No remarks were made about where the "gallant acts" took place.

While Brackett was moving toward the Rio Grande, some 800 miles to the north, Van Dorn was preparing to leave Camp Radziminski and embark upon his second major campaign against the heartland of the Comanches. It had been a busy winter at the Camp on Otter Creek, gathering supplies, caring for the wounded, and training recruits.[13] The bulk of the 2nd Cavalry, seven companies (A, B, C, F, G, H and K) were stationed here most of the winter. The men lived in crude shelters, tents with logs and sod piled up against the tent walls. While this arrangement kept out most of the rain and snow, it did little to stop the cold winter winds. Guards were posted 24 hours a day to watch the horses, as small parties of Indians were seen occasionally lurking in the distance.

---

trail used by the Indians returning north from Chihuahua after their raids and derived its name from the number of horse and mule skeletons lying on both sides of the Crossing. **Handbook, I,** p. 389.
[11] Quoted in **Price,** p. 79.
[12] **Ibid.,** p. 665. Two men were lost during the expedition. Private John J. Streeter was killed by Mexican guerillas on the march from Santa Rosa to Presidio del Norte and Private William R. Self deserted at the latter city. **Regimental Returns,** May, 1859.
[13] Twenty wagon loads of supplies were received, and 54 recruits reported in during the winter. **Mayhall,** p. 17; **Regimental Returns,** January, 1859; **Hartje,** p. 70.

Officers and enlisted men alike searched for ways to pass the long winter days and nights in this make-shift frontier post. The large number of poker chips and champagne bottles recently excavated at the site of Camp Radziminiski attests to how some of the time was spent.[14] Most of the officers visited Fort Belknap at one time or another during the winter to enjoy the creature comforts provided on a permanent post and see old acquaintances. Lieutenant James E. Harrison, however, had a special reason for returning to Belknap: he married the daughter of Matthew Leeper, Indian Agent for the Comanche Reserve, there.[15] Harrison would be wounded in the coming campaign against the Comanches.

By the end of April everything was in readiness to commence the campaign. Six companies of cavalry, some 300 troopers, and 58 Indian allies from the Brazos Agency composed Van Dorn's force. The seventh company which had wintered at Camp Radziminski, Company K, commanded by Captain Charles Whiting, had been reassigned in March to Camp Colorado. The Indian contingent was led by Jack Harry, a Delaware, and Shawnee Jim. The latter was a veteran of the Texas Revolution; he was intelligent, capable, spoke good English, and Van Dorn used him as his interpreter.[16]

The expedition rode out from Camp Radziminski on April 30, traveling light. They carried no tents, and rations were reduced to a minimum of pork, flour, coffee and salt. Van Dorn marched north toward the South Canadian River. Here he intended to establish an advanced supply base from which the cavalry could operate. With the Indian scouts riding ten miles to the front, the column followed Elk Creek, a tributary of the Red River, traveling "30 miles through herds of buffalo" to the Washita, which they reached on the second day out. On May 4, the scouts captured a Comanche boy, one of a party of three on their way south to steal horses in Texas. Shawnee Jim learned from the captive that there was a large Comanche Camp about two days journey north of the Cimarron.[17]

Van Dorn, taking the boy as a guide and promising to shoot him in case he gave false information, resumed the march, in the

---

[14] Hartje, p. 70.
[15] Mayhall, p. 17.
[16] Ibid.
[17] Ibid., Hartje, p. 70; Parks, pp. 96-97.

rain, toward the South Canadian River. The South Canadian was in flood stage and the Command camped some 30 miles below Antelope Hills to await the crossing. A supply base was established here for the wagons, surplus supplies and extra horses and a small guard left behind to secure it. After a day's delay, the South Canadian was crossed and Van Dorn continued on his march north across the North Canadian and the Red Fork of the Arkansas to the Cimarron. The horse soldiers splashed across the Cimarron River and into Kansas Territory on May 10. Soon after crossing into Kansas, the advance surprised a small band of Comanches out hunting and in a running fight one Indian was killed. Van Dorn then moved up a tributary of the Cimarron (probably Cavalry Creek) and on May 11 came upon a large recently deserted Comanche and Kiowa Village that stretched along the creek for miles. There were signs of recent habitation of some 2,000 Comanches. This was the encampment that the young prisoner had told about.[18]

While most of the Command rested and grazed their horses near the deserted village on May 11, scouting parties fanned out north and west looking for fresh trails. Lieutenant Royall located the enemy first. On May 12 he discovered a small band of Indians on a bluff nearby creeping up on the horse herd. Royall sounded the alarm and then gave chase hoping that the Indians would lead him to their village. This the fleeing Comanches proceeded to do. Van Dorn, upon hearing the alarm, had "Boots and Saddles" sounded and immediately put the companies in motion following Royall. After riding about two miles, the Lieutenant was found engaging three Indians in a fight along the steep banks of Crooked Creek; a short distance down the creek valley Van Dorn could see an Indian village, which his scouts estimated to number about 200.[19]

Van Dorn gave his attack orders after the Indians fighting Royall had been killed and all of the companies were up. He dismounted two companies (some 100 men) and had them advance on foot in a frontal attack against the village. The

---

[18] **Mayhall,** pp. 65-66; **Parks,** pp. 97-98.
[19] **Mayhall,** p. 66; **Price,** p. 80. Van Dorn referred to Crooked Creek as Small Creek and the engagement as the "Battle of Nescutunga" and this is generally what it is known by in military records. The village was located about 15 miles south of Old Fort Atkinson in present Ford County, Kansas, and near the Nescutunga, a tributary of the Arkansas.

remaining four mounted companies were ordered to seal off the valley on both ends of the village to prevent escape from the camp, a squadron of two companies at each end. The Indians occupied a strong defensive position near "a deep ravine, densely covered with a stunted growth of timber and brambles, through which a small stream with abrupt banks, meandered from bluff to bluff on either side."[20] The dismounted troops opened the attack, firing and yelling as they advanced, and soon drove the Indians from their village, and into the ravine close by where they had erected a breastwork of logs. The approach to the Indian's stronghold was only possible on foot and in open order as the undergrowth was almost impenetrable. The enemy could not be seen in the underbrush and were heard only by the twang of their arrows and noise from their rifles. The action at Crooked Creek was sharp, but short. No quarter was asked and none was given; Van Dorn in his report to General Twiggs stated that the "Comanches fought without asking or giving quarter until there was not one left to bend a bow, and would have won the admiration of every brave soldier but the intrusive reflection that they were murderers of the wives and children of their frontiersmen."[21]

Forty-nine warriors were killed and 36 were taken prisoners, including men, women and children. Only 5 wounded were found; many of the wounded probably crawled away or hid in the underbrush. One hundred animals were captured from the Comanches, and all of their camp supplies were either taken or destroyed.[22] The casualties sustained by the 2nd Cavalry were about the same that they had suffered at Wichita Village the year before. Four officers were wounded, Captain E. Kirby Smith, commander of Company B, and Lieutenants James E. Harrison (Co. H), Fitzhugh Lee (Co. B), and Manning M. Kimmel (Co. G).[23] Two enlisted men were killed, Private Willis Burrows (Co.

---

20 From Van Dorn's Official Report of the battle, dated May 31, 1859. As quoted in **Price**, p. 666. Hereafter cited as **Van Dorn's Report**, May 31, 1859; **Brackett**, pp. 199-200.
21 **Van Dorn's Report**, May 31, 1859.
22 **Hartje**, pp. 73-74; **Mayhall**, p. 66; **Crimmins** "Van Dorn", p. 126; **Price**, p. 80.
23 Kimmel, son of Governor Singleton M. Kimmel of Missouri, was graduated from West Point with the Class of 1857. Manning Kimmel had the distinction of fighting on both sides during the Civil War. When the 2nd Cavalry left Texas in the Spring of 1861 he accompanied it to Carlisle

G) and Sergeant William P. Leverett (Co. B), and eleven were wounded: 1st Sergeant John W. Spangler (Co. H); Sergeants Thomas Elliott (Co. A); and Peter Alba (Co. B); Corporal George Nicholls (Co. H); and Privates William Moore, Patrick Kenevane, Eugene Camus (Co. A), Isaac Chrisman, Benjamin Jones, William Hartley (Co. B), and Samuel Rorison (Co. H).[24] The friendly Indians also suffered some losses. Four of the Reservation Indians were killed and several were wounded. Although Van Dorn discouraged his Indians from fighting, Jack Harry and Shawnee Jim said that they would be dishonored if they did not fight so insisted on entering the battle. To distinguish themselves from the enemy, the Reservation Indians wrapped white cloths around their heads. Several of the Delawares and Shawnees killed their hated enemies, the Comanches, in hand-to-hand combat.[25] Surgeons James Simons and W. H. Babcock administered to the wounded cavalrymen and friendly Indians as well as to the wounded Comanches.

The most dangerously wounded was 2nd Lieutenant Fitz-hugh Lee,[26] nephew of Robert E. Lee. Lee led a charge against one of the flanks of the Indian position which resulted in taking prisoner a large number of women and children as well as several warriors. As the young lieutenant was returning with his captives, he was confronted by an armed brave. Lee fired his pistol, and the Indian shot his arrow at the same moment. The Comanche was hit directly between the eyes and expired instantly; his arrow struck

---

Barracks, Pennsylvania. Kimmel fought in the Federal Army as a company commander at the 1st Battle of Bull Run (Manassas) July 21, 1861. Soon, thereafter, he resigned his commission and joined the Confederate Army. He served in the Confederate Cavalry with distinction and rose to the rank of Colonel. Kimmel's son, Admiral Husband E. Kimmel, was in command at Pearl Harbor when the Japanese struck on December 7, 1941. **Price,** pp. 487-88; Burke Davis, **Our Incredible Civil War,** New York, Holt, Rinehart and Winston, 1960, p. 25.

[24] **Regimental Returns,** May, 1859; **Crimmins,** "Van Dorn", p. 126; **Mayhall,** p. 66.

[25] **Mayhall,** p. 66.

[26] Fitzhugh Lee was graduated from the U.S. Military Academy in 1856, and was assigned to the 2nd Cavalry, July 1 of that year. Lee was commended several times for his valor in engagements while the Regiment served in Texas. He served with the Confederate Army during the Civil War and rose to the rank of Major-General of Cavalry in the Army of Northern Virginia. Lee was elected Governor of Virginia in 1885 and served as the U.S. Consul General at Havana from 1893 to 1898. During the Spanish-American War, Lee served as a Major-General of Volunteers. He died at Washington, D.C. in 1905. **Price,** pp. 483-86; **Warner,** pp. 178-79.

Lee in the right side, passing through the rib cage and penetrating the Lieutenant's right lung. Blood streamed from Lee's mouth, and it was first thought that the wound was fatal; fortunately, however, the surgeons were able to staunch the flow of blood. He was transported the 200 miles back to Camp Radziminski on a litter between two mules. Lee suffered intensely from internal hemorrhaging for several weeks after the battle, and his recovery was painful and slow.[27]

The Commanders of the Army and of the Department of Texas both recognized the significance of the action at Crooked Creek and praised the gallantry of the troops engaged. General Scott wrote, "The fight was sharp and bloody and took place on foot in a thick jungle. The combat was highly creditable to the troops." (General Orders, No. 5, Hdqtrs., Department of the Army, November 10, 1859). Twiggs called it "A decisive victory, conspicious gallantry highly creditable to the troops." (General Orders, No. 13, Hdqtrs., Department of Texas, 1859). Van Dorn, in his official report of the action, dated May 31, 1859, was generous with his praise for his men,

> A too high meed of praise for gallantry and unflinching courage cannot be rewarded to the men who have achieved this success over so desperate a foe. It required the coolest and most undaunted individual bravery to advance upon the danger that presented itself in this fearful ravine. The troops of this Command moved, as it were, into darkness; and, with a courage that challenged admiration, felt for the danger they were called upon to encounter.

Following the engagement on May 12, the troops remained in the area for several days sorting through captured equipment and supplies and caring for the wounded. The command was divided into two groups for the march back to Otter Creek. Captain E. K. Smith, suffering from a flesh wound in the thigh, led one group directly back to Camp Radziminski, picking up the guard and wagons left at the temporary camp on the South Canadian on the way. Van Dorn commanded the other group composed of the healthiest men and the most serviceable horses. This group scouted to the Southwest on their return march hoping to locate other

---

[27] Col. Martin L. Crimmins, "Jack Hayes' Story of Fitzhugh Lee's Indian Fight;" WTHAYB, Vol. I, October, 1937, pp. 42-45. Hereafter cited as Crimmins, "Jack Hayes' Story."

parties of hostile Indians, but found nothing. Both contingents arrived back at Camp Radziminski on May 31. A few days after returning, Van Dorn was ordered to duty at San Antonio and Captain Smith took command of the troops on Otter Creek.[28]

Following his second complete victory over the Comanches at Crooked Creek, Captain Van Dorn was considered the outstanding Indian fighter on the Southwestern frontier and enjoyed "a greater distinction than any other mounted officer in his grade in the service."[29] He was a man of great daring and physical courage and appeared to invite danger. He was small, wiry and the embodiment of activity. Van Dorn was in his best element as a cavalry officer and a commander at brigade or division level. His subsequent career in the Civil War would bear this out.[30]

Captain E. K. Smith remained in command of Camp Radzminski until the post on Otter Creek was abandoned in September, 1859. It had served as the advance base for two successful expeditions against the Comanches and was garrisoned for nearly a year by from four to seven companies of the 2nd Cavalry. It was the northernmost post that the Regiment would occupy for any length of time and the only one outside of Texas durings its assignment to the Lone Star State. The last company to leave Camp Radziminski was Company B, commanded by Smith; it departed for Camp Cooper in early September. Prior to that Company A had been reassigned to Camp Colorado and Company C to Camp Cooper in July and Companies F, G, and H had marched to Camp Cooper in August.[31]

The summer of 1859 witnessed the termination of the Texas Indian Reservation Program. As noted in a previous Chapter,[32]

---

[28] Hartje, pp. 73-74; Mayhall, p. 66; Parks, pp. 98-99.
[29] Crimmins, "Van Dorn," p. 127.
[30] Early in the war Van Dorn was promoted to major general and placed in command of the Trans-Mississippi Department. After being defeated at Pea Ridge, Arkansas in April, 1862, he was transferred east of the River and placed in command of the Army of Mississippi. Van Dorn was badly defeated at Corinth, Mississippi, in October, 1862, and was replaced as Army Commander by John C. Pemberton. The high point of Van Dorn's Civil War career was his successful cavalry raid against Grant's large supply depot at Holly Springs in December, 1862. Ironically, the man who had escaped death in battle on numerous occasions was murdered by a Dr. Peters at Spring Hill, Tennessee on March 8, 1863. Peters claimed that Van Dorn had "violated the sanctity of his home." Thus died the brilliant cavalrymen at age 42. Crimmins, "Van Dorn", p. 128; Warner, pp. 314-15.
[31] Regimental Returns, July, August, September, 1859.
[32] See Chapter 5, pages 60-62.

two reservations were established for the Indians living in Texas. One for the peaceful Comanches, known as the "Comanche" or "Upper Reserve", was established on the Clear Fork of the Brazos and another for all of the other tribes living in Texas called the "Brazos Agency" or "Lower Reserve." Camp Cooper was built to guard the Comanche Reserve, and the Brazos Agency was protected by the garrison at Fort Belknap some 15 miles away. The 2nd Cavalry was deeply involved in this noble experiment. Companies of the Regiment built Camp Cooper in 1856, and occupied the Camp during its entire activation period, and, from time to time, companies of the 2nd Cavalry were stationed at Fort Belknap. When it was decided to end the reservation program and move the Indians north of the Red River, it was the 2nd Cavalry that was primarily charged with safeguarding the movement to the Choctaw and Chickasaw country.

From the very beginning the Indian Reservation program had its detractors and enemies, notably the "Indian-hating element" of Texas citizens. The system failed because of his antagonism and prejudice. The citizens in many cases were jealous of the Reservation Indians whom they considered the "pampered wards" of the Federal Government because they secured rations, arms, ammunition and other supplies free of charge and then, the frontiersmen believed, committed depredations against them.[33] John R. Baylor and Allison Nelson led the anti-reservation faction. The former, who had been deposed as the agent for the Brazos Reservation after 18 months of service, was particularly bitter against the system.[34] It was the contention of the Baylor-Nelson element that the Reservation Indians left the compound to conduct raids and then fled back to the reservation for protection.[35] Major Robert S. Neighbors, Indian Agent for Texas, was the single most important defender of the program. Neighbors was particularly bitter in his denunciation of Baylor, whom he claimed was fired as agent of the Brazos Reservation because he was "having a good time on the job." Neighbors also stated that "Baylor, Nelson and others wanted the offices held by Captain

---

[33] Koch, p. 113.
[34] Webb in his book, **The Texas Rangers,** wrote that after Baylor was discharged he "assumed the role of trouble-maker which he played with rare gift." p. 167; Koch, p. 118.
[35] Webb, pp. 166-169; Koch, pp. 113-115.

Shapely Ross [agent for the Brazos Agency] and Colonel Matthew Leeper [agent for the Comanche Agency] and himself."[36]

By the fall of 1858 the hopelessness of maintaining the Reservations was recognized by Neighbors, and as time passed conditions worsened. Incidents between the settlers and the Reservation Indians multiplied.[37] Public anti-reservation demonstrations were stepped up, and in late May 1859, a group of citizens headed by Baylor raided the Brazos Agency and terrorized the surrounding countryside.[38] The pleas from Governor Runnels to desist from such attacks and practices fell on deaf ears. Fearing a full scale war between the Texas citizens, the Army and the Reservation Indians, the Governor wrote the Secretary of the Interior on June 30, 1859, requesting that the Texas Indians be moved across the Red River "immediately." The Federal Government had hoped to leave the Indians on the reservations until late fall so that their crops could be harvested. This idea was abandoned, however, when Major Neighbors wrote Washington that it was necessary "for the good of all" to move the Indians as soon as possible. Consequently, Secretary for Indian Affairs Greenwood issued movement orders on June 11, stating that the Secretary of War would provide an escort.

Major George H. Thomas, Commander of the 2nd Cavalry, was in charge of the movement. Companies G and H of the cavalry from Camp Cooper and two companies of the 1st Infantry from Fort Belknap provided the military escort. Captain John Henry Brown and a company of Texas Rangers followed in the rear to guard against thefts by stragglers. Indian Agents Leeper and Neighbors accompanied the column north. Shapley Ross and other persons assigned to the two Reservations remained behind to guard government property; they were assisted in their duties by

---

[36] **Koch**, p. 119.

[37] On December 28, 1858 a party of Brazos Agency Indians were assailed by a group of Erath County settlers on Keechi Creek near the Reservation. In the fighting several braves and squaws were killed and wounded. **Koch**, p. 115.

[38] During the period of May 23-26, Baylor with some 250 armed citizens, defying U.S. Authority, attacked the perimeter of the Brazos Agency. They were reported to have killed and scalped several Indians, stolen horses, waylaid and robbed travelers and stopped the mails. **Koch**, p. 117; **Webb**, p. 170. Baylor was a noted Indian hater. During the Civil War as a Confederate Colonel he advocated the extermination of the Apache Indians by spreading blankets among them infested with cholera. For this proposed inhuman policy he was relieved of his commission by Jefferson Davis.

detachments of the 1st Infantry Regiment.[39]

On the morning of August 1, the cavalcade set out from Fort Belknap for the Red River. Most of the Indians walked, a few rode, alongside the wagons carrying their goods. It was a long column, 1,430 Indians (380 from the Comanche Reserve and 1,050 from the Brazos Agency), some 200 soldiers and 50 Rangers. Rations for 20 days were carried. The column crossed the Red River on August 8 and arrived at Fort Cobb, the designated receiving depot in Indian Territory, on August 16. Elias Rector, Special Agent for the Chickasaws, was on hand at Fort Cobb to officially accept the transfer. From here the Indians were escorted to the western part of the Choctaw and Chickasaw Country, the area designated as their new home. The transfer from Texas to Indian Territory was made without major incident.[40] There was no question now that any Indians found in Texas were unfriendly ones and would be hunted down by both soldiers and civilians.

Soon after Major Thomas returned to Camp Cooper from his escort duties he was assigned to command the "Cimarron Expedition," a major scouting movement to the north and west, seeking still more Comanche villages. The "Rock of Chickamauga" left Camp Cooper on October 1st with 5 companies of the 2nd Cavalry, C, D, F, G, & H, to reconnoiter the headwaters of the Red and Canadian Rivers.[41] It was to be one of the longer scouting expeditions that the Regiment would be involved in during its tenure in Texas. The command marched to a point 38 miles west of 100° west longitude,[42] struck an Indian trail there and followed it to the South Canadian where Thomas established an advance supply camp. The tracks were fresh, and it appeared to be a large body of Comanches returning from a raid in Mexico. The cavalrymen continued to follow the trail north but upon reaching the vicinity of the Cimarron River found it completely obliterated by a herd of buffalo, probably driven across the trail by the Indians to cover their tracks. Thomas, disappointed, returned to the supply camp on the South Canadian on October 31.[43] Here

---

[39] **Koch**, p. 112; **Regimental Returns**, August, 1859; **Price**, pp. 61-62.
[40] **Koch**, pp. 119-122; **Webb**, p. 171.
[41] Commanders of these companies were Lieutenants W. B. Royall (C), G. A. Cunningham (D), C. W. Phifer (F), Manning Kimmel (G) and R. W. Eagle (H).
[42] Probably in present day King County.
[43] **Price**, pp. 82-83.

the Command rested for a few days.

On November 5 Thomas resumed his reconnaissance south-west toward the headwaters of the Wichita. The Expedition passed along the eastern boundary of New Mexico and then south to Sweetwater Creek. Here Thomas divided his command into two groups in order to broaden the area of search. Lieutenant Royall commanding a squadron composed of Companies C and G marched east toward the headwaters of Sweetwater Creek, then south until he crossed the south branch of the Red River, thence directly to Camp Cooper. The main column under Thomas continued the march south across the several tributaries of the Red River, then marched east to Camp Cooper. Royall arrived at Camp Cooper on November 19 and Thomas three days later. The Cimarron Expedition was on scout for 53 days and had examined much of the country lying between the Brazos and Cimarron Rivers from 99° to 101° 30' west latitude. Although no Indians had been sighted much valuable geological and geographical information was obtained in regard to river crossings, wagon routes and terrain features.[44]

Although the Cimarron Expedition was perhaps the most extensive reconnaissance of the year, there were several other long range scouting forays worth mentioning. In June Companies I and E, under the command of Captain George Stoneman, scouted the Pecos River and Guadalupe Mountain areas before marching to Fort Stanton in the New Mexico Territory. Stoneman's Squadron returned to Camp Van Camp in late July having been absent almost two months. In November and early December Company G went on two expeditions, one to the headwaters of the Rio Frio and one to the headwaters of the Sabinal. As in the case of Thomas' Cimarron Expedition, no hostiles were sighted in either the march to Fort Stanton or the scouts to the headwaters of the Rio Frio and the Sabinal.[45]

The year 1859 closed with a flurry of action along the Indian frontier and the Rio Grande. Corporal Patrick Collins with a detachment from Company I left Camp Ives in early December in

---

[44] Ibid.; Colonel M. L. Crimmins, "Camp Cooper and Fort Griffin, Texas", WTHAYB; Vol. XVII, October, 1941, p. 36. Hereafter cited as **Crimmins, "Camp Cooper"**; Wilber Thomas, **General George H. Thomas, The Indomitable Warrior,** New York: Exposition Press, 1964, p. 113. Hereafter cited as **Thomas.**

[45] **Price,** pp. 82, 84.

pursuit of a band of Comanches reported to be raiding in the area.[46] Collins finally overtook the marauders on the north branch of the Guadalupe River on December 14 and scattered them after a running battle. Four of the Indians were killed, and practically all of their animals and camp supplies were taken. The cavalrymen suffered no casualties. Collins was given an "Honorable Mention" in Headquarters of the Army General Orders which stated that he had "conducted the scout with discretion and energy." In the same order for the same engagement, both Privates Matthew Kennedy and Henry Weiss were "specially mentioned" for their conduct and the command, as a whole, was extolled for "behaving in the best manner."[47] This was another case of a noncommissioned officer providing an excellent example of leadership.

During the winter of 1859-1960, a Mexican National, Juan Nepomucino Cortinas (or Cortina), a rogue and a rascal, living in Brownsville, provoked the U.S. military forces in Texas as well as the Texas Rangers into action along the Rio Grande. Cortinas born in Camargo, State of Tamaulipas, fought in General Cos' Army during the War between the United States and Mexico. Following the war he settled with his mother and brother on a ranch they owned a few miles west of Brownsville on the left bank of the Rio Grande. Cortinas, although uneducated and illiterate, was a natural born leader. He promoted the cause of the Mexicans in Texas, then became the champion and idol of the humble Mexicans on both sides of the River. By the late 1850's Cortinas had a well armed following estimated as high as 1,000 men, but probably no more than 400 or 500 at any one time. His first serious trouble with Texas authorities occurred in July, 1859 when he wounded the City Marshal of Brownsville and then rode off with the Marshal's prisoner, one of Cortinas' former servants. Following this incident Cortinas moved across the River to Matamoras, and used this city as his base of operations for raids in Texas along the Lower Rio Grande.[48]

---

[46] Camp Ives, a sub-post of Camp Verde, was established by Lieutenant Wesley Owens, Company I, 2nd Cavalry on October 2, 1859. It was located on Turtle Creek about 4 miles north of Camp Verde in eastern present Kerr County. **Handbook,** I, p. 282.

[47] **Price,** p. 666, quoting General Orders No. 11, Headquarters of the Army, November 23, 1860.

[48] J. Fred Rippy, "Border Trouble Along the Rio Grande, 1848-1860." SWHQ, Vol. XXIII, No. 2, October, 1919, pp. 104-05. Hereafter cited as

General Twiggs, aware of the depredations being committed by Cortinas was finally goaded into action on September 28, 1859, when the renegade captured Brownsville, killed several citizens, and occupied the deserted barracks at Fort Brown. Upon learning this startling news, the commander of the Department of Texas took immediate action, issuing Special Orders No. 103 and setting in motion a series of troops movements to the Rio Grande. Twiggs, per the Special Order, appointed Major Samuel P. Heintzelman of the 1st Infantry Regiment and later Civil War fame as the commander of the "Brownsville Expedition," whose objective would be to hunt out and destroy Cortinas. The Special Order directed several companies of the 1st Artillery Regiment, the 1st and 8th Infantry Regiments and the 2nd Cavalry Regiment to rendezvous at old Fort Merrill on the Nueces and then move on to Brownsville.[49] The Order also stated that Cortinas should be brought to battle and be pursued, if necessary, to the Rio Grande, but that U.S. troops were not to cross the River "unless in hot pursuit."[50]

Major Thomas, upon receipt of Twiggs' order, started companies of the 2nd Cavalry south toward posts on or near the Rio Grande. Company E, under Captain Stoneman at Camp Hudson on the Devil's River, was immediately dispatched to Brownsville. At the same time detachments of Companies A, I, and K were ordered to old Fort Merrill to join the artillery and infantry companies assembling there. Companies C and F were ordered to Brownsville, Company G to Fort Inge, Company D to Camp Verde, Company H to Eagle Pass, and Company K to Camp Wood. This left only Company B and elements of Companies A, I, and K to guard the 1,500 mile upper Rio Grande and the western and northern frontiers against the Indians. Of the cavalrymen sent south, only Captain Stoneman's Company E saw action against the free booters.[51]

Cortinas' followers were no match for the U.S. Regulars and the Texas Rangers. Two actions were fought against the Mexican

Rippy; Price, p. 84; **Handbook,** I, pp. 416-17.
[49] Fort Merrill, located on the right bank of the Nueces River in present Live Oak County, was established in March, 1850 at the point where the road from San Antonio to Corpus Christi crossed the river. It was abandoned in March, 1853. **Handbook,** I, p. 629.
[50] Lyman L. Woodman. **Cortina, the Rogue of the Rio Grande.** San Antonio: Naylor, 1950, p. 32. Hereafter cited as **Woodman.**
[51] **Price,** p. 84; **Regimental Returns,** December, 1859.

marauders during December. On December 14, Heintzelman, commanding a force of 150 Regulars, including Company E of the 2nd Cavalry, and 125 Rangers, met and easily dispersed an "army" of some 450 men and two cannons under Cortinas. The engagement took place 12 miles up the river from Brownsville and was known as the battle of La Ebronal, the name being derived from the barricade of ebony logs erected by the Mexicans. The casualties at La Ebronal were eight of the enemy killed, an unknown number wounded, one Ranger mortally wounded and two Regulars wounded. Heintzelman pursued the fleeing Cortinas several miles up the river but lost contact and returned to Fort Brown the following day.[52]

After the affair on the 14th, Cortinas, operating from the Mexican side of the Rio Grande, engaged in sporadic raiding north of the River. Heintzelman, following several futile attempts to bring Cortinas to battle, finally caught up with him at Rio Grande City near Ringgold Barracks. The Major, with a force of some 350, including 200 Rangers under Major Rip Ford and Captain Stoneman's Company of the 2nd Cavalry, struck the Mexicans on December 27 and routed them completely, forcing Cortinas and his 20 man bodyguard to swim across the Rio Grande. The Texas Rangers who led the attack at Rio Grande City had some 17 men wounded, the only casualties suffered by Heintzelman's force. It was a complete defeat for Cortinas. He lost much equipment and ammunition, his baggage weapons and both of his artillery pieces. However, as subsequent events would prove, Cortinas was far from through raiding in Texas.[53]

Following the victory at Rio Grande City the Commander of the Department of Texas cancelled the further movement of the cavalry to old Fort Merrill and Fort Brown. Thus Company G remained at Fort Inge, Company H at Eagle Pass, Company I at Camp Verde and Companies C and F, which were destined for Brownsville, were reassigned to Camp Lawson and Fort Mason, respectively.[54] Company E under Captain Stoneman had been the only company of the 2nd Cavalry to participate in the Brownsville Expedition, and its role was primarily that of pursuing a defeated

---

[52] **Price**, p. 85; **Rippy**, p. 107; **Woodman**, pp. 42-43; **Webb**, p. 184.
[53] **Webb**, p. 186; **Woodman**, pp. 44-45; **Rippy**, p. 107; **Price**, p. 85.
[54] **Regimental Returns**, December, 1859.

enemy. However, Stoneman was not through chasing the "Rogue of the Rio Grande". Cortinas would continue to harass the border until the spring of 1860, and several more companies of the Regiment would become involved in the Cortinas War.

CHAPTER TEN

1860 – LEE TAKES COMMAND

His [Lee's] appearance was dignified, without hauteur, grand
without pride, and in keeping with the noble simplicity
characterizing, a true republican. He evinced an imperturbable
self-possession, and a complete control of his passions.
To approach him was to feel yourself in the presence of a
man of superior intellect, possessing the capacity to
accomplish great ends, and the gift of controlling and
leading men.[1]

Lieutenant-Colonel Robert E. Lee returned to Texas in February, 1860, after an extended leave of absence of some 28 months, and found himself in command of the Department. Major General Twiggs, the 69 year old Commander of the Department of Texas, had requested and received sick leave back to Georgia the previous November, "before the December rains set in."[2] During the period between Twiggs' departure and Lee's arrival, Lieutenant Colonel Washington Seawell, 8th Infantry Regiment, temporarily commanded the Department. Lee, during his tenure as Department Commander would be faced with a multitude of problems, the most serious being increased Comanche and Kiowa raids on the northern and western frontiers and the continuation of the Cortinas War along the Rio Grande.

Although Cortinas and his irregulars had been badly beaten and scattered at the fight near Rio Grande City, in late December, 1859, the bandit chief would continue to harass the border until the spring of 1860. Although the Mexican Government had

---

[1] The famous Texas Ranger John S. "Rip" Ford's impression of Lt. Col. Robert E. Lee. The two met for the first time during the Cortinas War in the spring of 1860. Quoted in **Webb**, p. 193.

[2] David Emanuel Twiggs, a colorful and controversial officer of the pre-Civil War Army, had distinguished himself in both the War of 1812 and the Mexican War. He commanded the 2nd Dragoons during the latter conflict and was made a brevet major general for his part in the storming of Monterey. He was known by two nicknames, "The Horse" and the "Bengal Tiger". In December, 1860 Twiggs was one of four general officers of the line in the U.S. Army, the others being Winfield Scott, John E. Wool, and William S. Harney. Twiggs, a Georgian and southern secessionist, was appointed a major general in the Confederate Army, but was too infirm to command in the field. He died in 1862. Warner, **Gray**, p. 312; **Woodman**, p. 33.

promised to cooperate in the suppression of the activities of Cortinas, it appeared to Lee, Heintzelman and the company commanders of the 2nd Cavalry involved in the Cortinas affair that only lip service was being rendered. If the outlaw was to be captured, it was clear that the Americans would have to take the initiative and, if needed, conduct a "hot pursuit" into Mexico.

Early in 1860 rumors persisted along the lower Rio Grande Valley that the Mexican marauder was preparing for another major invasion of Texas. His whereabouts were reported in a dozen different towns along the river and he was rumored to have as many as 1,500 followers. All of this was designed, of course, to keep the Federal and Texas troops in a state of confusion. Lee, sensitive to the Cortinas affair, as soon as he reached San Antonio on February 20, started planning a campaign against the free booter.

In early March, Lieutenant Manning Kimmel left Fort Inge with Company G (64 troopers) for Fort Brown, headquarters for the Brownsville Expedition, as the force designated to hunt down Cortinas was called. Kimmel arrived on March 7 and proceeded up the Rio Grande where he camped above Captain Stoneman and Company E (62 troopers) who had bivouacked near Las Cruces. Upon Kimmel's arrival both companies were combined into a squadron commanded by Stoneman and assigned the duty of closely guarding some 100 miles of the Rio Grande. This was an impossible assignment for some 125 men. The river was fordable everywhere, and it was an easy matter to raid into Texas after the patrols had passed. It would take more than two companies of cavalry and a few companies of Texas Rangers to adequately protect the Rio Grande area from Mexican incursions. On March 15, word reached Stoneman that Cortinas was at La Mesa, Mexico, with a large number of his command. Stoneman, after consulting with Kimmel, decided it was worth the risk of invading Mexico to capture the outlaw. La Mesa was close by, just across the River from the area that the squadron was patrolling, and the rumor that Cortinas and his men were there had been passed on to the Captain from an "unimpeachable source.[3]

On the night of March 16, the two companies of the 2nd Cavalry accompanied by Rip Ford and about 75 Texas Rangers

---

[3] Price, p. 86; **Regimental Returns**, March, 1860

crossed the River and at daybreak of the 17th rode into La Mesa from four sides and carried it by assault. The Americans killed and wounded several Mexicans and captured 300 armed men. At first Stoneman was elated with what appeared to be the capture of Cortinas and most of his force. However, the joy soon turned to consternation when it was discovered that the troopers and Rangers had captured members of the Mexican National Guard who were garrisoning the town.[4] Viewing the ludicrous situation after the fact, Ford turned to Stoneman and remarked, "Well, Captain, we have played Old Scratch, whipped the Guardia Nacional, wounded a woman and killed a mule." Unfortunately, the woman later died, and at least 4 of the Mexican soldiers were killed. As for the dead mule, Lieutenant Nolan of the Rangers took credit for this feat, proclaiming that it was dark and he had mistaken the mule for a Mexican.[5] Apologies were made, the prisoners were released, and Stoneman's Command, along with the Rangers, left La Mesa and searched the countryside for 20 miles into Mexico unsuccessfully looking for Cortinas. The elusive Mexican had won another round and the Americans returned north of the Rio Grande on March 20, "after a long and tedious march."[6]

Department Commander Lee, at about the same time that Stoneman and Ford attacked La Mesa, took the field in person in an effort to put an end to the trouble along the border. Lee left San Antonio with a small escort on March 15 for Ringgold Barracks. He was joined on the way by Captain Brackett with Company I from Camp Verde, and Lieutenant Eagle with Company H joined the command at Eagle Pass. Lee and the two companies after enduring a violent sleet storm at Laredo on March 26, arrived at Ringgold Barracks on March 31. The sleet storm encountered near Laredo was of great intensity, so severe in fact that Privates Thomas Gaskin and Richard Keegan of Company I were "chilled to death because of exposure ... in the intensely cold weather."[7] From Ringgold Barracks the command continued south down the River to Edinburg where it arrived on April 7.[8]

[4] Price, p. 87
[5] Webb, p. 101. Ford was of the opinion that part of the National Guard captured at La Mesa had fought with Cortinas. Ibid.
[6] Price, p. 87; Regimental Returns, March, 1860.
[7] Price, p. 666
[8] Price, p. 88

While on the march from San Antonio to Edinburg, Lee maintained a strict schedule: reveille at 4 A.M., start of the day's march at 5:30 A.M., and a final halt at 2 P.M. to make camp and graze the horses before dark. It reminded some of the old timers of the march from Jefferson Barracks to Texas in late 1855.

When the Department Commander arrived at Edinburg, he found the community in a state of great excitement. On the morning of his arrival Mexican troops and Texas Rangers had exchanged shots across the Rio Grande at Reynosa, the Mexican town across the River from Edinburg. Lee, on being told that the Mexicans had initiated the firing sent Captain Brackett across the River with a white flag to consult with the local authorities as to the reason for the shooting and to ask about Cortinas. The town presented a warlike appearance. Brackett found the streets of Reynosa barricaded, artillery in place in front of the courthouse and four companies of infantry under arms in the plaza. The Captain learned that more troops were expected hourly from Camargo and Matamoros. Lee, with four companies (E, G, H and I) of the 2nd Cavalry (Companies E and G had joined Lee at Edinburg) and Major Ford's Texas Rangers awaited the results of Brackett's mission. Fortunately, the Reynosa authorities apologized for the firing, declared it would not happen again, and said that Cortinas and a group of his followers had fled into the interior. The *alcalde* and local military commander gave Brackett their word that if the bandit leader appeared again he would be turned over to American authorities. With this assurance of future cooperation, Brackett withdrew and reported back to Lee.[10]

An ugly situation was avoided at Reynosa, for had the Mexicans insisted on continuing their fire and harboring Cortinas and his band, Lee would have assaulted the town and, if required, invaded the interior of Mexico. The Virginian had specific orders from Secretary of War Floyd "to stop Mexican depredations, and, *if necessary* pursue the Mexicans beyond the limits of the United States."[11] Lee, an aggressive commander, would not have hesitated to carry out these orders if the situation had called for it.

Following the Reynosa incident, Lee proceeded to Fort

[9] Carl Coke Rister. **Robert E. Lee In Texas.** Norman: University of Oklahoma Press, 1946, p. 118. Hereafter cited as **Rister.**
[10] **Price,** p. 88; **Rister,** p. 124
[11] **Webb,** p. 192; **Rippy,** p. 108

Brown. However, he left the two squadrons of cavalry under Captains Brackett and Stoneman posted near Edinburg where they were in position to watch the Lower Valley from Fort Brown to Ringgold Barracks. While at Fort Brown, Lee opened up communications with Mexican General Guadalupe Garcia, commander of the Matamoros garrison. Garcia assured the American commander that "he would vigorously seek out and put in jail those raiders within his jurisdiction."[12] Although Lee took the assurances of cooperation that he had received from both the Mexican officials at Reynosa and Matamoros with a pinch of salt, he concluded that there was little more that he could personally do to restore order along the River. Cortinas and his men were reported to be hiding in the Burgos Mountains some 100 miles in the interior of Mexico,[13] and 40% of the strength of the 2nd Cavalry was deployed along the Lower Rio Grande. Consequently, Lee left Fort Brown for Department Headquarters at San Antonio on May 6, arriving there on the 13th.[14] While enroute north he reported to Washington that he considered Cortinas had abandoned the Rio Grande, surmising that the bandit saw nothing to gain in attracting more U. S. Troops and Rangers to the River, as it interferred with his rustling operation, so he withdrew to the interior of Mexico awaiting developments.

Although the Cortinas affair had been the main concern of both Texas and Federal officials during the early months of 1860, the north and western frontiers were far from quiet.[15] Both

---

[12] Rister, p. 124

[13] Rippy, p. 110. During the so-called Cortinas War, 15 Americans and 80 friendly Mexicans were killed and numerous others wounded. Cortinas was estimated to have lost some 150 men. The Lower Rio Grande Valley was left in ruins, most of the ranches and farms were abandoned and the towns deserted. Damage claims by American citizens alone amounted to over a third of a million dollars. Cortinas surfaced again during the American Civil War to plague the Rio Grande Valley once more, offering allegiance to both the Federal and Confederate forces. Later he became a general in the Mexican Army, served as Governor of the State of Tamaulipas, and amassed a fortune estimated at a half million dollars. Webb, p. 193. Cortinas, however, never quite achieved the fame of his 20th century counterpart Pancho Villa.

[14] Rister, p. 124

[15] Governor Sam Houston in the spring of 1860 persisted in his efforts to have Lee and Secretary of War Floyd place on the Federal payroll ten companies of Texas Rangers. Houston, who had a distaste for Federal troops wrote Floyd and Lee that the cavalry was inadequate to protect the frontier, that they did not like to fight Indians and that their horses were tenderfooted and had to be grain-fed and there was no grain on the Indian frontier. Houston's pleas were in vain. Webb, p. 201; Rister, p. 137.

January and February were active months for the companies of the 2nd Cavalry stationed at Camps Colorado and Lawson and at Fort Mason. At midnight on January 14 a settler brought word into Camp Colorado that a Comanche raiding party had stolen 24 horses and mules from farmers within 16 miles of the Fort. Lieutenant Fitzhugh Lee, who that same evening had returned from attending the inauguration of Governor Sam Houston in Austin, volunteered to lead a detachment against the thieves. A blue norther was blowing and drifting snow made progress slow for Lieutenant Lee and his detachment of 12 men from Company B. Finally at daylight on January 15 the command came to the area where the rustling had occurred and were fortunate enough to pick up the trail that was all but obliterated by the blowing storm. As the pursuit progressed south out of the snow area, the trail became plainer.

The young Lieutenant tracked the marauders all day of the 15th and, after riding 18 hours without halting, stopped for the night. No fires were allowed, and the men "feasted on hard tack and frozen pork." When the time came to mount their horses, some of the men were so cold and stiff they had to be helped into their saddles.[16] On the morning of January 17, Lee continued his pursuit. The sun was out, melting the snow, and made the trail easy to follow. In mid-afternoon the detachment caught up to the Indians as they were driving a herd of animals up Pecan Bayou in present Callahan County. Lieutenant Lee immediately ordered an attack. With drawn pistols the cavalrymen charged the unsuspecting Comanches, who, wrapped in their blankets, were not aware of their pursuers. Too surprised to make a stand, the Indians broke for a nearby stand of timber and succeeded in escaping except for two warriors at the rear of the herd. One of these was killed by the troopers before he could reach the timber, but the other in defiance to Lee turned and fired two arrows at the Lieutenant, his bugler, and a trooper, who were in close pursuit.[17]

Now unfolded one of the most bizarre episodes of individual combat engaged in by a member of the 2nd Cavalry while the Regiment was in Texas. The account is related by Bugler Jack Hayes of Company B, who accompanied Lee during the pursuit

---

[16] Crimmins, "Jack Hayes' Story," p. 44
[17] Ibid., p. 45; Price, p. 89

and subsequent fight.[18] Lee was determined to catch his adversary, and he followed the Comanche closely for "about 7 miles", losing him in the timber and then catching sight of him again in the clear spaces. Finally the woods gave way to prairie altogether, and here the Indian's tracks could be easily seen and followed. The Comanche, catching sight of the soldiers who were rapidly approaching him, abandoned his pony and sought safety on foot in a rocky ravine. The Lieutenant and bugler entered the ravine on foot, the trooper holding the horses. Lee was armed with an "old fashioned muzzle loading carbine" and a Navy Colt revolver and was wearing his heavy army overcoat and cape. The two searched the ravine carefully and as Lee approached a rocky ridge near the end of the ravine, the Indian suddenly jumped out and shot an arrow at short range directly at him. The Lieutenant jumped aside and the arrow passed through the left sleeve of his coat and his cape and shattered the stock of the carbine he was carrying. The warrior was on him in a flash, and as Lee attempted to use his revolver, the Indian grasped the barrel and turned it aside as the gun fired. In the struggle for the pistol it dropped to the ground and was temporarily lost by both sides. Then ensued a "desperate hand-to-hand struggle," the Indian using his knife and the cavalryman trying to avoid the thrusts and slashes. Finally Lee, in a quick manuever, placed his foot behind the Comanche's heel and succeeded in throwing him backward to the ground with Lee on top. As luck would have it, the revolver was within reach of the Lieutenant who freed his right arm, cocked the pistol and shot the Indian through both cheeks. A second shot, better aimed, killed the warrior instantly.[19]

Bugler Hayes recalled that after Lee had killed the Comanche,

> He arose to his feet and commenced to feel over his body for knife or arrow wounds, but unfortunately though his clothing was cut in many places, his skin was not touched. This was due to the heavy clothing he had on, especially to the overcoat, the material of which was unusually thick and heavy.

[18] Hayes was commissioned during the Civil War and fought with distinction in the Federal Army. Following the War he served with various cavalry regiments. He retired in 1903 as a colonel and commander of the 13th U.S. Cavalry. Crimmins, "Jack Hayes' Story," p. 40.
[19] Crimmins, "Jack Hayes' Story," pp. 46-47

Later on when Hayes inquired of Lee how he succeeded in throwing the Indian, the Lieutenant replied,

> He the Indian was very strong, as far as brute strength went, but he knew nothing of the science of wrestling. For a time though, I thought that he would get me, when I happened to think of a trick in wrestling which I learned during my school days in Virginia. It was known as the "Virginia back heel". I tried it on him and *fotched* him down.[20]

While Lieutenant Lee himself was highly commended for his leadership and bravery in both Department and Army Orders he, in turn, praised several of his men for their conduct in his report of the engagement. Included in General Orders, Number 11, Headquarters of the Army, dated November 23, 1860, was the following, "Specially noticed for good conduct" at Pecan Bayou, January 16, 1860, "Bugler Edward M. Hayes, Privates Benjamin Jones, Robert W. Turner and William McLean" and "commended for soldierly behavior, Corporal John M. Smith and Private Francis M. Alexander."[21]

Shortly after Lieutenant Lee's encounter at Pecan Bayou, 1st Sergeant R. H. Chapman left Fort Mason on a scout with a bugler and 9 men of Company A. Chapman left the Fort on January 25 and on the second day out discovered a war party of 18 Comanches camped near the head of Kickapoo Creek in present Schleicker County. The Indian camp was protected by steep bluffs on one side and a dense chaparral on the other. Regardless of the odds against him and the strong position that the Indians occupied, Chapman attacked the camp. Several charges were made both mounted and on foot in an effort to dislodge the Comanches. Darkness finally put an end to the fighting, and the Indians escaped, losing 4 killed, several wounded, and 13 of their horses captured. The detachment had two horses killed and the Sergeant's horse and three others were badly wounded. Miraculously none of the troopers were killed or wounded. Chapman in his report to the company commander mentioned the valuable services of three local citizens who volunteered to accompany him, J. B. Riley, T. B. Ives and Robert Casey.[22] Ives was slightly

---

[20] Ibid., p. 47
[21] Price, p. 666
[22] Colonel M. L. Crimmins, "Colonel Robert E. Lee's Report on Indian

wounded. Sergeant Chapman was mentioned in Army General Orders for "conduct greatly commended."[23]

Yet another engagement occurred in January, 1860, involving outstanding enlisted leadership. On January 27, Sergeant Alex McK. Craig, a corporal, and 13 men of Company C left Camp Lawson in pursuit of a band of Comanches who had been stealing horses from settlements along the Leona River.[24] On the second day out, Craig's command was joined by several citizen volunteers and on the following day, January 29, a party of 8 comanches was encountered camping along the Rio Frio. Craig immediately ordered a charge, the Indians mounted their ponies, and a running battle of several miles took place. Four Comanches were killed, two badly wounded and 21 horses captured. Private Joseph Blythe and Michael Flinn of Company C were wounded. Lieutenant Royal, Commander of Camp Lawson, in his report to the Department Commander gave "great credit to Sergeant Alex McK. Craig and his whole party for energy in the pursuit and bravery in the combat" at Rio Frio, January 29, 1860. This comment was made a matter of public record when it was included in General Orders, Number 11, Headquarters, U. S. Army, issued the following November.[25]

On January 30, Captain Richard Johnson left Fort Mason on a routine scout to the headwaters of the North Concho with a detachment of 40 men from Companies A and F and 20 days rations. After several days of fatiguing march in bad weather and sighting no Indians, Johnson decided to return to his home station by the way of Fort Chadbourne. At Chadbourne the Captain decided to send 20 men "whose horses were lame or partially broke down" directly back to Fort Mason while he took the remaining 20 troopers to "make a circuit in another direction hoping to come up with a small party of Indians."[26] On February 10, when Johnson was two days out from Fort Chadbourne he came across a fresh Indian trail of 14 horses. The cavalrymen immediately took up the pursuit. After three days of hard riding,

Combat in Texas." SWHQ., Vol. XXXIX, (July, 1935), P. 27. Hereafter cited as **Crimmins**, "Lee's Report."
[23] **Price**, p. 666
[24] Camp Lawson was located in present LaSalle County, some 75 miles southeast of Fort Inge.
[25] **Crimmins**, "Lee's Report," p. 27; **Price**, p. 666
[26] Johnson **Reminiscences**, pp. 124-25

averaging 60 miles a day, the command, near sunset of February 13, came upon a party of Comanches camped in a dense chaparral between Brady and Kickapoo Creeks in present Concho County. Although the number of Indians was estimated at 40, twice Johnson's number, he decided to attack. Not being able to approach the position mounted, the cavalrymen attacked dismounted and kept up a brisk fire against the Indians until dark, killing at least three. During the night a violent rain and wind storm came up, enabling the Comanches to escape into the brush, but most of their horses were left behind. Private A. J. O'Neill of Company F was wounded. Johnson, in his report of the affair, stated that he was of the opinion that there were white men with the Comanches, as when "he first charged the position he heard two men speaking English much too fluently for Indians." After resting a day at the scene of the engagement, the detachment took up the march for Fort Mason. However, prior to reaching the Fort their rations gave out, and the command had to subsist on mule meat for several days.[27]

Johnson's guide on the North Concho reconnaissance was the famous Delaware scout employed by the 2nd Cavalry, John McLoughlin, the same man who had accompanied Hood in 1857 to Devil's River. In fact, McLoughlin accompanied most of the major scouting expeditions to leave from Fort Mason during the time that the 2nd Cavalry was in Texas. He was one of the best scouts on the frontier; he was brave, could not be lost and "he always knew by the character of the country where to seek for food, water and grass." Too, he was a tracker *par excellence* and could speak several Indian tongues. The Delaware, however, had one great weakness: a fondness for whiskey. When informed that he was to go on a scout he would go through a regular ritual. He would prepare his rations, carefully arrange his clothing and supplies and then go on a drinking spree. McLoughlin would become so drunk that he would be unable to move out with the command but he would always overtake it the next day and remain stone sober for the entire expedition. One day Captain Johnson asked the scout why he always got drunk before starting on field service, McLoughlin replied, "Maybe so for, Captain, thirty days before I can get some more whiskily." The army

---

[27] Ibid.; Price, pp 90-91; Crimmins, "Lee's Report." pp. 27-28

overlooked the Indian's friendship with John Barleycorn because of his devotion, scouting skills and good conduct when removed from temptation. McLoughlin remained in Texas when the Regiment left the State in the spring of 1861, and his career thereafter is unknown.[28]

Major Thomas, the Regimental Commander, during the summer of 1860 conducted a major scouting expedition to the headwaters of the Concho and Colorado Rivers. This expedition was reminiscent of the extended reconnaissance he had conducted the previous autumn to the Cimarron River country. Thomas left Camp Cooper on July 23, accompanied by Lieutenant William W. Lowe and a detachment of 7 men from Company D.[29] Thirteen members of the Regimental Band also left for field duty with Thomas.[30] The command rode south from Cooper to Camp Colorado where it arrived on the 27th and was joined here by Lieutenant Fitzhugh Lee with Company B. Thomas marched to Kiowa Creek, reaching there on July 31, where Captain Johnson with Company E and Lieutenant A. Parker Porter with Company A, both from Fort Mason, joined the expedition.[31] The command

---

[28] Johnson, **Remininscences**, p. 112; Price, p. 91. McLoughlin, like most Indians would not kill a snake. Whenever he would see one, he would point it out to Johnson and say in his broken English, "For Captain, a snattlesake." Johnson would then dispatch the reptile with his Navy Colt. On one occasion Johnson recalled he shot a rattler in two parts and while the first half crawled away, the second half continued to rattle as if nothing had happened. Johnson, **Remininscences**, pp. 114-115.

[29] Lowe was graduated from the U. S. Military Academy in 1853. After short assignments in both the 1st and 2nd Dragoons, Lowe was assigned to the 2nd Cavalry when it was activated, March 3, 1855. He was appointed Adjutant of the Regiment in May, 1858, and was involved in several engagements with the Indians while the 2nd Cavalry was in Texas. Lowe served with the Federal Army during the Civil War and had a distinguished record. At the end of the War he was a colonel in the cavalry. Lowe resigned from the army in 1869 to engage in civilian pursuits in Omaha, Nebraska.

[30] Due to the fact that four companies of the Regiment were still stationed on the Rio Grande, all available manpower had to be utilized when conducting major scouting expeditions. With few men left at Camp Cooper to enjoy the evening band concerts, Thomas, who placed little emphasis on military bands, turned the tooters into shooters. This is the second instance known of the Regimental Band participating in a scout or expedition. On February 17, 1860, when numerous animals were stolen near Camp Cooper, the Band was sent out in pursuit of the Indians and succeeded in recovering a large number of the stolen horses. **Freeman**, p. 405; Letter from Captain Richard Johnson to Colonel Albert Sidney Johnston, date line Fort Mason, Texas, November 3, 1857 (Mason, Barrett Collection, Tulane University); **Price**, p. 91.

[31] Lieutenant A. P. Porter was graduated from West Point in 1856 and

proceeded to march west toward the headwaters of the Concho without encountering hostile Indians. Thomas continued his reconnaissance until August 20 and discovering no fresh trails disbanded the expedition. Companies A, B and F returned directly to their duty stations at Camp Colorado and Fort Mason, while Major Thomas with the Regimental Band and the detachment of Company D under Lieutenant Lowe followed the stage road back to Camp Cooper.[32]

On the morning of August 25 Thomas' Delaware guide, Doss, came across an Indian trail about 25 miles east of Mountain Pass, in present Taylor County. The wagons were immediately sent to Camp Cooper, and the command with pack mules started in pursuit in a northwest direction, marching 40 miles before nightfall. Thomas continued the pursuit at daylight on the 26th and at 7 A.M. Doss discovered a band of 13 Indians, breaking camp on the Salt Fork of the Brazos, about a mile and a half away. Thomas, as soon as he received the scout's report, started his command at a gallop and arrived at the Indian encampment a few minutes after the Comanches had left. Now a running battle took place with the Indians having a half mile lead. For over three miles the pursuit continued, the soldiers following the Indians so closely that they abandoned their loose horses. As the chase continued one warrior, "an old Comanche", dropped off of his horse and armed with only a bow and arrows and a lance defied the pursuers. In their eagerness to dispatch the lone Indian the cavalrymen (and bandsmen) pressed too closely, and consequently several of his arrows and lance thrusts took effect. Major Thomas was hit in both the chin and chest by arrows, but a thick beard and stout chin and heavy hair on his barrel chest fortunately turned both barbs, although leaving painful cuts. The venerable Comanche before he fell managed to wound Privates William Murphy and Hugh Clark of Company D, Chief Bugler August Hausser and bandsmen John Zito and Casper Siddel. Murphy, who later died of his wounds, Zito and Siddel were all struck by

---

assigned to the 2nd Cavalry. Porter engaged in numerous Indian fights with the Regiment and was commended for bravery on several occasions. He remained with the Federal Army during the Civil War and rose to the rank of major. Porter died at Little Rock, Arkansas in 1866. **Price**, pp. 481-83.
[32] **Price**, pp. 92-93; R. C. Crane, "One Indian Faced Twenty Soldiers." **Frontier Times**, Vol. 3, No. 2, May, 1925, p. 13. Hereafter cited as **Crane**; **Crimmins**, "Lee's Report," p. 21.

arrows, as was Thomas. Clark and Hausser were wounded by weak lance thrusts administered by the warrior after he had been shot "twenty or more" times.[33] No greater example of self-sacrifice is recorded in the annals of Indian warfare on the Western frontier.

Thomas was of the opinion that had their pursuit not been stopped by the old warrior, his command could have caught and brought to justice the 12 other fleeing Comanches. The cavalry-men, however, did capture 28 horses. On the night of August 26, Thomas and his men rode back to the abandoned Indian camp on the Salt Fork and spent the night. The wounded were treated by Lieutenant Lowe, and the column started for Camp Cooper on the 27th in a rain storm. After traveling three more days in the rain, the command arrived back at their home station on the 30th. George H. Thomas, the famed "Rock of Chickamauga," saw much front line action during the 2nd Seminole, Mexican and Civil Wars, but a solitary old Comanche warrior near the Salt Fork of the Brazos in Texas on August 26, 1860, gave him his only "battle" wounds.[34]

While Thomas was pursuing the band of horse thieves in the vicinity of present Sweetwater and Abilene, Texas, in late August, 1860, Corporal John Rutter was on the same type of mission at about the same time in present Comanche County. Rutter left Camp Colorado on August 25 with a detachment of 8 men from Company B and a guide, Mr. Mulkey. They were in pursuit of a party of Indians who had stolen horses from farmers within five miles of the post. Trailing the Indians for two days in rain and mud, Rutter's small command approached the Sabano River, swollen by recent rains. The Corporal elected to cross the flooded stream, and in doing so his men and their arms and ammunition were thoroughly soaked. Upon gaining the opposite bank, Rutter found himself close to the Indian camp. He immediately ordered a charge, but unfortunately only a few of the carbines and pistols would fire. The Comanches, discovering the condition of the soldier's arms, took the offensive, forced their way through the line of cavalrymen and made their escape. Two warriors were

[33] Crane, p. 13; Price, p. 667
[34] Crane, pp. 13-14; Price, p. 92; Richard O'Connor. Thomas: Rock of Chickamauga. New York: Prentice Hall, 1948. pp. 96-97; Wilbur Thomas. General George H. Thomas, The Indomitable Warrior, New York; Exposition Press, 1964. pp. 113-114.

wounded, and all of the stolen horses recovered. One enlisted man, Private James Cunningham, was killed and two horses were wounded. Both Corporal John Rutter and Private William McLaughlin of Company B were mentioned in General Orders. The former was commended for his leadership and "persevering in pursuit during the heavy rainstorm" and the latter was given "honorable mention" for his performance in battle.[35]

As the year 1860 drew to a close the Naconi Comanches under their chief, Peta Nacona, staged a series of raids through Jack, Wise, Parker and Palo Pinto Counties, murdering, raping, looting and stealing horses. The incensed citizens of these counties elected J. H. Cureton, a seasoned frontier captain, to form a "citizens company" to pursue the marauders. At the same time, Governor Sam Houston ordered Texas Ranger Rip Ford to recruit a company of 75 men in the vicinity of Waco and then proceed to Fort Belknap to chastise the raiders. Ford and Cureton joined forces at Belknap in early December, and this force was soon augmented by a detachment of 20 cavalrymen from Company H under 1st Sergeant John W. Spangler. Company H had been reassigned from the Rio Grande area to Camp Cooper in October.[36]

Ross moved out from Fort Belknap with his Rangers, Cureton's citizens and Spangler's troopers in mid-December. The command rode northwest from Belknap and found the trail of the marauders just north of Camp Cooper. The column with Ross and Sgt. Spangler forming the advance party and Cureton's group several miles to the rear, struck the Pease River and followed it to its confluence with Mule Creek near the present town of Crowell in Foard County. Here, the Rangers and the cavalrymen surprised a party of Comanches and routed them, a running battle taking place. Ross, in personal combat singled out and killed Chief Peta Nacona. One of Ross' lieutenants, Thomas Kelleher, after a two mile chase overtook what he thought was a brave but what turned out to be a squaw with a two year old baby. In reporting his capture to Ross, Kelleher, in his Irish brogue, said, "Captain, I ran

---

[35] Price, pp. 92-93, 667; Colonel M. L. Crimmins, "The Military History of Camp Colorado," WTHABY, Vol. XXVIII, October, 1952, p. 79.
[36] Richardson, Rupert N. The Frontier Of Northwest Texas, 1846 to 1876. Glendale (Cal.); A. H. Clark Co., 1963. pp. 209-10. Cited hereafter as Richardson, Frontier. Rister, pp. 146-157.

me horse most to death and captured a damned squaw."[37] However, the "damned squaw" turned out to be Cynthia Ann Parker, a legendary figure in Texas history.[38] Comanche losses were 14 killed, several wounded, three warriors and several squaws and children captured and 45 horses taken. Ross' command suffered no losses.[39] Company H participated in the battle and played a prominent part in routing the Comanches. Spangler was given an "honorable mention" in General Orders for his efforts on the Pease River. He was later commissioned in the 3rd Cavalry Regiment during the Civil War and for his "gallantry and meritorious service" at Gettysburg received a brevet captaincy.[40]

The battle on the Pease River, December 19, 1860, was the last engagement in which the Regiment participated during its assignment on the Texas Frontier.

General Twiggs returned from sick leave on December 13 and relieved Robert E. Lee of command of the Department of Texas. Six days later, after settling up all of his accounts and bidding his friends goodbye, Lee set out for Fort Mason to resume command of his old regiment. On the way north a blue norther hit with its cold winds and freezing rain. Camping for the night by the roadside gave the Virginian little relief and the sharp wind, when he was riding, knifed through his heavy woolen overcoat. Lee reached the warmth of Fort Mason on December 23 amid the holiday festivities and assumed command of the 2nd Cavalry the following day, Christmas Eve, 1860.[41]

[37] Richardson, **Frontier**, p. 211.
[38] Cynthia Ann Parker was captured in a Comanche raid on Fort Parker in present Limestone County, on May 19, 1836 when she was 9 years old. She married the Comanche Chief Peta Nacona and had two sons by him that later became Comanche chiefs, Pecos and Quanah Parker. When captured she was carrying her two year old daughter, Prairie Flower. Ross, knowing that they had captured a white woman because of her blue eyes and fair complexion, took her back to Camp Cooper where she was positively identified by a relative as Cynthia Ann Parker. In 1861, the State of Texas granted her a pension and a league of land. Cynthia Ann Parker died in 1864, shortly after the death of her daughter. The United States Government voted in 1910 to remove her body from Anderson County, Texas to Post Oak Cemetery near Cache, Oklahoma. **Handbook,** II, p. 335.
[39] Price, p. 93.
[40] Francis B. Heitman. **Historical Register and Dictionary of the U.S. Army.** 2 volumes. Washington: Government Printing Office, 1903. Reprint. I, p. 909.
[41] **Rister,** pp. 149-50. In Lee's absence the Regiment had been commanded, except for a short period of time, by Major Thomas. **Price,** pp. 549,619.

CHAPTER ELEVEN

1861 - EXODUS FROM TEXAS

By the direction of the President of the United States,
it is ordered that Brigadier General David E. Twiggs,
major-general by brevet, be, and is hereby dismissed
from the Army of the United States, for his treachery
to the flag of his country, in having surrendered on the
18th of February, 1861, on demand of the authorities of
Texas, the military posts and other property of the
United States in his department and under his charge.[1]

The year 1861 opened with much foreboding concerning the continued existence of the Federal Union. South Carolina had already seceded and during the first month of the new year, the old Palmetto State would be joined by the rest of the "deep south" — Mississippi, Florida, Alabama, Georgia and Louisiana, in that order. A Texas convention on February 1 would vote overwhelmingly (166 to 8) to leave the Union. This action of the Secession Convention was confirmed a few days later by the Texas Legislature and by the electorate later in the month. The nation was rapidly being torn apart, and the 2nd Cavalry, posted as it was in a state that would secede, was much involved in the momentous events occuring around it.

Since December 27, 1860, General Twiggs had repeatedly asked Washington for instructions on what course of action to take in case Texas left the Union. He had stated in his numerous letters to Adjutant General Samuel Cooper that he did not assume that the government desired him to carry on civil war in Texas and that he consequently would turn over the army property in his department to the government of the state after Texas seceded.[2] On January 13, Twiggs, an ardent secessionist, asked to be relieved of command of the Department of Texas, but the order relieving him of duty was not issued until January 28 and not received at

---

[1] General Orders, No. 5, War Department, Washington, March 1, 1861. **The War of the Rebellion: Official Records of the Union and Confederate Armies.** 128 Volumes. Washington: Government Printing Office, 1880-1901, Series I, Vol 1, p. 597. Hereafter cited as **ORA.**
[2] Ibid., p. 582.

San Antonio until February 15.[3] While the orders were in transit, the Department Commander was completely in the dark concerning the War Department's policy.

Soon after the Texas Secession Convention adjourned in early February, Twiggs was approached by representatives of the State in regard to the transfer of United States property to Texas. In these negotiations the Department Commander followed the policy that he had written Cooper that he would pursue. He appointed three commissioners, Majors David H. Vinton (Quartermaster) and Sackfield Maclin (Paymaster) and Captain Robert H. K. Whiteley (Ordnance Department) to negotiate the surrender terms with Thomas J. Devine, Sam A. Maverick and P. N. Luckett, who were members of the Texas Committee of Public Safety.[4] Negotiations were almost completed when Twiggs received the order relieving him of his command. He was replaced by Colonel Carlos A. Waite, Commander of the 1st Infantry Regiment, the next senior officer in the Department. Waite arrived at San Antonio on February 19, and at this time assumed command from Twiggs.[5]

The Texans, however, before negotiations had been completed, surmising that Waite, a New Yorker, would not surrender Federal property rode into San Antonio before daylight on February 16 and siezed the government stores. Twiggs made no attempt to prevent the takeover. This seizure was carried out by Colonel Ben McCulloch and some 1,000 of his so called "buffalo hunters." McCulloch had been designated as the interim commander of Texas troops by the Committee of Public Safety. After this dramatic turn in events, Twiggs, before Waite could reach San Antonio from Camp Verde and physically assume command, issued on February 18, Department of Texas, General Orders No. 5. This order delivered all Federal military posts and property within the limits of the Texas Military District to the State of Texas. Order No. 5, which was transmitted to all Federal posts in

[3] Ibid., p. 584
[4] Harold B. Simpson, **Texas in the War, 1861-1865**, Hillsboro: Hill Jr. College Press, 1965, p. 189. Hereafter cited as Simpson, **Texas in the War.**
[5] ORA. Ser. I, Vol., p. 591. The selection of Colonel Waite by Washington was a last minute attempt to organize some type of Federal resistance in Texas. However, Waite found the task impossible, due primarily to the large extent of country over which the troops were scattered and so advised the Adjutant General that "it was his duty to comply with the agreement entered into by General Twiggs." Ibid., p. 521.

Texas, also stated that the troops would "march out of Texas by the way of the coast."[6] Few, if any, of the Federal commanders in the field were aware of the fact that Twiggs had been relieved of command and had been replaced by Colonel Waite, so considered the order as legal and binding. Thus Twiggs with one stroke of the pen surrendered to State authorities. 21 Federal military posts, ordnance, commissary and quartermaster supplies worth somewhere between 1.5 million and 3 million dollars and about $23,000 in cash. The amount of cash taken would have been greater, but for the fact that 1st Lieutenant Kenner Garrard, Company K, secreted $20,000 on his person when he left Texas.[7]

In an effort to forestall the movement of the Federal troops from Texas via the coast, Assistant Adjutant General Lorenzo Thomas sent a message to Colonel Waite on February 15 (received by Waite on March 1) advising him that General Scott wanted the United States troops in Texas to march to Fort Leavenworth in Kansas. To accomplish this the Federal units would rendezvous at four locations in Texas, Forts Stockton and Clark, San Antonio and Camp Cooper. From these locations they would march to Fort Belknap, then to Fort Arbuckle above the Red River, thence through the Indian Territory and west of the state of Arkansas to Fort Leavenworth. The order of February 15 also advised Colonel Waite to use all available transportation possible to move Federal property to Fort Leavenworth, even employing the camels stationed at Camp Verde. Although several company commanders of the 2nd Cavalry gave some consideration to Scott's order,[8] it was found impractical to move the command this great distance because of the lack of transportation, forage and subsistence. Waite, feeling bound by Twiggs' surrender agreement, and the fact that some of the units were already bound for the coast chose not to enforce the order.

As early as mid-January Texans with secessionist leanings had begun to organize informal bodies of men for the ultimate purpose

---

[6] Simpson, **Texas in the War**, p. 195. This order was referred to as the "Order of Exercises" by the pro-Federal officers of the Regiment. **Price**, p. 281.

[7] **Price**, p. 346. Soon after Garrard arrived in the North he turned the money into the U.S. Treasury. **Ibid.**

[8] Captains Stoneman (Company E), Oakes (Company C) and Whiting (Company K) met at Fort Inge to consider uniting their companies and march north out of the state. **Price**, pp. 282, 316, 332; **Rister**, p. 162.

of taking over the Federal posts and seizing Federal property. Some of these groups disguised their real aims and identity by calling themselves "buffalo hunters." The Knights of the Golden Circle, a secret, para-military, radical secessionist organization with headquarters at San Antonio, had established "castles" in many towns in Texas and boasted publicly that in four days they could put 8,000 fully armed men in the field.[9] At most camps and forts in the Department, strange and suspicious looking men lurked about,[10] disappearing as fast as they appeared and causing the post commanders to make plans for defense and take steps to safeguard public property.

Robert E. Lee, commanding the Regiment and also Fort Mason where the Regimental Headquarters was located, was concerned with these happenings. Richard Johnson, Commander of Company F stationed at Fort Mason, said in his *Reminiscenses* that Lee called him in one day in early February to discuss the defense of the Fort with him. The Virginian said that he was determined *to defend Fort Mason at all hazards* and asked Johnson, a Kentuckian, if he, Lee, could rely on Johnson's support. After an affirmative answer "which seemed to please the Colonel very much," said Johnson, Lee "divulged to him his plan of fortifying the post."[11] However, before Lee could begin to carry out his plan, he was transferred out of the Department.

Unfortunately, Lee's plan is not known, for neither he or Johnson put it in writing. Lee, we know was a Union man, a non-slave holder and against the process of secession. On numerous occasions to his family, his friends and in public statements he made clear his stand on disunion. In a letter to his son, Custis, written from Fort Mason on January 23, 1861, Lee stated that "secession is nothing but revolution".[12] He also made clear, however, that his first loyalty was to his state, Virginia. Douglas Southall Freeman, Lee's biographer, stated that Lee had little sympathy with the "cotton state extremists" and that while "his mind was for the Union; his instinct was for the State of Virginia."[13]

---

[9] Freeman, I, p. 414.
[10] Johnson, Reminiscences, p. 132.
[11] Ibid, p. 133.
[12] Freeman, p. 420.
[13] Ibid., p. 416.

In the midst of this turmoil the Commander of the 2nd Cavalry, on February 4, received a message from General Twiggs relieving him of duty with the Regiment and ordering him to report to General Scott at Washington no later than April 1. With Lee's departure the Regiment was without a commander. Lee was the only field grade officer of the 2nd Cavalry present for duty as Major Thomas was on extended leave and Major Van Dorn had resigned his commission.[14] The Virginian left Fort Mason on the morning of February 13 for San Antonio. As he was departing, Captain Johnson went to the ambulance in which Lee was riding and said to him. "Colonel, do you intend to go South or remain North? I am very anxious to know just what you propose to do." Lee replied to Johnson, "I shall never bear arms against the United States — but it may be necessary for me to carry a musket in defense of my native state, Virginia, in which case, I shall not prove recreant to my duty."[15] The driver cracked his whip, the ambulance was off and as it rolled away, Lee thrust his head out of the window and said, "Good-bye, God bless you." This is the last time that Johnson saw Lee, and Fort Mason was Lee's last duty station in the Federal Army.

Knowing Lee's character and feelings, there is little doubt that if he had still been in command of the 2nd Cavalry and Fort Mason when Texas state troops demanded its surrender in late March, he would have resisted the attempted take over. Lee would have protected Federal property for which he was responsible and he undoubtedly would have encouraged his other company commanders to do the same. There were two companies of cavalry stationed at Fort Mason and three other companies within a two or three day ride of the Fort. Being mounted units, the three companies stationed at Camps Cooper and Colorado could have assembled at Fort Mason on Lee's order, and along with two companies already there, would have given Lee over 250 well trained and well armed soldiers, a force large enough to resist a much greater body of undisciplined "buffalo hunters." If, on the other hand, Lee had been commander of the Texas Military Department, he would have not hesitated to obey War Department

---

[14] First Lieutenant W. W. Lowe, Adjutant of the Regiment, was left in charge of the Regiment records, the non-commissioned officer staff, and the band.
[15] Johnson, **Reminiscences**, p. 133.

Orders. He certainly would have refused to surrender government property and resisted surrendering it to a group of irregulars whose authority to act for Texas was highly questionable. Conceivably, if Lee had been in command of the 2nd Cavalry or the Department of Texas when the troops representing the Committee of Public Safety took over the Federal installations, the Civil War may have started in Texas in February or March, 1861, rather than a half continent away at Fort Sumter in April.

When Lee reached San Antonio on February 16, the day that McCulloch seized the Federal installations there, he was appalled at what he saw and what had happened. The state troops attempted to arrest Lee and prevent his leaving for Washington pursuant to his orders. After being detained a day or two and humiliated he was permitted to go to Indianola to board a ship for New Orleans. The treatment Lee received at San Antonio strengthened his views against secession, and it was not until he arrived in Virginia, talked to his family and friends, and witnessed the secession of "his State," that he could come to support disunion.

However, even during this period of uncertainty and unrest while the Federal forces in Texas awaited word from San Antonio as to their future course of action, the Regiment continued to vigorously protect the frontier. Scouting parties were dispatched regularly during January and February from all of the posts garrisoned by companies of the 2nd Cavalry and during the latter month, the last recorded field service conducted by the Regiment in Texas took place.[16] In mid-February, 1861, Lieutenant A. K. Arnold[17] and a detachment from Company C left Fort Inge in pursuit of a band of hostile Comanches who were raiding settlements between Camp Wood and Fort Inge in present Kinney

---

[16] **Regimental Returns**, January, February, 1861.
[17] Abraham K. Arnold was graduated from the U.S. Military Academy with the Class of 1859, and was assigned to the 2nd Cavalry. After serving at Carlisle Barracks, (Pennsylvania) for a year, Arnold joined his Regiment in Texas, December, 1860. He served in the Federal Army during the Civil War and saw much action in Virginia with the Army of the Potomac. Following the war Arnold served at various posts on the Western Frontier with the 6th Cavalry Regiment. During the Spanish-American War he was promoted to brigadier-general. **Price**, pp. 363-65; **Register of Graduates**, p. 150. Arnold, as a captain and company commander, won the Medal of Honor in 1864 on the North Anna River "by a gallant charge against a superior force of the enemy, extricated his command from a perilous position in which it had been ordered." **Medal of Honor, 1863-1968**. Washington: U. S. Government Printing Office, 1968. p. 21.

County. Arnold caught up with the raiders and pursued them so closely and so vigorously that they were forced to abandon several of their horses and flee across the Rio Grande to safety. Thus, as the biographer of the Regiment wrote, "to the very last hour the Regiment discharged its duty to the State, even when the citizens had renounced the flag of their country. . ."[18] In sending Arnold against the Indians Captain James Oakes, Commander of Company C and Fort Inge, received a vote of thanks inscribed upon parchment by the Secession Convention. It is interesting to note that in performing this service, Oakes was reprimanded by his Department Commander, Colonel Waite.[19]

At the time that Twiggs issued his surrender order in mid-February, companies of the 2nd Cavalry were scattered along a thousand miles of frontier. Along with the Regimental Headquarters and Band, Companies A and F were at Fort Mason, Companies D and H garrisoned Camp Cooper, Company B was stationed at Camp Colorado, Company C at Fort Inge, Company I at Camp Verde,[20] and Company K at Camp Wood. Both companies E, under Captain Stoneman, and G, commanded by Lieutenant Kimmel, were still stationed along the Lower Rio Grande.[21] According to the agreement that Twiggs had made with the Texas Commissioners of Public Safety, the Federal troops would be allowed to keep their arms and the "necessary means for regular and comfortable movement, provisions, tents, etc., etc., and transportation,"[22] as they marched or rode to the coast in their exodus from Texas. The various Federal commanders in the State, cavalry, infantry and artillery, were to leave their posts on specified dates for the coast. "These dates were so arranged," wrote Captain Richard Johnson, "that not more than one

[18] Price, p. 96.
[19] Ibid., p. 283.
[20] Lt. Col. Waite, 1st Infantry, commanding Camp Verde, on January 28 wrote Twiggs that he was ordering Captain Brackett's Company I from indefensible Camp Ives to Camp Verde in order to better defend the latter post. It is interesting to note that Waite, in his letter to Twiggs, listed his 53 camels, which he valued at $20,000, as the most valuable public property at Camp Verde. ORA, Ser. I, Vol. I, pp. 589-90.
[21] Price, pp. 619-621, 623, 626, 628, 630, 633, 636, 638, 641, 644, 647.
[22] Simpson, Texas in the War, p. 195. Federal troops were to leave behind all personal property that could not be carried on their person. Captain E. Kirby Smith, commander of Company B and a dedicated sportsman, lamented the fact that he had to leave behind at Camp Colorado his two bird dogs, "Nell" and "Ugly." Parks, p. 117.

thousand men would be at any point at the same time," thus minimizing the risk of armed resistance.[23] Once at Indianola, supplies, transportation and arms would be turned over to State authorities. Major Fitz-John Porter, Assistant Adjutant General of the Department of Texas, was designated to superintend the embarkation of troops at Indianola and to provide and schedule ships for the voyage north.[24]

The Regiment was much depleted of officers when it commenced its withdrawal from Texas. As of March 31, 1861, of the 36 officers assigned to the 2nd Cavalry but 14 were present for duty.[25] Many of the officers were on leave, and several had already resigned or were in the process of resigning their commissions. Major Earl Van Dorn, an avowed secessionist, was the first officer of the Regiment to resign from the United States Army, doing so on January 3, 1861. In late March, as a colonel in the Provisional Army of the Confederate States, he was assigned to Texas. Van Dorn's mission was to convince as many officers of the 2nd Cavalry as possible to resign their commissions and join the new Confederacy. In this he was unsuccessful: the North and South were not yet at war and the officers still on duty with the Regiment preferred to stay with the Federal Army under existing conditions.[26] Captains E. Kirby Smith and Nathan "Shanks" Evans and Lieutenant John B. Hood, who were present for duty with the Regiment when Twiggs issued the surrender order, resigned their commissions before the 2nd Cavalry left for the North.[27] Most of the officers on leave at the time of the exodus from Texas never rejoined the Regiment but tendered their resignations during April and May, 1861, and joined the Southern Army.

It was a simple matter for the officers to resign their commissions. This privilege was accorded commissioned officers

---

[23] Johnson, **Reminiscences**, p. 148.
[24] Ibid., p. 149.
[25] **Regimental Returns**, March, 1861.
[26] Hartje, p. 76. Van Dorn, however, was successful in preventing the departure of Federal troops from Texas after the **Empire City** sailed on April 12. On April 16 he captured the steamer **Star of the West** (with troops on board) at Indianola. In late April and early May, Van Dorn, at the head of 800 men captured 7 companies of the 8th Infantry and 6 companies of the 1st Infantry on their way to Green Lake. **Price**, p. 276; ORA, Ser. I, Vol. I, pp. 562-564, 568-570.
[27] **Price**, pp. 278, 335, 472.

with no punishment and with very little stigma attached. For the enlisted men, it was an entirely different matter. If the enlisted man failed to complete his three year term in the army and left the service without an approved cause, for the convenience of the government, he was listed as a deserter. Non-commissioned officers and privates could not resign. Although the senior sergeants of the 2nd Cavalry were offered numerous enticements to desert, they remained loyal to the flag except in a few cases.[28] Even though some of the Officers "who went South," like John Bell Hood, encouraged the enlisted men "to remain faithful to their obligation," well over 100 of them (about 15% of the regimental strength) deserted during the spring of 1861, before the Regiment left Texas.[29] Of the enlisted men who deserted during this period almost all were privates; a few, however, were corporals and low ranking sergeants; only one was a senior non-commissioned officer, 1st Sergeant John N. Smith of Company B.

The companies of the 2nd Cavalry began leaving their posts in late February for the trek to the coast. They were to rendezvous at Green Lake some 10 miles from the coast in western Calhoun County, and then march the 30 miles to Indianola for transportation north. Colonel Rip Ford had been designated by the Committee of Public Safety to take the surrender of the Federal posts in the southern half of the state and Colonel Henry McCulloch was designated to conduct the takeover of the posts in the northern half of Texas. The first two posts to be abandoned were Camps Verde and Cooper on February 21.[30] Camp Colorado was turned over to State authorities five days later.[31] The four companies (B, D, H, and I) marched from Camps Colorado, Cooper and Verde to Green Lake, arriving there in early March. These four companies were joined in late March by the two companies, E and G, stationed on the Lower Rio Grande. Company E, camped just west of Brownsville, and Company G in camp near Edinburg, left their stations on March 20 and were transported to Brazos Santiago near the mouth of the Rio Grande on the steamboat *Mustang*. At Brazos Santiago they boarded the

---

[28] Ibid., p. 98. Eleven senior non-commissioned officers of the Regiment were commissioned as officers in the Federal Army during or just after the Civil War.
[29] **Regimental Returns**, February, March, April, 1861.
[30] Price, pp. 628, 638, 641.
[31] Ibid., p. 623.

steamship *Arizona* for Indianola where they arrived on March 22, marching to Green Lake the following day.[32] The six companies of the 2nd Cavalry bivouacked at Green Lake were under the command of the senior captain present, Innis N. Palmer, commander of Company D.[33]

A tragic event occurred on the night of March 20 while Company E was on board the *Mustang* waiting to transfer to the *Arizona.* First Lieutenant James B. Witherell, who had been a member of the Regiment since its activation in March, 1855, and who had engaged in numerous Indian combats with Company E, was drowned. He fell overboard during the early morning hours of March 21 and was carried out to sea. His body was never recovered. Witherell was near sighted and the *Mustang* was a ship of light draught with the deck close to the water and was without guard rails. It was surmised the Lieutenant was asleep on the deck and either rolled or stepped overboard during the night.[34]

The battalion of six companies under Captain Palmer was the first contingent of the 2nd Cavalry to leave Texas. Palmer's command moved from Green Lake on March 30 to Indianola where they boarded the *USS Coatzacoalcos* the following day and sailed for the East Coast. Proceeding by the way of Key West to take on water and food and Havana, to pick up the mail, the battalion reached New York on April 11, the day before Fort Sumter was fired upon.[35]

The second and last contingent of the Regiment to leave the Lone Star State was composed of the Headquarters and Companies A, C. F, and K. The Regimental Headquarters and the above companies abandoned Forts Mason and Inge and Camp Wood during the last two weeks in March; Captain Whiting and Company K left Camp Wood on March 15; Captain Oakes and Company C left Fort Inge on the 19th; and Captain Johnson left Fort Mason with the Headquarters and Companies A and F on March 29. Ironically, Fort Mason was both the first and last post in Texas to be occupied by the 2nd Cavalry. The four companies marching by the way of San Antonio, reached the rendezvous

---

[32] Ibid., pp. 97, 630, 636; Regimental Returns, March, 1861.
[33] Price, p. 285.
[34] Ibid., p. 479.
[35] Ibid., p. 97; Official Records of the Union and Confederate Navies in The War of the Rebellion. Washington: Government Printing Office, 1884-1927. Ser. I, Vol. 4, p. 106.

point, Green Lake, in early April. Under the command of Captain Whiting, the senior officer present and commander of Company K, the second contingent of the Regiment, marched to Indianola on April 12, and boarded the *USS Empire City* for the trip north. Whiting's Battalion, also sailing via Key West and Havana, where they replenished their supply of water and fuel and picked up mail, reached New York City on April 20.[36]

When the companies of Whiting's detachment of the 2nd Cavalry reached San Antonio on their way to the coast the State troops were flying the Texas flag over the Alamo. The next morning when Whiting and his men marched through the city and passed the Alamo on their way to Green Lake, they carried the regimental standard and the company guidons and the band played "Yankee Doodle" and "Hail Columbia." A large number of citizens followed the troops out of the city and on the outskirts presented the Captain with a large United States flag. The next afternoon when the battalion arrived at Goliad, a "Secession flag" was flying from the principal flagstaff in town. A group of the enlisted men, without the knowledge of the officers, proceeded to rip the banner down and then cut it into pieces to make head streamers for the train mules as they marched through town.[37]

The officers who left Texas on the *Coatzacoalcos* and the *Empire City* were Captains Brackett, Johnson, Palmer, Stoneman and Whiting, and Lieutenants Arnold, Chambliss, Harrison, Jenifer, Kimmel, Lowe, Porter and Royall.[38] Of this group Jenifer and Kimmel eventually resigned their commissions after accompanying the Regiment North, the former within a few weeks after reaching the East Coast and the latter after he had participated as a Federal officer at the 1st Battle of Bull Run (Manassas), July 21, 1861.[39]

The 2nd Cavalry could be proud of its five years of dedicated service on the Texas frontier and border. The Regiment left behind a proud military heritage. It had driven the Indians far beyond the fringes of settlement and had attacked the hostile Comanches deep in their heartland. Too, the Regiment had assisted the Texas Rangers in neutralizing the efforts of the

---

[36] **Price**, p. 97.
[37] Ibid., p. 98
[38] Ibid.
[39] Ibid., pp. 467, 484.

Mexican outlaw, Juan Cortinas, and in bringing peace to the Lower Rio Grande Valley. Thorough in reconnaissance, persistent in pursuit and successful in battle, the 2nd U. S. Cavalry Regiment made a significant contribution to Texas frontier history.

EPILOGUE

God and the soldier all men adore,
in times of war, but not before.
When the war is over and all things righted,
God is forgotten, and the soldier is slighted.

After the return of the 2nd Cavalry to New York, it was assigned to Carlisle Barracks, Pennsylvania, for re-equipping and reorganization. Major Thomas, acting commander of the Regiment, met the first contingent of the unit (Companies B, D, E, G, H, I) when they arrived and moved with the companies by rail to Carlisle Barracks, which they reached on April 13. From here Companies D and H were ordered to Washington, D. C. arriving there on the 17th. The second battalion or contingent of the Regiment (Headquarters and Companies B, C, F and K), after docking at New York City on April 20, also proceeded to Carlisle Barracks by rail, arriving there on the 27th.[1]

On the trip from New York City to Carlisle Barracks the train had to pass through a village of Dunkers in eastern Pennsylvania. The Dunkers, like the Quakers, are conscientious objectors in wartime but they do not hesitate to comfort and supply food to combatants. In this particular Dunker community a committee had been formed to board troop trains and pass out sandwiches and lemonade to the soldiers passing through. The committee members boarded the train in which the second battalion of the Regiment was traveling and inquired of Captain Johnson what state the troops were from. Johnson, in a loud voice replied, "This is the 2nd Cavalry from Texas." The word "Texas" seemed to startle the Dunkers, who looked around wildly to see if Texas had captured the Union and then with a rush picked up their sandwiches and drinks and leaped off the train. The Dunkers had no food for soldiers from Texas even if they were fighting for the Union.[2]

Several of the companies of the 2nd Cavalry saw action in the early fighting of the war. The first company to be engaged was E. Kirby Smith's old command, Company B, now under Lieutenant

---

[1] Price, p. 97. On April 25, Thomas was promoted to lieutenant colonel and on May 3 to colonel and commander of the Regiment. **Ibid.**, p. 101.
[2] Johnson, **Reminiscences**, p. 159.

Charles H. Tompkins. Tompkins with 50 men of the company, many of whom had served in Texas, charged three times through Fairfax Courthouse, Virginia, on June 1, 1861, and completely routed a Confederate force occupying the town. The Southerners suffered a loss of 25 men killed and wounded; Tompkins had but five casualties.[3] This was the first Federal cavalry success in the Old Dominion State.

An act passed by Congress on August 3, 1861, called for all mounted units in the army to be designated as cavalry and for renumbering them as such by seniority of authorization. Thus, the 1st and 2nd Dragoons became the 1st and 2nd Cavalry, the Mounted Rifles were redesignated as the 3rd Cavalry and the numbers of the original 1st and 2nd Cavalry Regiments were changed to the 4th and 5th Cavalry, respectively. The original 3rd Cavalry, which had been authorized by Congress as a new mounted regiment on July 29, 1861, was renumbered as the 6th U. S. Cavalry Regiment.[4] These were the only Regular Army Cavalry Regiments to fight in the Civil War.

The original 2nd U. S. Cavalry Regiment had an activation span of only six years and five months — March 3, 1855 to August 3, 1861. However, during this relatively short period of time, the Regiment made a significant contribution, not only to Texas and frontier history, but also to United States Military history as well. Its horses, its equipment and its arms were the best obtainable at the time. Its private troopers appeared to be better than the average horse soldiers of that day, its non-commissioned officers were of high caliber and its officers were outstanding.

No other regiment in the United States armed forces, before or after, has produced, in so short a period of time, so many general officers. Sixteen (37 percent) of the 43 officers who served with the Regiment while it was in Texas were promoted to general officer rank and "with few exceptions" the others gained field-officers' commissions. Of the 16 generals, 11 served in the Southern army and five in the Northern army. Four of the 11 that served the Confederacy rose to the rank of full general — Albert Sidney Johnston, Robert E. Lee, E. Kirby Smith and John Bell Hood. Thus, the 2nd U. S. Cavalry Regiment provided Jefferson Davis with one-half of his full generals. One, William J. Hardee,

[3] Price, p. 101.
[4] Ibid., pp. 103-04.

was promoted to lieutenant-general, and three, Earl Van Dorn, Charles W. Field and Fitzhugh Lee, served as major-generals. Nathan "Shanks" Evans, James P. Major and George B. Cosby were Confederate brigadier-generals.[5] Four of the five officers of the Regiment who became generals in the Federal Army attained major-general rank; George H. Thomas, Kenner Garrard, George Stoneman, Jr., Richard W. Johnson. It must be remembered that except for Ulysses Simpson Grant, no Federal general rose above major-general rank during the war. Innis N. Palmer was a brigadier-general.[6]

Many of these generals held important commands during the Civil War. All four full generals of the Confederate Army, as the rank would indicate, played a major role in the war. Albert Sidney Johnston, the ranking field general in the Southern Army,[7] had what probably would have been a brilliant career cut short with his untimely death early in the war. "Sid" Johnston, commanding the Confederate armies in the West, was killed at Shiloh on April 6, 1862, while directing reserves into the front lines. Robert E. Lee's exploits in the war are legendary. He was probably "the great hero" of the war. Lee commanded the Army of Northern Virginia from June 1, 1862 to April 9, 1865, and he commanded all of the Southern armies the last three months of the war. E. Kirby Smith, after a brief career with the armies in the Eastern and Western Theaters of Operations, was assigned to command the Trans-Mississippi Department. Smith did a good job in a difficult assignment. His department was often referred to as "Kirby Smithdom" because of its isolation from Richmond and the blanket authority given him to conduct administrative and military affairs. John Bell Hood commanded the famous Texas Brigade early in the war, a division in Longstreet's Corps at Gettysburg, and in late 1864 the Army of Tennessee. Hood, along with Forrest and Cleburne, was perhaps the most aggressive battlefield commander in the Southern Army.

William J. Hardee, "Old Reliable," commanded a corps in the Army of Tennessee from 1862 to 1864, and his *Rifle and Light*

---

[5] Warner, **Gray**, pp. 64, 84, 87-88, 124, 142-43, 159-60, 178.
[6] Ibid., **Blue**, pp. 167-68, 253-54, 358, 481-82, 500-01.
[7] Samuel Cooper, Adjutant and Inspector General was the highest ranking general officer in the Provisional Army of the Confederate States of America.

Infantry Tactics, written before the war, was used as a manual by both sides. Charles W. Field commanded Hood's old division the last year of the war, and Fitzhugh Lee commanded a cavalry division under Jeb Stuart and later Wade Hampton in the Cavalry Corps of Lee's Army. As noted elsewhere Earl Van Dorn held several major army commands early in the war. His greatest single exploit prior to his murder in May, 1863, was the destruction of Grant's forward supply base at Holly Springs, Mississippi in December, 1862.

On the Federal side, both George H. Thomas and George Stoneman, Jr., particularly the former, made notable contributions to the Union war effort. Thomas with his determined stand, saved Rosecrans' Army at Chickamauga in September, 1863, and earned himself the sobriquet "Rock of Chickamauga." Later, as commander of the Federal Army at Nashville, Tennessee, in December, 1864, Thomas routed the Confederate Army of Tennessee under his fellow officer of the old 2nd Cavalry, John B. Hood. Thomas, who also acquired the nicknames of "Slow Trot" and "Granny" because of his methodical and slow movement of troops and his personal conservatism, nevertheless hit hard when he struck. His reputation as a general during the war was second to none. Stoneman, who had chased Cortinas back and forth across the Rio Grande on several occasions while he was with the 2nd Cavalry in Texas, was the Chief of Cavalry of the Army of the Potomac during 1861 and 1862; later he commanded the Cavalry Corps of the Army of the Ohio.

The original 2nd U.S. Cavalry Regiment (1855-1861) was studded with stars, a total of 41 in the Civil War and three later in the Spanish-American War.[8] It would be a long time, if ever again, before America would see another regiment as elite as "Jeff Davis's Own."

---

[8] Fitzhugh Lee would serve as a Major-General of volunteers and Abraham Arnold as Brigadier-General during the Spanish-American War.

APPENDIX

PART ONE

Officers Assigned to The 2nd
U.S. Cavalry, 1855-1861.

PART TWO

Enlisted Men Assigned to the
2nd U.S. Cavalry, 1855-1861
And Commissioned Later as
Officers in the U.S. Army.

PART ONE
Officers Assigned to the 2nd U.S. Cavalry, 1855-1861

Name	Place of Birth	Appointed From	Remarks
Anderson, Geo. B.	North Carolina	Regular Army (USMA, 1852)	Aptd. 2Lt., 2Cav., 3/5/55; Declined Aptmt. 4/18/55; B-Gen., CSA; Died of wounds, 10/16/62.
Arnold, Abraham K.	Pennsylvania	Regular Army (USMA, 1859)	Aptd. BVT2Lt., 2Cav., 6/28/60; Jnd. Regt., 12/2/60; USA, Civil War.
Brackett, Albert G.	New York	Civilian Life (Mex.War Vet.)	Aptd. Capt. 2Cav., 3/5/55; Cmdr., Co. I; USA, Civil War.
Bradfute, William R.	Tennessee	Civilian Life (Mex.War Vet.)	Aptd. Capt., 2Cav., 3/5/55; Cmdr., Co. G; CSA, Civil War.
Chambliss, Wm. P.	Virginia	Civilian Life (Mex. War Vet.)	Aptd. 1Lt., 2Cav., 3/5/55; USA, Civil War.
Colburn, Albert V.	Vermont	Regular Army (USMA, 1855)	Aptd. BVT2Lt., 2Cav., 7/1/55; Jnd. Regt. 9/30/55; Aptd. 2Lt., 1Cav., 10/11/55.
Cosby, Geo. B.	Kentucky	Regular Army (USMA, 1852)	Aptd. 2Lt., 2Cav., 3/5/55; B-Gen. CSA, Civil War.
Cross, Alexander H.	Washington, D.C.	Civilian Life (Mex.War Vet.)	Aptd. 1Lt., 2Cav., 3/5/55; Resgnd., 5/1/56.
Cunningham, Geo. A.	Georgia	Regular Army (USMA, 1857)	Aptd. 2Lt., 2Cav., 10/1/58; CSA, Civil War.
Eagle, Robt. N.	New York	Civilian Life (Mex. War Vet.)	Aptd. 1Lt., 2Cav., 3/5/55; USA, Civil War; Resgnd. comm., 1/15/62.

Evans, Nathan G.	South Carolina	Regular Army (USMA, 1848)	Aptd. 1Lt., 2Cav., 3/5/55; B-Gen. CSA, Civil War
Field, Charles W.	Kentucky	Regular Army (USMA, 1849)	Aptd. 1Lt., 2Cav., 3/5/55; M-Gen. CSA, Civil War.
Garrard, Kenner	Kentucky	Regular Army (USMA, 1851)	Aptd. 1Lt., 2Cav., 3/5/55; M-Gen. USA, Civil War.
Gibbs, Wade H.	South Carolina	Regular Army (USMA, 1860)	Aptd. BVT2Lt., 2Cav., 7/1/60; Did not join Regt.; Resgnd. comm., 1/1/61.
Hardee, Wm. J.	Georgia	Regular Army (USMA, 1838)	Aptd. Maj., 2Cav., 3/5/55; Transfd. June, 1856; Lt-Gen. CSA, Civil War.
Harrison, James E.	Virginia	Civilian Life (U.S. Revenue Service)	Aptd. 2Lt., 2 Cav., 6/27/56; USA, Civil War.
Hartwell, George	Vermont	Civilian Life	Aptd. 2Lt., 2Cav., 3/5/55; Did not join Regt.; Resgnd., 8/21/55.
Jenifer, Walter H.	Maryland	Civilian Life (Mex.War Vet.)	Aptd. 1Lt., 2Cav., 3/5/55; CSA, Civil War.
Johnson, Richard W.	Kentucky	Regular Army (USMA, 1849)	Aptd., 1Lt., 2Cav., 3/5/55; M-Gen. USA, Civil War.
Johnston, Albert S.	Kentucky	Regular Army (USMA, 1826)	Aptd. Col., 2Cav., 3/5/55; Transfd., July 28, 1857; Gen, CSA, Civil War; K. Shiloh, Apr., 1862.
Kimmel, Manning M.	Missouri	Regular Army (USMA, 1857)	Aptd. 2Lt., 2Cav., 8/18/58; USA & CSA, Civil War.
Lee, Fitzhugh	Virginia	Regular Army (USMA, 1856)	Aptd. BVT2Lt., 2Cav., 7/1/56; Transfd., 12/29/60; M-Gen. CSA, Civil War.

Lee, Robert E.	Virginia	Regular Army (USMA, 1829)	Aptd. Lt-Col., 2Cav., 3/5/55; Regmtl. Cmdr. July, 1857 & Dec. 1860; Gen. CSA, Civil War.
Lomax, Lunsford L.	Rhode Island	Regular Army (USMA, 1856)	Aptd. BVT2Lt., 2Cav.; 7/1/56; Did not join Regt.; Transfd., 9/30/56.
Lowe, William W.	Indiana	Regular Army (USMA, 1853)	Aptd. 2Lt., 2Cav., 3/5/55: USA, Civil War.
McArthur, Jos. H.	Missouri	Regular Army (USMA, 1849)	Aptd. 1Lt., 2Cav., 3/5/55; USA, Civil War.
Magruder, John T.	Virginia	Regular Army (USMA, 1857)	Aptd. BVT2Lt., 2Cav., 7/1/57; Transfd. to 1Cav., 4/24/58; Died 6/28/58.
Major, James P.	Missouri	Regular Army (USMA, 1850)	Aptd. BVT2Lt., 2Cav., 12/1/56; B-Gen. CSA, Civil War.
Merrifield, Edwin R.	New York	Civilian Life (Mex.War Vet.)	Aptd. 2Lt., 2Cav., 3/5/55; Declined Aptmt.
Minter, Jos. F.	Virginia	Civilian Life	Aptd. 2Lt., 2Cav., 3/5/55; CSA, Civil War.
Oakes, James	Pennsylvania	Regular Army (USMA, 1846)	Aptd. Capt., 2Cav., 3/5/55; Cmdr. Co. C; B-Gen. USA, Civil War.
O'Hara, Theodore	Kentucky	Civilian Life (Mex.War Vet.)	Aptd. Capt., 2Cav., 3/5/55; Cmdr., Co. F; Resgnd., 12/1/56.
Owens, Wesley	Ohio	Regular Army (USMA, 1856)	Aptd. BVT2Lt., 2Cav., 1/7/56; Transfd., 11/9/60; USA, Civil War.
Palmer, Innis N.	New York	Regular Army (USMA, 1846)	Aptd. Capt., 2Cav., 3/5/55; Cmdr. Co. D; B-Gen., USA, Civil War.
Phifer, Charles W.	Tennessee	Civilian Life	Aptd., 2Lt., 2Cav., 3/5/55; CSA, Civil War.
Porter, A. Parker	Pennsylvania	Regular Army (USMA, 1856)	Aptd. BVT2Lt., 2Cav. 7/1/57; USA, Civil War.

Royall, William B.	Virginia	Civilian Life (Mex.War Vet.)	Aptd. 1Lt., 2Cav., 3/5/55; USA, Civil War.
Radziminski, Charles	Poland	Civilian Life (Mex.War Vet.)	Aptd. 1Lt., 2Cav., 3/5/55; Died 8/18/58.
Shaaff, John T.	Washington, D.C.	Regular Army (USMA, 1851)	Aptd. 1Lt., 2Cav., 3/5/55; CSA, Civil War.
Sweitzer, Nelson B.	Pennsylvania	Regular Army (USMA, 1853)	Aptd. 2Lt., 2Cav., 3/5/55; Declined Aptmt.; Remained with 1st Dragoons.
Smith, Edmund K.	Florida	Regular Army (USMA, 1845)	Aptd. Capt., 2Cav., 3/5/55; Cmdr. Co. B; Gen, CSA, Civil War.
Stoneman, George, Jr.	New York	Regular Army (USMA, 1846)	Aptd. Capt., 2Cav., 3/5/55; Cmdr. Co. E; Maj-Gen. USA, Civil War.
Sweet, John J.	Illinois	Regular Army (USMA, 1860)	Aptd. BVT2Lt., 2Cav., 7/1/60; Never joined Regt.; Sick at Ft. Leavenworth.
Thomas, George H.	Virginia	Regular Army (USMA, 1840)	Aptd. Maj., 2Cav., 5/12/55; Cmdr. Regt., 10/21/57 to 11/12/60; Maj-Gen., USA, Civil War.
Travis, Charles E.	Texas	Civilian Life (Texas Ranger)	Aptd. Capt., 2Cav., 3/5/55; Cmdr. Co. H; Dismsd. from service, May, 1856.
Van Camp, Cornelius	Pennsylvania	Regular Army (USMA, 1855)	Aptd., 2Lt., 2Cav., 7/1/55; killed in action, 9/15/58.
Van Dorn, Earl	Mississippi	Regular Army (USMA, 1842)	Aptd. Capt., 2Cav., 3/5/55; Cmdr., Co. A; Maj-Gen., CSA, Civil War.
Wheeler, Junius B.	North Carolina	Regular Army (USMA, 1855)	Aptd. BVT2Lt., 2Cav., 7/1/55; Transfd. to Topographical Engrs., 6/27/56; USA, Civil War.

Whiting, Charles J.	Massachusetts	Civilian Life (USMA, 1835)	Resgnd. Reg. Army, 5/31/36; Aptd. Capt., 2Cav., 3/5/55; Cmdr. Co. K; USA, Civil War.
Williams, John	Ireland	Regular Army	1Sgt., Mtd. Rifles; Aptd. 2Lt., 1 Dragoons; Assgd. 2Cav. May 1855; Killed June 30, 1855, before joining Regt.
Witherell, James B.	Michigan	Civilian Life	Aptd. 2Lt., 2Cav., 3/5/55; Drowned, 3/21/61.
Wood, Robert C., Jr.	Minnesota	Civilian Life (West Point Cadet)	Aptd. 2Lt., 2Cav., 3/5/55; Resgd., 1/1/58; CSA, Civil War.

PART TWO

Enlisted Men Assigned to the 2nd U.S. Cavalry, 1855-1861 and Commissioned Later as Officers in the U.S. Army

Name	Place of Birth	Highest Grade Held in 2nd Cav.	Remarks
Baden, James T.	Maryland	1st Sgt. Co. F.	Aptd. 2Lt., 5 Cav. 7/17/62; 1Lt., 11/2/63; Resgnd., 9/12/64
Baker, Henry	England	Regimental Sgt-Maj.	Aptd. 2Lt., 5 Cav., 7/17/62; 1Lt., 4/13/63; Dropped from rolls, 1/12/66.
Burns, James	Ireland	Regimental Comsy-Sgt.	Aptd. 2Lt., 5Cav. 8/9/65; 1Lt., 7/28/66; Capt., 3/1/72; Died, 1874.
Denney, Jeremiah C.	Ireland	Regimental QM-Sgt.	Aptd., 1Lt., 5Cav., 7/17/62; Capt., 7/28/66; Died, 1869.
Dwyer, Phillip	Ireland	Regimental QM-Sgt	Aptd., 1Lt., 5Cav., 7/17/62; Capt., 7/31/66; Died, 1872.

Hayes, Edward M.[1]	New York	Musician, Bugler, Cos. H & B	Aptd. 2Lt., 5 Cav., 2/23/66; 1Lt., 8/20/66; Capt., 8/15/74; Maj., 7Cav., 4/7/93; Lt.Col., 4Cav., 7/1/99; Col., 13Cav., 2/17/01; B-Gen., 1/15/03.
Henley, Joseph P.	Ireland	1st Sgt. Co. G	Aptd., 2Lt., 5 Cav., 4/22/63; 1Lt. 3/30/64; Killed, Trevillian Sta., VA, 6/12/64.
Jones, Henry	Ireland	Sergeant Co. G	Aptd., 2Lt., 5 Cav., 7/17/62; 1Lt., 10/10/62; Dropped from rolls 11/19/63.
Kane, John H.	Ireland	Sergeant Co. D	Aptd. 2Lt., 5 Cav.,2/19/63; 1Lt., 11/19/63; Capt., 12/22/68; Resgnd. 8/31/70 at own request.
Maley, Thomas E.	Ireland	Regimental QM-Sgt.	Aptd. 2Lt., 5 Cav., 4/22/62; 1Lt., 7/17/62; Capt. 7/28/66; Retd as Lt. Col. 3/3/73. Brevetted for bravery 3 times during Civil War. Died, 1896.
Montgomery, Robert H.	Pennsylvania	Sergeant Co. C.	Aptd. 2Lt., 5 Cav., 11/29/62; Dismsd., 11/19/63; Reinstd., 2/6/65; Capt. 1/3/70; Maj. 10Cav., 3/8/91. Brevetted for bravery 3 times during career. Retired 4/8/92.
Spangler, John W.	Kentucky	1st Sgt., Co. H	Aptd., 2Lt., 3Cav., 5/14/61; 1Lt., 10/2/61; Capt. 7/28/66; Died, 1867.
Urban Gustavus	Prussia	Regimental QM-Sgt.	Aptd., 1Lt., 5Cav., 7/17/62; Capt., 7/28/66. Brevetted twice for bravery during Civil War. Died, 1871.

---

[1] Hayes enlisted in Co. H, 2nd U.S. Cavalry as a bugler in 1855 at the age of 13.

BIBLIOGRAPHY

PRIMARY SOURCES

Government Documents

Annual Returns of the Alterations and Casualties Incident to the Second Regiment of the U. S. Cavalry during the years, 1855-1860. Microfilm Copy No. M-744, Roll No. 51. National Archives, Washington, D. C.

Post Returns, Camp Cooper, June, 1856. Microfilm Copy No. M-617, Roll No. 253, National Archives, Washington, D. C.

—————, Camp Hudson, July, 1857. Microfilm Copy No. M-617, Roll No. 495 National Archives, Washington, D. C.

—————, Fort Chadbourne, June - August, 1856. Microfilm Copy No. M-617, Roll No. 195, National Archives, Washington, D. C.

—————, Fort Inge, April, June-July, 1857. Microfilm Copy No. M-617, Roll No. 5517, National Archives, Washington, D. C.

—————, Fort Mason, June, 1856; February, July, 1857. Microfilm Copy No. M-617, Roll No. 759, National Archives, Washington, D. C.

Proceedings of the Court in the Case of Captain Charles E. Travis, 2nd Cavalry, Record Group 153, Records of the Office of the Judge Advocate General, HH626. National Archives, Washington, D. C.

Regimental Returns, 2nd U. S. Cavalry. Microfilm Copy No. M-744, Roll No. 51, Oct., 1855; July-Sept., Dec., 1856; Mar.-April, Aug.-Sept., Nov., 1857; Jan.-Feb., June-Nov., 1858; Jan., Mar., July, Sept., 1859; Mar., Oct., 1860; Jan.-April, 1861. National Archives, Washington, D. C.

Report of the Secretary of War, Dec. 1, 1853, 33rd Congress, 1st Session, Ex. Doc. No. 1, National Archives, Washington, D. C.

—————; Dec. 4, 1854, 33rd Congress, 2nd Session, Ex. Doc. No. 1, National Archives, Washington, D. C.

—————, Dec., 1857. "Report of Lieutenant John B. Hood", Sen. Ex. Doc. No. 1, 35th Congress, 1st Session, No. 11, National Archives, Washington, D. C.

United States Navy Dept. *Official Records of the Union and Confederate Navies in the War of the Rebellion,* Washington: Govt. Printing Office, 1884-1927, 31 Vols., Series 1, Vol. 4.

United States Senate. *Medal of Honor, 1863-1968.* Washington: Govt. Printing Office, 1968.

United States War Department. General Orders Nos. 4, 13 (1855) No. 6, (1856); No. 5 (1861). National Archives, Washington, D. C.

—————, *The War of the Rebellion: Official Records of the Union and Confederate Armies,* Washington: Govt. Printing Office, 1880-1901, 128 Vols., Series 1, Vol. 1.

Books

Johnson, Richard W. *A Soldier's Reminiscences in Peace and War.* Philadelphia: J. B. Lippincott, 1886.

Scott, Winfield. *Memoirs of Lt.-Gen. Winfield Scott., LLD.* New York: Sheldon & Co., 1864.

Davis, Jefferson. *The Rise and Fall of the Confederate Government.* (2 Vols.). New York: Thomas Yoseloff, 1958, (re-print).

Articles

Crimmins, Colonel Martin L. (ed). "Colonel J. K. F. Mansfield's Inspection Report of Texas," *SWHQ*, Vol. 42, No. 4 (April, 1939), pp. 351, 379.

_____, "Colonel Robert E. Lee's Report on Indian Combat in Texas." *SWHQ*, Vol. 39, No. 1 (July, 1935), pp. 21-31.

_____, "Jack Hayes' Story of Fitzhugh Lee's Indian Fight," *WTHAYB*, Vol. 13, (1937), pp. 42-45.

_____, "Robert E. Lee in Texas: Letters and Diary." *WTHAYB*, Vol. 8, (1932), p. 6.

Roland, Charles P. and Richard C. Robbins, "The Diary of Eliza (Mrs. Albert Sidney) Johnston." *SWHQ*, Vol. 60, No. 4 (April, 1957), pp. 463-500.

Rost, H. G. "Desperate Fight on Devils River," *Frontier Times.* Vol. 21, p. 142.

SECONDARY SOURCES

Books

Adams, Henry. *The War of 1812.* Washington: The Infantry Journal, 1944.

Brackett, Albert G. *History of the United States Cavalry.* New York, Argonaut Press, 1965. (re-print).

Cavalry ROTC Manual. Harrisburg (PA): The Military Service Publishing Co., 1935, 6th Edition, p. 343.

Davis, Burke. *Our Incredible Civil War,* New York: Holt, Rinhart and Winston, 1960.

Eaton, Clement, *Jefferson Davis.* New York: The Free Press, 1977.

Frazer, Robert W. *Forts Of The West.* Norman (OK.): University of Oklahoma Press, 1965.

Freeman, Douglas Southall, *Lee's Lieutenants.* New York: Charles Scribners Sons, 1944. Vol 3.

_____, *R. E. Lee, A Biography* New York: Charles Scribner's Sons, 1934. (4 vols), Vol. 1.

Gruver, Rebecca Brooks, *An American History,* Reading (Mass.): Addison-Wesley, 1976.

Hartje, Robert G. *Van Dorn: The Life And Times Of A Confederate General.* Nashville: Vanderbilt University Press, 1967.

Heitman, Francis B. *Historical Register And Dictionary Of the U. S. Army.* Washington, D. C.: Government Printing Office, 1903.

Henry, Robert Selph *The Story of the Confederacy.* Indianapolis: Bobbs-Merrill Company, 1936.

Herr, John K and Edward S. Wallace. *The Story Of The U. S. Cavalry.* Boston: Little, Brown and Co., 1953.

Hood, J. B. *Advance and Retreat.* New Orleans: G. T. Beauregard, 1880.

Hughes, Nathaniel Cheairs, Jr. *General William J. Hardee.* Baton Rouge: Louisiana State University Press, 1965.

Johnston, William Preston *The Life Of Albert Sidney Johnston.* New York: D. Appleton and Co., 1879.

Lesley, Lewis B. *Uncle Sam's Camels.* Cambridge (Mass.): Harvard University Press, 1929.

Merrill, Jas. M. *Spurs To Glory, The Story Of The United States' Cavalry.* New York: Rand McNally & Co., 1966.

O'Connor, Richard. *Thomas: Rock Of Chickamauga.* New York: Prentice Hall, 1948.

Parks, Joseph H. *General Edmund Kirby Smith.* Baton Rouge: Louisiana State University Press, 1962.

Perkins, Dexter & Glyndon Van Deusen. *The United States Of America: A History.* New York: The McMillan Company, 1962.

Powell, William H. *List Of Officers of The Army Of the United States From 1779 To 1900.* New York: L. R. Hamersly & Co., 1900.

Price, George F. *Across The Continent With The Fifth Cavalry.* New York: Antiquarian Press, 1959. (re-print).

Register Of Graduates and Former Graduates, United States Military Academy 1802-1946. New York: The West Point Alumni Foundation, Inc., 1946.

Richardson, Rupert Norval. *The Frontier Of Northwest Texas 1846-1876.* Glendale (Cal.): A. H. Clark Co., 1963.

—————, *Texas: The Lone Star State.* Englewood Cliffs (N. J.): Prentice Hall, Inc., 1958

Rister, Carl Coke *Robert E. Lee in Texas.* Norman: University of Oklahoma Press, 1946.

Roland, Charles P. *Albert Sidney Johnston, Soldier Of Three Republics.* Austin: University of Texas Press, 1964.

Simpson, Harold B. "Fort Mason", *Frontier Forts Of Texas.* Waco: Texian Press, 1966.

—————, "The Kiowas", *Indian Tribes Of Texas.* Waco: Texian Press, 1971.

—————————, (ed). *Texas In The War, 1861-1865.* Hillsboro (TX): Hill Jr. College Press., 1965.

—————————, "John Salmon Ford", *Rangers Of Texas.* Waco: Texian Press, 1969.

Steffen, Randy *The Horse Soldier, 1776-1943.* Norman, Okla.: University Of Oklahoma Press, 1978, Vol II.

Strode, Hudson *Jefferson Davis; American Patriot, 1808-1861.* New York: Harcourt, Brace and Co., 1955.

Spaulding, Oliver L. *The United States Army In War and Peace.* New York: G. P. Putman's Sons. 1937.

Thomas, Wilber. *General George H. Thomas, The Indomitable Warrior.* New York: Exposition Press, 1964.

Utley, Robert M. *Frontiersmen In Blue: The U. S. Army And The Indian, 1848-1865.* New York: Macmillan, 1967.

Van Horne, Thomas B. *The Life Of Major-General George H. Thomas.* New York: Charles Scribner's Sons. 1882.

Warner, Ezra J. *Generals In Gray.* Baton Rouge: Louisiana State University Press, 1959.

—————————, *Generals In Blue.* Baton Rouge: Louisiana State Press, 1964.

Webb, Walter Prescott (ed.). *The Handbook Of Tesas.* Austin: Texas State Historical Association. 1952. Vol. II.

—————————, *The Texas Rangers.* Austin: University Of Texas Press, 1965.

Woodman, Lyman L. *Cortina, The Rogue Of The Rio Grande.* San Antonio: Naylor, 1950.

Wormser, Richard *The Yellowlegs, The Story of the United States Cavalry.* Garden City (N. Y.): DoubleDay & Co. 1966.

Upton, Emory. *The Military Policy of the United States.* Washington, D. C..: Government Printing Office, 1912.

Articles

Crane, R. D., *"Robert E. Lee's Expedition in the Upper Brazos and Colorado Country." WTHAYB,* Vol. XIII, Oct. 1937, pp. 54-58.

—————————, "One Indian Faced Twenty Soldiers". *Frontier Times,* Vol. III, No. 2, May, 1925, p. 13.

Crimmins, Colonel Martin L. "Camp Cooper and Fort Griffin, Texas." *WTHAYB,* Vol. XVII, October, 1941, p. 36.

—————————, "First Sergeant John W. Spangler, Company H, 2nd U. S. Cavalry". *WTHAYB,* Vol. XXVI, Oct., 1950, p. 75.

—————————, "Major Van Dorn in Texas". *WTHAYB,* Vol. XVI, Oct., 1940, p. 123.

—————————, "The Military History of Camp Colorado" *WTHAYB,* Vol. XXVIII, Oct. 1952, pp. 71-80.

Holden, W. C. "Frontier Defense, 1846-1860". *WTHAYB,* Vol. VI, June, 1930, pp. 35-38.

Hunter, J. Martin. "Battle With Indians on Devil's River." *Frontier Times.* Vol. III, No. 6, (March, 1926), p. 14.

——————, "General John B. Hood's Victory." *Frontier Times,* Vol. IV, No. 7, (April, 1927), p. 16.

Koch, Lena Clara, "The Federal Indian Policy in Texas, 1845-1860," *SWHQ.,* Vol. XXIX, No. 1, (July, 1925), p. 19; Vol. XXIX, No. 2, (Oct. 1925), pp. 98-107, 119.

Mayhall, Mildred. "The Battles of Wichita Village and Crooked Creek." *True West,* Jan.-Feb., 1972, pp. 14-15.

Mueller, Richard E. "Jefferson Barracks: The Early Years". *Missouri Historical Review,* Vol. LXVII, No. 1. (October, 1972), pp. 1, 13-14.

Rippy, J. Fred. "Border Trouble Along the Rio Grande 1848-1860." *SWHQ,* Vol. XXIII, No. 2 (October, 1919), pp. 104-105.

KEY

SWHQ — Southwestern Historical Quarterly

WTHAYB — West Texas Historical Association Year Book

INDEX

G

Gaensleve, John J., 116.
Garcia, Guadalupe, 144.
Gardner, Thomas, 81-82.
Garrard, Kenner, 44, 157.
Garrison, James E., 114f.
Gaskin, Thomas, 142.
Gates, Fort, 22f, 49, 55.
Gehring, Louis, 100.
Gettysburg, Battle of, 84f, 103.
Gibson, Fort, 38, 40, 45-46.
Gordon, Bishop, 114f.
Gordon, Henry, 69, 123.
Graham, Fort, 22f, 55.
Grant, Ulysses Simpson, 169.
Green, Nathaniel, 2, 46.
Groghan, Fort, 22f, 55.
Gruver, Rebecca Brooks, 54f.
Guadalupe Hidalgo, Treaty of, 10, 13.

H

Hampton, Wade, 5, 170.
"Hardee Hat," 29.
Hardee, William J., 23-24, 28-33, 36, 39, 48, 57, 75f, 118, 168-169.
Harney, William S., 8, 51-52, 140.
Harrison, James E., 22, 112, 114, 126, 128, 165.
Hartley, William, 129.
Hausser ————, 152.
Hawks, Howard, 38.
Hayes, Edward M., 147.
Hayes, Jack, 145-147.
Hays, John C. "Coffee Jack", 11, 52-53, 108f.
Heintzeman, Samuel P., 137-138, 141.
Henderson, James P., 52f-53.
Henley, Joseph D., 83-84f, 88.
Higgins, ————, 105.
Hill, G. W., 61.
Hinckley, ————, 114f.
Hood, John Bell, 21f, 83-92, 98, 162-163, 168, 170.
Hopkins, Dick, 85.
Horshoe Bend, battle of, 6.
Horton, Albert C., 52.
Houston, Sam, 7, 17, 145, 153.
Howard, George, 62.
Howard, Henry, 114f.
Howe, William, 2.
Hudson, Camp, 63, 90-91, 107, 122-123.
Hughes, Thomas, 105f.
Humes, Samuel, 46.

I

Inge, Fort, 55, 57, 62, 77,

93, 94-96, 137-138, 141, 157f, 160-161, 164.
Iron Jacket (Comanche Chief), 108.
Ives, Camp, 135-136f.
Ives, T. B., 147.

J

Jack, Harry, 126, 129.
Jackson, Andrew, 6, 7, 44-45f.
"Jeff Davis Hat," 29.
Jefferson Barracks, 8, 21, 27, 31-35, 37, 39-40, 44, 48, 66, 70-72, 143.
Jefferson, Thomas, 5, 32.
Jenifer, Walter H., 27, 76, 79, 95-96, 165.
Jessup, Fort, 9f.
Johnson, Andrew, 98f.
Johnson, Richard W., 6, 24, 26, 30f, 32-33, 37-40, 47, 65f, 74, 78-80, 94, 103, 118-120, 148-150, 158-159, 161, 164-165, 167, 169.
Johnston, Albert Sidney, 21f, 22-23, 26-28, 32-33, 35-37, 39-40, 42-43, 48-49, 62-63, 65, 67, 70-71, 74-75, 96-97, 106f-107f, 168-169.
Johnston, Eliza (Mrs Albert), 35-36, 39-40, 43f-45, 47f, 49, 59, 66, 72-73.
Johnston, Joseph E., 21f, 66.
Jones, Benjamin, 129, 147.
Jones, Henry, 85.

K

Katumse, (Comanche Chief), 62.
Kearney, Stephen Watts, 8-13, 36.
Keegan, Richard, 142.
Kelleher, Thomas, 153.
Kenevane, Patrick, 129.
Kennedy, Mathew, 136.
Kimmel, Husband E., 129f, 161.
Kimmell, Manning, 128-129f, 134f, 141.
Kimmell, Singleton M., 128f.
Knights of the Golden Circle, 158.
Kuhn, John, 68.

L

Lamb, Timothy, 82.
La Ebronal, battle of, 137-138.
La Mesa, battle of, 141-142.
Lancaster, Fort, 63f, 122.

Lawson, Camp, 138-145, 148.
Leavenworth, Fort, 9, 11-12f, 32-34, 39f, 106, 157.
Lee, Fitzhugh, 128-130, 145, 150, 169-170.
Lee, Henry "Light Horse Harry," 2, 4, 23.
Lee, Robert E., 2, 21f, 23, 26-27, 32, 39, 75-77, 97, 129, 140-144, 146-147, 154, 158-160, 168-169.
Leeper, Mathew, 62, 126, 132.
Leverett, William P., 96, 129.
Lewis, H. M., 71.
Lincoln, Fort, 55, 57.
Little Turtle, (Miami Chief), 5.
Lowe, William H., 27, 150, 152, 159f, 165.
Luckett, P. N., 156.
Lundy's Lane, Battle of, 6.

M & Mc

Maclin, Sackfield, 156.
Major, James P., 98, 114f, 169.
Maley, Thomas, E., 61.
Mansfield, J. K., 77-78.
Marcy, R. B., 60.
Marion, Francis, 2-4.
Marshall, Humphrey, 11.
Martin, John, 94.
Martin Scott, Fort, 55.
Mason, Fort, 43, 49-50, 57, 63, 65f, 67-69, 72-77, 79, 80, 82-85, 87, 90, 92-93, 95f, 97, 107, 138, 145, 147-151, 154, 158-159, 161, 164.
Mason, James, 21.
Mason, Richard B., 35.
Maverick, Sam A., 156.
McArthur, Joseph H., 37.
McCarty, John, 99.
McClellan, George B., 21f.
McCulloch, Ben, 23, 156, 160, 163.
McDonald, Walter, 94, 102, 104-105.
McDonald, William, 102.
McEnery, John, 123.
McIlraith, –, Maj., 3.
McIntosh, Fort, 55, 57, 82, 94, 97-98, 100, 106.
McKavett, Fort, 22f, 57, 62, 65, 94, 95f.
McKim, Jim, 82.
McLane, Allan, 2.
McLaughlin, William, 153.
McLean, Eugene E., 71.
McLean, William, 147.
McLellan, Curwin B., 114f.
McLoughlin, John, 84-85, 87, 93, 149-150.
McNamara, ————, 114f.